From Here
to
Maturity

CONFESSIONS OF A KID AT HEART

Deborah Paul

Guild Press of Indiana, Inc.

GUILD PRESS OF INDIANA, INC.
10665 Andrade Drive
Zionsville, Indiana 46077

ISBN 1-57860-096-0
Library of Congress Catalog Card Number 20-01092397

Interior and text design by Sheila G. Samson

Printed and bound in the United States of America

To my family — especially Steve and the boys — who have graciously allowed me to wear their hearts on my sleeve.

Contents

Foreword

ON MY MOTHER'S closet shelf sits a ribbon-bound packet of love letters, most written from the lobby of the Claypool Hotel, where my father— enjoying the air-conditioning—would put his amorous notions to paper. When my sister, Judy, and I were girls, we would camp out on the floor by the upstairs hall closet and pore through the letters, weeping reverently, praying that someday romance such as this—more honest than love songs, more transcendent than simple poetry—would someday be ours. Sixty-five years later and six years after his death, his confessions of love are still too private for my mother, now ninety-two, to share.

My father was an eloquent speaker and an even better listener. "There's a reason God gave us two ears and one mouth," he would say. But most of all he could write. Had he graduated from high school rather than worked to support his family of nine, who knows what he might have become? The last of his four children, I inherited his proclivity for the written word; I composed letters to my grandmother in Cincinnati, overwrought passages in my diary, missives to boys at summer camp. In the high school newspaper, I wrote a personal column called "Debris," which I hoped was more a nod to my name than the content. Later, I collaborated with my friend, Judy Kammins, on another column, "Frank and Earnest"; the experience was as dismal as what was published. Unlike birth or sex, the act of writing really requires only one, even if her subject is no more profound than the school cafeteria.

Forsaking these weekly forays into immortality, as well as front-page features in the Indianapolis daily newspaper's Saturday tabloid section, *The Teen Star*, I traded my avocation for something more pragmatic: a college degree in education. In the sixties, a girl needed something to fall back on should husband-hunting take an unfortunate turn. I later returned to the fold in a quarterly column, "A Spoonful of Sugar," for the Junior League publication, *Pen and Inklings*. The monikers alone should provide a glimpse of the journalistic reputability of both the message and the messenger. Desperate for a byline, I assembled a packet of these columns and sent them to small-town newspapers around Indiana, offering my literary services for free. Only the editor of the Martinsville paper responded, saying if he weren't so old and set in his ways, he probably would have published them.

I doubt that my father's unrecognized talent was what prompted my mother to pay my tuition to Butler University when I was thirty-one years old and myself the mother of two. More likely, she was simply tired of hearing how sorry I was not to write. In my journalism class I met the editor of the burgeoning local magazine, *Indianapolis Home and Garden*, who, less impressed by my talent than my enthusiasm, assigned me a monthly column about unique shops around town. The title, "Perspicacity," is a word few can spell and fewer can define, which doubtless had something to do with the magazine's brief dip into bankruptcy before it was ultimately rescued and turned into *Indianapolis Monthly*. The magazine will enjoy its twenty-fifth anniversary in 2002.

In it, I have penned "Comment" for twenty years. For eighteen of those, I was the magazine's editor-in-chief, which gave me the credibility (not to mention the space) to write what I wanted. And that I have done. Like my father, I don't consider an experience or an emotion fully developed until it is shared. This collection of favorite columns is a testament to his legacy.

The honeymooners, 1935

Wives and Lovers

I think I married him because of the way he made me feel when we danced.

Kids at Heart

GIVEN THE CIRCUMSTANCES, most people don't cry on their honeymoons. I guess that's what surprised the cabbie who drove the young newlyweds from the airport to the Fairmont Hotel, which was in 1969 San Francisco's poshest accommodations.

But as I sat in the backseat of that cab, jostling occasionally against my new husband, it was all I could think to do. It wasn't that I was sad—maybe a little scared—but definitely not unhappy. It was merely that I was young. Barely twenty-one, I was already somebody's wife, and I had just come from being somebody's child. As the landscape passed by in fits and starts, the sobs increased, prompting my husband, Steve, to tighten his grip around my shoulders, and begging the obvious question from the driver: "You kids here on your *honeymoon?*"

I couldn't define the emotion at the time, but twenty-eight years later, I can. I was homesick, pure and simple. When most couples marry, they leave behind an empty apartment, a lonely existence, plenty of time to weigh the alternatives. When I married, still in my senior year of college, I left behind a family, a two-story house, and a bedroom recently redecorated to reflect the tastes of a young adult. My closet was full of all the outfits a girl could want, and black-and-white snapshots were stuck into the edge of the mirror over the curved vanity table. Because someone had always called me to dinner, I had no idea what the refrigerator held or why. And when I suddenly considered myself married, not just the object of a sorority candlelight ceremony marking the glory and wonder of engagement, the truth set in. I wasn't yet finished being a kid.

I loved my husband then and do still. But my reasons for marrying him at such a tender age hardly reflect good judgment or respectable life planning. After a childhood romance and an off-again-on-again courtship of six years, it seemed like the appropriate thing to do. With my college years almost behind me, it was as logical a next step as the education major I pursued at the close of high school, even though I hadn't the least desire to be a teacher. In the sixties, nice girls didn't move into their own apartments or begin careers. They studied teaching as something to fall back on, and stalked husbands with the determination of a deer hunter.

For me, however, the quest was nothing like that of my girlfriends. I merely had to say yes. A loyal suitor, my husband always knew what he wanted and was steadfast in his pursuit. We met as children in the truest sense of the word. I was dressed in a white blouse and black felt skirt with an applique of a clock and the embroidered inscription DATE TIME, when I spied him at seventh-grade dance class. I guess it was his height that attracted me, and the rosy places on his cheeks. I remember his bending over to talk into my ear, and the way he held me: tightly, with a warm, steady palm spread against my narrow back. The romance grew around dancing: dancing in class, at preteen and high school club dances, and at college parties. If we didn't share the same interests or reach for the same stars, it didn't matter because when we danced, life as we knew it disappeared.

To the strains of "Moon River" or "Sixteen Candles," we clung to each other—sometimes for hours—until the crick in my neck that resulted from our height difference and the way he mashed his chin against my forehead grew so intense I wanted to cry. When the record "Our Day Will Come" dropped onto the turntable, the longing became almost unbearable. And when I was sick with fear and indecision just the night before our wedding, all he had to do was gather me up in his arms, glide me around the dance floor, and croon his rendition of Dean Martin's "You're Nobody Till Somebody Loves You" to melt away my doubts and defenses. I think I married him because of the way he made me feel when we danced.

We didn't live in "married student housing," mostly because of the institutional nature of both the label and the building. Our little, furnished, below-ground-level apartment pleased us but displeased my father, whose hopes and dreams did not include his daughter living in a basement. On Sundays my parents came to visit bearing not just gifts, but Sunday dinner and at least a week's worth of prime provisions from the butcher. A savvy shopper, my mother usually included in her bounty a pretty outfit or two to ensure that I not only ate well, but looked at least as fine as my prior lifestyle had allowed. Maybe it was as hard for her to accept me as an adult as it was for me to actually be one.

We were as snug in our relationship as we were in our home, although my fleeting youth tugged unexpectedly and often. I felt uncomfortable and out of place at the laundromat and supermarket, and at class registration, the same homesickness that plagued me on my honeymoon overcame me once more as I glanced longingly at the table reserved for last names that began with "D," not the "P" that seemed to belong to a stranger. It's one thing to conform to marriage, but it's another to adjust to being an adult at the same time.

Miracles have ensued in the twenty-eight years that have passed since then. Two strong, glorious boys have made our lives complete, and we are probably closer than most couples in that we haven't just shared our lives, we've grown up together. Granted, we didn't sow any wild oats before our marriage, and for that we'll probably wonder forever. Others have looked tempting, but never tempting enough. Our history might not be as wide as some, but it is deeper than most.

When we recently visited our first apartment, I stood blankly on the concrete path in front of the door, unable to summon the feelings I had before. Nothing looked familiar, not even the windowsill where our first cat, Benjamin, used to sit, peering curiously up at ground level. Whenever I enter a hospital or nursing home, just the smell brings rushing back all the terrible emotions surrounding my father's dismal period there. This time, however, even the exact locale couldn't trigger a sensation, because I was a different person then, in a different life.

Now that our children have left the nest, we have a chance to start again, maybe even to recapture all the silly reasons we got together in the first place. We're adults now, with the ability to reason and plan and rationally consider all the options. We have everything we didn't have at twenty-one, but the spark that caused our hearts to meld together as one on the dance floor has been replaced with fiscal responsibility, parental good judgment, and mutual respect. With an empty house and a fresh perspective, maybe this second life will afford the opportunity to light the fire anew, and allow us to love most the one we loved first. *Venus, if you will, please send a little girl for me to thrill . . .*

—February 1997

The only tangible memory that remains from our weeklong honeymoon is an eight-by-ten photograph of us dining at Caesar's Palace. He was all boyhood hope; I was all bangs and Twiggy-white eyeliner. The last time I saw the two rolls of developed film was when I shared the photos with my sister-in-law more than twenty years ago. There is no good explanation for what became of them.

Night Stalker

IT WAS THAT STILL, black hour just before dawn when the birds are quiet and everyone is in a delicious dead sleep.

My eyes opened abruptly and I glanced at the clock: four-fifty. Why was I awake? Why was my heart pounding, and why did I feel such shock? Then my confusion ebbed, and it became clear and real. There was someone in the hall, scattering papers and tap-tapping his feet on the hardwood floor. My eyes wide open, I could see nothing in the blackness—no great figure of a man wearing a bandit's mask and dropping silver trays into a Santa Claus bag, no gun pointed toward my head.

Nonetheless, he was there—not talking, not visible, but there, walking and rustling my possessions and deciding—yes, deciding—what to take and what to leave, who should live and who should die. My mind raced: Be sensible. Feign sleep. Do not let him know you hear him.

With barely a movement, I poked a long forefinger into the shoulder beside me and whispered, "There's someone in the hall." He listened, motionless, to the scattering of belongings, the scraping of something across the floor, the drum roll of fingers on the wall, and confidently, with masculine finesse, took control.

"Oh, my God," he whispered. "There's someone in the hall."

Like two prisoners about to be thrown to the lions, we shook uncontrollably and mouthed imperceptible orders to one another.

"Don't move," he warned. "Lie still."

"We're going to die," I responded.

"Maybe it's one of the children," he offered.

"Couldn't be. No one's up yet. Oh, my God—the children. Call the police."

"He'll hear me," he reasoned. "Then he'll shoot us for sure. Besides, he's probably cut the phone lines."

Doomed and frozen with fear, we lay there, listening to the rattling and scraping, unable to act, unable to think. No one appeared in the black doorway, no one threw open the drawers to ransack my jewelry box, no one clapped a burly hand over my mouth. Straining to see the clock without moving, I checked the time: five-twenty-four. It would be light soon, and he would leave—with my VCR, electric typewriter, and wedding china—but he would leave, and it would be over.

"Turn on your light," the protector ordered. "Now."

He had snapped. I should turn on my light and then be blown away, blood spattering the wall, headlines reading HUSBAND WITNESSES WIFE DIE IN PREDAWN SHOOTING.

I couldn't take it anymore. I had to confront the ransacker, rescue my sleeping children, and then die. Like a gazelle in the wild, I leaped from the bed, cracking my knee on the nightstand and dashing for the bathroom. Once inside, I slammed and locked the door, leaned against it, and commanded from within, "Get him!"

"You can come out now," a familiar voice responded calmly. "There's nobody here."

I cracked the door and peered out. The lights were on, and no one was bound or gagged. The police had not come, and only a man wearing pajamas and brandishing a needlepoint footstool occupied the scene.

Obviously frightened by the commotion, the intruder, of the animal species, we decided, quieted. Reborn, I threw open the shutters and let the early morning light wash over me. I hadn't died, and my flatware was still in the drawer. I had acted sensibly and won. Whatever the alien, he had guessed who was boss and left.

Or so we thought. Three days later, a rank odor seeped from the closet—a smell of a threatened skunk or a cat litter box that hasn't been emptied in a month. Like the bandit, it wasn't in the closet, and it wasn't in the hall. It was coming from the wall, and it reeked worse with each passing hour. Not only had whatever rodent that dared trespass in our home scared us all into last rites, it had had the nerve to expire in the insulation.

Searching for help, I summoned the good-natured serviceman who came with the house. Sunday morning, eight o'clock: "Hello, Leon?"

"Yes?"

"Something died in the wall, and I think you should come right over and get it out."

Not exactly the stuff of which Sunday morning dreams are made.

"The thing'll dry out pretty soon—three, four days at the most—and you won't smell it anymore," Leon said.

Great. Something to look forward to.

It still spooks me to imagine the tiny, dehydrated carcass, but at least the ordeal made it easy to come up with an answer for a nine-year-old who aimed a poorly timed request in my direction.

"Mom, Michael's gerbil had babies. Please, oh please, can we have one?"

"Who needs another rat?" I answered without hesitation. "We've already got one in the wall."

—April 1986

Shortly after this column appeared, my husband, Steve, tried a case before the Indiana State Tax Court. Presiding Judge Thomas R. Fisher called him before the bench and said, "Scared of mice, huh?" So much for credibility.

Together Forever

MIKE AND LINDA ARE in love. They display it in all the ways you see in movies: She marvels at his lips as he speaks, he gazes at her with bedroom eyes. As she pokes at her entree at a fashionable Northside restaurant, he holds her close, leaving himself only one hand with which to wrestle his bread and pasta. No matter. Food for the soul comes first.

We, too, are present: old folks whose first marriage, it seems likely, will be our last. We feel uncomfortable amidst their quiet giggles, private glances, and caresses of hands. My hand is still held, on occasion, when a patch of ice must be crossed or when dragged down an airport concourse if our departure time looms. Unlike them, whose love is new, we do not gaze lovingly at anything during dinner, except dessert.

Unhappy in his first marriage, Mike has found his second love, a dark-eyed, dark-haired wisp of a woman who is as brilliant a lawyer as she is a beautiful bride-to-be. Before she arrives, he confides that he won her over by finding homes for her grown dogs when she moved, saving her the trauma of having them put to sleep. That explains the pure-breed puppy that awaits her for Christmas, along with the custom-made diamond earrings that will grace her adoring face.

I think of my own holiday request for professional cookware and sigh deeply. Never again will a surprise ring await me in a fortune cookie; nevermore will my heart skip a beat when I hear our special song. In all likelihood, I shall never again enjoy the newness of love, the joys belonging to the second wife.

The dinner show proceeds on course: they the performers on their heavenly stage, we the confused audience, part jealous, part relieved that we can relax, free of the trappings of first impressions. When away from each other for five days, the loving couple hid greeting cards—one for each day, and to announce himself on her beeper, he leaves a secret string of numbers that spell out I LOVE YOU. In their respective homes they held a dinner cook-off, each trying to outdo the other. His consisted of stuffed green peppers at the kitchen table; hers featured a lace tablecloth and candelabra, and no one knows who won.

During the infrequent moments between bites of luscious garlic mashed potatoes and grilled lamb, my husband and I catch one another's eye and go back to our more tangible feast, neither of us knowing if the other would like a divorce so that he or she too can experience such unbounded joy. We each shift imperceptibly in our seats, brushing away such thoughts but wondering about them just the same.

As dinner plates are cleared and the loving couple whispers over the dessert menu, we have time to think. Ironically, we just celebrated our twenty-fifth anniversary (still weeks away at the time of the dinner). We share the same children, who considered a gift of silver but decided instead on a tree sapling for the yard and a cappuccino maker for fireside nights. He does not put tiny, sparkling gifts into my movie popcorn, but he knows where I sit in the theater, even without asking. He does not order for me in French, but if his entree looks better than mine I know he will switch. When a party gets dull, we know how to back out of a room, in perfect synchrony, and head for the car. At school plays and graduations, we bawl in unison, and an "A" on a report card might as well be our own.

Mike and Linda are far from alone. In this age when marriages seem to constantly end and begin, we have seen many find happiness the second time around. A former neighbor left Post-it note love messages on her new spouse's windshield and kept a coffee pot and microwave in their bedroom. Another, smiling broadly with newly capped teeth, shows off his glamorous young spouse at restaurants and parties. And yet another secretly shares late Sunday morning breakfasts at Shapiro's Deli, oblivious to old friends and the drudgery of familiarity.

On the way home, shivering as we waited for the car heater to kick on, I asked him flatly, "Do you wish you were Mike?"

"No," he said simply. "Hell, no."

"Good," I responded, thinking of the two of them nuzzling, eyelashes barely brushing each other's cheek. "I'm too tired, too."

—February 1994

I unexpectedly saw Mike's first wife at an airport just days after this column appeared. Even ravaged by multiple sclerosis and imprisoned by a wheelchair, she appeared beautiful and dignified. I was sorry if I had added to her pain.

Big Night

AFTER TWENTY-EIGHT YEARS of marriage, the man has found a hobby. Thankfully, he never took up golf or other women, and I came to accept the insistent workout regimen and voracious reading, except when I was asked to run the treadmill or benefit from the self-help books myself. But this time was different. At the tender age of fifty, he wanted to learn to cook.

We all have a favorite cuisine, although most of us are content to eat it in a restaurant. His is Italian, translated to mean any combination of tomatoes, garlic, and olive oil. A little veal or scaloppini of chicken doesn't hurt, but most of all he favors pasta. So, for his landmark birthday, his sons dreamed up the gift to end all gifts: Italian cooking lessons with Patrick Aasen, the master chef/proprietor of Arturo's restaurant. Patrick willingly complied, perhaps unaware that he was to become an accessory to a crime.

The ultimate feast began innocently enough at O'Malia's market, the one place this husband of mine was sure he could find the gourmet ingredients necessary to try out what he had learned the day he came home from Arturo's with a song in his heart and garlic on his breath. He had stood at Patrick's elbow, imitating his proficient moves like a little boy learning how to shave. Patrick taught him the art of chopping and dicing, pounding and mixing, leaving his protege drooling with anticipation.

He unpacked the groceries with the skill of a surgeon, setting each precious item on the counter, where he could stare at it longingly as the daytime hours stretched into night. The menu was simple: caprese (sliced tomatoes and fresh buffalo mozzarella drizzled with olive oil and basil), capellini alla puttanesca (thin spaghetti with tomatoes, capers, and calamata olives), ciabatta bread (Italian flat bread from the Lake Como region), salad in a bag with fat-free Caesar dressing, and Diet Coke. Every so often I caught him admiring the can of imported plum tomatoes as if it were a rare jewel, whiling away the remaining hours assembling the necessary ingredients, as well as assorted spoons, skillets, and lids.

The exercise struck me oddly: Here was a man whose culinary accomplishments included coffee so strong it really didn't require a cup, and torn lettuce washed thoroughly enough to satisfy both the soup and salad course. And he was making the leap to a preparer of fine Italian cuisine, nudged on by a chef of local renown. It seemed a bit like a sixteen-year-old being taught to drive by NASCAR superstar Jeff Gordon, but the beauty, I suppose, is not in the skill, but in the dream.

Resonant Italian music began to blare through the stereo speakers as night fell, and there at the sink he stood, draped in a too-small white apron and backward baseball cap. "Why the cap?" I questioned, expecting a hair net like those worn by school cafeteria workers. "Because it's cool," he replied, his voice smooth, his mood mellow, his uniform right. The grinding and chopping began without delay, his movements becoming faster with each new task. I sat silently on a kitchen stool, thinking he might turn into butter, like the tigers in *Little Black Sambo*. As the music swelled ("*Ey mambo, mambo Italiano . . .*"), the cooking became a frantic dance, with him twirling in place, tossing olives in the direction of the pan, and making mad dashes from one side of the unfamiliar territory to the other.

Horror-struck by this unlikely behavior, I couldn't move, much like the time a neighbor's dog charged me, freezing me in my tracks. I was summoned once from my stupor to fish an olive pit out of the garbage disposal, but otherwise left him alone. Imitating his instructor, he smashed garlic with the side of a knife and scraped the skillet furiously on the burner, attempting to flip the tomatoes into the air before being caught and disciplined like a schoolboy. This was definitely a case of style over substance.

Looking like he'd just completed forty minutes on the exercise bike, he finally called me to the table, where I sat uncertainly, fighting not to look in the direction of the tomatoes on the ceiling and bread crumbs in the drawers. Aside from the repetitious nature of the caprese and the pasta puttanesca (What can I say? The man likes tomatoes.) the meal was, well, tolerable. Next time, he assures me, he will drain the beloved can of plum tomatoes, which surely will result in more of a pasta sauce and less of a hot gazpacho. The garlic will be minced into tinier pieces that one will not remember into the following week, and *al dente* will lean a little more toward cooked. Diet dressing, which slides off the lettuce but leaves the aftertaste of library paste, will perhaps be replaced with balsamic vinaigrette, and a nice Merlot will put us all in a better mood for the cleanup.

I keep hoping the novelty will wear off, like that of a kid with a new puppy, but I have glimpsed him eyeing the meat mallet. I know, therefore, that a repeat performance is a certainty. More important than dinner, this is a fulfillment of a promise made to himself as he begins to leave middle age behind: a vow to grow and improve and live life to the fullest. In Gabriel Garcia Marquez' profound novel, *Love in the Time of Cholera*, the Nobel Prize-winning author shares that human beings are not born once-and-for-all on the day their mothers give birth to them, but that life obliges them over and over again to give birth to themselves.

Personally, I'm content to keep doing what I've done so many times before, hoping I'll get better at it. The same age as my husband-turned-chef, I don't long to play the violin or learn to sail. I view life differently than I did even a decade ago, but I hope the rebirth that Marquez so eloquently describes will occur comfortably, while I maintain the day-to-day activities I continue to love. In the meantime, I know my husband will appreciate the gift all wrapped and ready for his fifty-first birthday: a Guy Buffet print of a lovely, fat French chef, entitled *Monsieur Paul*. Besides, Luciano Pavarotti wasn't available to teach opera, and a baby grand piano wouldn't fit through the front door.

—October 1997

To date, the pasta dinner was a one-night stand. Oddly, he speaks of opening an Italian restaurant upon his retirement. The chef remains to be selected.

First Wives Club

WHEN WE ENTERED the restaurant and saw them sitting there, I was instantly struck with the profound notion of the continuum of life. The couple, well into their eighties if not nineties, were sitting on the same side of the booth, leaving the opposing bench empty. It might have been my imagination run wild, but I believe they may even have looked alike, both stooped over their plates, their thin faces and bony hands speckled with the brownish battle scars of age. Her fork danced across his plate, arranging things to suit her, and ultimately, him. And like musicians performing an elegant symphony, they lifted their coffee cups in unison, sipping slightly from the rims.

It was obvious that they'd spent their lifetimes together, so long that one's thought became the other's action. They sat shoulder to shoulder, I surmised, not for the thrill it once provided, but for the comfort and strength it now allowed. I remembered my own parents together sixty years and how their height eventually matched, how her arm fit naturally inside the crook of his. Two little puffs of white hair, my sister would remark as she saw them approach, a poster couple for the marriage vow, "Till death do us part."

Reaching that point is harder now. Resisting temptation is barely even an option, and I've seen all manner of trade-ins. Two times I've witnessed a foursome of best friends in which the husband from one couple and the wife from the other have paired up together. A man I know went back to his high school sweetheart after decades with his wife, and two families were broken forever when an office romance became too torrid to control. Maybe all involved in these scenarios ended up happier, and I'm the one stuck: stuck with the same man I've known since high school, stuck with the sameness of conversation and intimacy, stuck with a daily routine we know by heart.

I am, after all, a card-carrying member of the First Wives Club. We're the ones who put our mates through school, lived in the basement apartment, and gave birth to their babies. For us, there are fewer highs and lows than enjoyed by our counterparts in new relationships, but probably more middles. The younger second and third wives I've observed have bigger diamonds and smaller hips, and no matter how hard we veterans try to tighten our faces and darken our hair, we're still the original models, not as sleek in black capri pants and little Lycra tops. We trade for ease the somber realization that more romance is behind us than in front of us: the way we can be ourselves in worn warm-up suits, eat too much dinner and then groan in bed, replace lengthy conversations with just a nod and a look.

When we are young, we flirt with the idea of starting over, as irritating habits and differing opinions drive us crazy. All that history makes us more accepting, however, and settles us more deeply into the grooves our bodies have worn in the mattress. I'm not so far gone as to ask him to carry my purse in the mall, but I do notice we say, "Huh?" more often and read each others' menus when bifocals are forgotten. Unlike our friends in the Second Wives Club, when we talk of times per week, it's *Seinfeld* reruns to which we refer, and he knows when I'm hot, I've forgotten my estrogen tablet again.

On a recent business trip a good male friend also in a long marriage asked me some leading questions. Do I regret having been with only one man? Do I wonder if I'm still attractive? (When you're over fifty, the term "still" always precedes "attractive," like asking if the moldy cheese in the refrigerator is "still" good.) Would I behave more boldly with a new man? Yes, on all counts. But as mature adults, we don't act on our temptations for the same reason we don't gobble up a batch of potato chips in a fit of hunger. We recognize the cause, but we fear the effect. A diversion would feed our ego but starve us of our self-respect.

A woman I like is now with one of our old friends, long since divorced. At a recent get-together, she confided that he advised her only slightly kiddingly that her butt was falling. A sharp retort quickly followed, but I'm sure she looked over her shoulder to assess the damage. Now, my husband knows that if he ever brought such a thing to my attention, I'd make Lorena Bobbitt look like a rank amateur, but that isn't why he'd never say it. It wouldn't come up because it's not what brought us together in the first place. I was attracted to his calmness and warmth, and he to my spirit and energy. If we're declining physically, either neither of us notices or neither of us cares. Soul mates rely on each other's souls, which is how it should be. In his best-selling novel *A Man in Full,* author Tom Wolfe describes a first wife as someone who marries you for better or for worse, and a second wife as somebody who marries you for better. Maybe for all us old-timers, all those years of worse make us appreciate the better.

Life isn't as exciting as it could be, but I'll happily trade that for the knowledge that he'll still want to sit beside me when I'm eighty, with nothing left of my butt at all. Even then, we'll remember how we danced the stroll as teens, watched *Our Miss Brooks*, and swooned when Dean Martin sang "You're Nobody Till Somebody Loves You." And I guess that beats wondering if the guy who left his first wife would leave you, too.

—April 1999

Vanity

What would Botticelli and Rubens think, to know that the artistic swell of a woman, that glorious curve adorning the world's most cherished masterpieces, has been rendered obsolete?

Keeping Abreast

THEY HAVE DISCONTINUED my bra. It is the bra I have worn for twenty years, comfortable all over and lacy in the right places. As with many bras of its generation, adjustable slides adorn its satiny straps, and double hooks fasten in one of three options in the back. That bra was something I didn't have to think about, along with who cuts my hair and what doctor I see. In more ways than one, it was my support.

Frantic at my inability to replace the few shabby ones left in my drawer, I stormed in and out of intimate apparel departments, demanding to know why the display had been removed. No more pretty options in white, blush, and black dangled from their little plastic hangers, twice-yearly sales treating me to one free for every two I purchased. In their place hung stiff replacements with hard underwire cups, unfriendly demons that threatened to poke and dig, ruining my mood along with my rib cage.

I surfed the Internet in obscure places, hoping against hope to find a stash of them boxed up at some online lingerie shop like so many Princess Diana books at Amazon.com. I spent thirty-three dollars in Chicago hotel room charges calling nearby factory outlets, and, in desperation, dug through a bin of leftovers at Filene's Basement like a stray dog rooting through the trash. There I found all manner of shiny purple contraptions nobody wanted, as well as a red velvet number with gold braided trim, like one of those pillows on which only a poodle will perch.

And then, frustrated and exhausted, I broke down and called Olga. Only there is no Olga, just some conglomerate that owns and markets designer clothing along with its female foundations. The representative was kind but firm: The bra had gone out of style because, apparently, no one wants a pretty, natural slope to her breasts anymore. "Soft cups," as they are known, have given way to underwires: hard, metal curves like an lopsided letter "c," unyielding bases that round, uplift, and allow mounds of bosom to cascade over the bra's demi tops, reducing us to the likes of serving wenches in *Taming of the Shrew*. In the year 2000, something as classic and revered as the shape of a woman's breast has been redefined. What would Botticelli and Rubens think, to know that the artistic swell of a woman, that glorious curve adorning the world's most cherished masterpieces, has been rendered obsolete? Gravity and the obsession with surgically augmented breasts have caused styles to change. Now, women want softballs under their sweaters, and underwires—those chastity belts for the chest—will oblige.

On one level, I haven't given up. In my drawer now are five or six new styles, some worn only once before I pulled them out of my sleeve in misery, sometimes stomping on them dramatically before I threw them away. On another level, I am in mourning: grieving that as we face the new millennium, a whole generation of us is going out of style along with our breasts. We are certain to become tourists in the next century, interlopers who look on from the sidelines, old women clinging to their soft-cup bras while a new citizenry populates the planet and decides that we read Harry Potter books, watch *Buffy the Vampire Slayer*, and wear midriff tops and skirts below our knees. Perhaps those of us who will face old age in the early part of the next millennium will be reduced to laughingstocks, like the bespectacled fashion diva in the Old Navy commercials, an anachronism turned into a prop.

My father was born in 1900 to a mother who would have seven children and only two burners on her stove. As she stacked pots one on top of another, he sold newspapers on the corner at the age of five, rode a streetcar to Indianapolis Traction Terminal to carry rich men's bags for a nickel tip, and gave up his high school education for the shallower rewards of the workplace. The letters he left behind proved not just his talent, but his genius, and we, his sons and daughters, heard but didn't listen to his stories, concentrating instead on our transistor radios, princess telephones, and color TVs. I knew that he completed his schoolwork on a pickle barrel and that his father drove a milk wagon over cobblestone streets, but I had no use for such reminiscences. We probably regarded him the way the seventeen-year-old salesgirls in Victoria's Secret view me, someone too mature for the merchandise, boring another generation with what-used-to-be's.

The older one gets, the more effort is required to stay current. It is easier to slip into our comfortable ways, using such passe terms as "charge-a-plates" and "icebox," and sauteeing salmon croquettes instead of grilling sea bass. While recently evaluating a photographic composite of a male model in contention for a magazine cover, I described him as a "smokin' hottie." Even though that was the preferred term, the group looked at me as if Howdy Doody had just spewed the "F" word at Clarabell. Sometimes it is better to maintain the dignity of one's years, even in the face of contemporary culture.

I'm lucky to have five great-nieces and nephews, the youngest of whom, Abby, slipped in just before the end of the century. When I look at her adorable face, her brows raised with curiosity above quizzical dark eyes, I wonder what her century will provide. She giggles at my vocal rendition of "Six Little Ducks," but when she is old enough to talk, she'll probably reject it as old-fashioned, like me. I am an intruder in her millennium, and she will doubtless dismiss my wisdom as out of date. Our generation will fade in her eyes the way the white-haired workforce is all but absent on city streets, overtaken by twentysomethings in black Lycra skirts, buzzing about branding, while pressing double mocha lattes in cardboard cups inside their fists.

Anyway, I'm not alone. Even my cat, Woody, the old, furry girl, knows what it's like to be left in the dust. At about the same time the cruel retail forces changed society's perception of the female form, the cat food companies stopped making her ocean whitefish and tuna dinners, the kind she has enjoyed since kittenhood. As I dumped newfangled sliced chicken and gravy out of a resealable pouch, she stared into her bowl with disappointment and disbelief. How do I explain to her that no one cares what an old cat wants, that younger cats prefer their food another way? We both have experienced our millennium metaphors, even if only one of us understands what lies ahead.

In the end, I just want to enjoy as much of the next thousand years as I can, and conceal my obsolescence the way our generation has stained the roots of its hair. I must contend with the fact that the very essence of breasts is no longer in vogue, and shape myself to conform to the times.

—December 1999

As an aftermath of this column, I received a call from the manager of an Olga factory outlet store, offering to locate the remaining bras. A nationwide plea resulted in my receiving twenty-six leftover bras,

21

eighteen blush-colored, eight white. I was embarrassed only once, when my assistant, Brad, opened the package and draped the contents over my desk chair.

Face Value

EMMA, AN INTELLIGENT professional woman whom I trust and admire, recently shared a story about having run into an old friend who confided that she needed to talk. The friend, it seems, had made an important discovery, which Emma assumed must have been at the very least metaphysical. But when the meeting took place, the subject was hardly profound. She had discovered a great new skin cream that really *did* diminish the appearance of lines and wrinkles. "Colored Vaseline," Emma shrugged, disappointed as much in the product as the supposed epiphany.

Even among learned women, women of valor, sisterhood pioneers, it keeps coming down to wrinkles. At a recent fiftieth birthday party for an old friend, I experienced a rare and uncomfortable inability to find anyone with whom to share a conversation. Every cluster of lovely women seemed immersed in the subject of cosmetic surgery: who was getting what "done," and how good or bad they looked after. Having no interest in nips and tucks, I skittered about the restaurant wishing for somewhere to light. Finally, I hightailed it for the door, exasperated by the old high school feeling of unpopularity, and fitting in about as well as Bob Knight at a baby shower.

On the way back to my office, I comforted myself that I really hadn't lost touch with my gender, I just like my face the way it is. Over an alarmingly short period, I've watched numerous friends and acquaintances change before my eyes, as they clip their noses more dramatically than their hair, tug their eyelids up into their brows, and hide face-lift staples in their scalps. Soft necks that should age gently into Katharine Hepburn turtlenecks are stretched like canvas over a tent pole, and hips that once spilled generously into the next larger size are sucked into liposuction tubes and squeezed into jeans better suited for twenty-one-year-olds at a singles bar.

Like most woman, I have experimented in my makeup mirror, pulling my cheeks toward my ears and raising my eyebrows in mock surprise. I have coaxed the skin on my neck downward into my collar and practiced walking with my head tilted upward, like the QTπ girls in high school, in whose sorority I did not belong. Fearing that I will resemble Carol Channing—or worse yet, Rich Little impersonating Carol Channing—I succumb to gravity and consider filling my head instead of the crevices that have formed on my face.

This spirit of nonconformity will doubtless cause me to stand out in wrinkled splendor, but I am not totally alone. An ally assures our counterparts that she will exist as their portrait of Dorian Gray, deteriorating in age as they travel the time line in the opposite direction. In less literary moments, however, both of us admit that we're chicken: Anyone who has experienced surgery can relate to the sick feeling of unprotected skin against the cold steel side of a gurney, or the dreaded approach of the anesthesiologist. Some mornings, half awake in that gray space at dawn, when I collect my jumbled thoughts and consider the unsavory tasks that lie ahead, I console myself that at least I'm not scheduled for surgery at seven A.M.

In a recent newspaper ad a golfer boasts an improvement in his game now that eye surgery has eliminated his need for glasses. "Come view a live laser surgery," the ad reads, a prospect less inviting to me than, say, digging up earthworms. Probably the only thing worse than having surgery is watching it, and I decide instead to consider the Weber grill demonstration advertised at Sullivan hardware.

Braver souls might be tempted by the promise of new beauty, but I'd rather leave well enough alone. Like accumulating wealth, the more you have, the more you want, and today's eye lift can too easily become tomorrow's full-body liposuction. A model I know had Gore-Tex strips threaded into her lips twice before she felt beautiful enough, later adding large breast implants to her delicate frame. To be fair, many women look ravishing after surgery, like a former college classmate who in her early fifties looks different but probably prettier than before. Knowing my luck, however, I'd resemble those too-old Palm Beach women with skin pulled tautly over their hard cheekbones, the excess falling into crepey bundles on either side of their mouths like the puddled drapes on my living room floor.

A new flap that suddenly appeared over my left eye the day after my fiftieth birthday provoked a call to beauty maven Mary Miller, the luscious-lipped, creamy-skinned proprietor of the spa/salon David & Mary. Her usual advice to wear a lighter shade of foundation, sparingly adding color and using that makeup sponge to blend, blend, blend didn't compare to her overall perception of the aging process. "Aren't you prettier than you were ten years ago?" she asked, to which I flatly replied, "No." Arguing my response, she confided that even with her new sags and bags, she treats people better the older she gets, and finds a greater sense of self-respect. "I have more confidence and a real sense of style," she admitted, "and I don't make the same mistakes I made twenty years ago." From a woman who makes her living selling goods and services for our outsides, I was heartened by her attention to what lies within.

I once spent seventy-five dollars on a skin cream made from the placenta of sheep, and aside from a thinner wallet, saw no discernible results. Since that day, I have vowed to accept who I am and, as Miller advises, decide what I'm going to bring to these next twenty years. I understand how frightening it is to watch yourself become someone else in the mirror, but even when we mess with Mother Nature, we won't ever turn into what we were. Too often, we become like photocopies made from photocopies, losing our detail and our identity. Julie Andrews doesn't look like Julie Andrews anymore, and even with her expertly crafted face, Mary Tyler Moore will never be the giddy, young TV housewife we once adored. Like it or not, we become different people even if we don't accomplish it surgically. As Miller says: "Getting older isn't the end of the world. Let's age beautifully."

—June 1997

Black by Popular Demand

It was on Rush Street in Chicago that I learned the importance of wearing black. In the city for a getaway weekend, we stood outside a trendy restaurant awaiting a table when I saw her: my old friend Susan. She stood a few feet away, talking excitedly, waving her hands with every exclamation. All at once our eyes met, and, almost imperceptibly, we gave each other the once-over. After all, it had been at least ten years, and we needed to know if time had treated us well.

She was wearing a black, skintight velour top; black silky slacks; a narrow black belt; black hose; chunky black suede shoes; and a black nylon backpack slung over one shoulder. Her obviously colored, dramatic auburn hair and pale makeup made the look complete. As if in slow motion, we approached one another, and I couldn't help but catch the horror in her eyes. Her once-with-it pal from Indiana was dressed in a pale blue tunic-length sweater trimmed in white and paired with white knit slacks and matching white sandals (well, it was summer). I looked like a seed corn salesman.

As I searched for the nearest available manhole to serve as an escape hatch, I realized the error of my ways. In a big city, you wear black. Always. Without exception. In entirety. The hipper the locale, the more black you wear; it is a proven mathematical equation. Since then, I have paid closer attention to the fashion mantra, and I like what I see. Women look better in black: slimmer, smarter, sharper. And after you get used to wearing it, anything else makes you feel like Mimi, the gaudy clown-like secretary on *The Drew Carey Show.*

These days I could attend a funeral at the drop of a hat, and my closet is beginning to look like the backstage wardrobe room for *La Dolce Vita.* Every pair of shoes and handbag I own is black, as well as most of my suits, slacks, and dresses. Considering the lack of variety, my coworkers probably think I never change my clothes. A lovely turquoise suit I bought last spring was worn exactly once, and I felt like a Kewpie doll the entire day.

According to Beverly Rice, Jacobson's senior vice president of fashion and merchandising strategy, I'm not alone. Black is camouflage, she says, meaning it in a good way. It's safe and comfortable, flattering and functional. Like our etiquette instructors once taught us, it goes easily from day to night with the addition of a simple strand of pearls.

As for my turquoise suit, Rice says I jumped in too suddenly, resulting in culture shock. To get out of the black syndrome, she advises, you ought to start by throwing in some colorful accessories, and then eventually emerge from the black addiction like a peacock. That sounds like a twelve-step program to me, a warning against any sudden moves. Though her advice is legitimate, I'm not sure I want to act like a heroin addict. Since most stylish black outfits are worn bare-legged, maybe our spider veins can add the "pop" of color fashion experts suggest.

In fact, it isn't just fashion-conscious women who are parading around city streets and cocktail parties in black. It has extended to bridesmaids, little girls in party dresses, and teenagers at the prom. For that landmark event decades ago, I wore a floor-length white chiffon dress with see-through sleeves. A perfect viney yellow flower wound its way from hem to waist, where it delicately disappeared into the sheer, square-necked bodice. A dreamy inscription in my high school yearbook from Rick Tucker, a boy I secretly adored, read, "I'll never forget how you looked at the prom." I doubt that I would have made such an impression had I looked like every other black-garbed vixen in the gym.

Rice, who hopes we don't start dressing our infants and toddlers in black, expresses a theory on the trend that extends even deeper. She thinks maybe it's a respite from all the violence and noise we're exposed to in TV and movies. It makes us quieter, less aggravated. Black, she says, doesn't shout. The person has to come through.

Maybe there's something to that. When we're garbed entirely in black, what begins to count are our faces, our attitudes, even our sensuality. In Europe, women in black slink along busy streets, their formfitting blouses left open to reveal just a hint of black lace demibra, their clinging slacks showing only the line of thong underwear. Shape, not color, becomes important, and sexiness is inherent. There, much of black is satin or lace, so it doesn't cover as much as it reveals, like the best sexy scenes in movies. What's left to the imagination is almost universally better than the real thing.

Expression takes on new importance, too, so that even if your color never changes, your mood can. You convey who you are with what you say, and what your feelings say, without a word being uttered. More crassly, maybe that's why the whiteness of our teeth has taken on such importance: The contrast is our only means of decoration.

Sometimes I wonder if this absolute trend toward black is a step backward on our evolutionary path, but maybe I'm thinking too hard about it. Perhaps eventually we'll go back to colorless animal skins, every now and then flashing a sinewy thigh to attract the male of the species.

After all, hasn't the same thing occurred with cars? In my teenage years, a bright yellow Trans Am or a turquoise T-bird showed everyone on the road who was boss. Now most new cars are silver or champagne, with an occasional black or wine-colored one leaving the showrooms. Like their drivers in black, automobiles are forced into fancy taillights, intricate computer systems, and soft interiors to proclaim their individuality.

Or maybe all this is just so much empty philosophizing. Diane Abdellah, Jacobson's regional public relations and special events manager, a knockout herself who wears black day-in and day-out, has a more practical explanation. "The other day I wore a yellow suit, and sure, I got lots of compliments," she shares. "But like every time I wear a light color, I got stuff all over myself. Black is better; it hides the dirt."

—December 1997

Never Say Diet

IT'S FINAL. TOMORROW I start my diet. It's one thing to expand to Zsa Zsa Gabor proportions, but it's another to fixate on food every waking moment.

As a kid, I never really cared much for food. When God passed out moms, however, he gave me one who whiled away what little spare time she had making raspberry-filled, twenty-four-layer French pastry; daily home-baked fruit pies; and fat, hand-cut french fries that sizzled cheerfully in bubbling pots of cooking oil. While everyone in the house was remarkably satisfied with all this, no one got fat. It was a miracle.

Actually, if the truth be told, I can't name one item I really liked. It was all just there like so much homework waiting to be done. I endured a lifetime of nagging by outsiders: How could I stay so thin? Didn't I have to watch my weight? The fact was, I wasn't ever hungry.

In a foolhardy attempt to fatten me up, they ganged up on me with tall, chilled glasses of chocolate milk, peanut butter and jelly sandwiches without their crusts, bags of potato chips at every turn. Since restaurant-grilled hamburgers caught my fancy, they picked me up from school at noon, delivered me to the nearest Borky's or the Huddle restaurant, and watched like Cheshire cats as I nibbled quarter-pound hamburgers or broasted chicken.

At one point, fearing for my very life, a camp director actually phoned home to report that after a six-day stay no one had seen me eat anything and wouldn't they please come for me? Like I said before, it was nothing to get alarmed about: I simply wasn't hungry.

I am now, and in revenge, the cleaners have shrunk all my clothes. It's hard for those who knew me then to fathom. Is this adult person seen sniffing around church fish fries and walking whole city blocks out of her way on the scent of onion rings the same kid who turned up her nose at warm apple pie? Before I even get to work, the temptation of my sack lunch on the car seat beside me is simply too much, and I've been known to disassemble the entire thing before eight.

I have to reacquaint myself with this evil twin who goes to movies she doesn't even like just for the popcorn or sets the office record by spending fourteen dollars on a lunch of prime rib and creamed corn. Who is this vagabond who stalks the office hallways at ten forty-five A.M. for some other loon already hungry for lunch? And, like the cleaners, they're all torturing me, albeit with chocolate-covered Oreos, white birthday cakes, bags of M&Ms, and morning doughnut runs.

But with the present metabolism of a steamroller, I respectfully decline. I'm not taking this expanding girth sitting down. A national health columnist recently decreed that if a person maintained his diet but walked two miles a day, he'd lose fourteen pounds a year, and I'm holding him to his word. If I leave tomorrow, I figure, I'll be in Duluth sometime before Thanksgiving.

I don't discourage easily either. On a recent weekend I walked eleven miles and ate nothing but ice cubes and rice cakes, which, to the uninitiated, are glued-together puffed rice patties that sound and taste like a Big Mac box, and gained two pounds. I'll lick this thing, though I'd rather do the same to a nice, melty scoop of mint chocolate chip.

My greatest fear, actually, is that my mother-in-law, who is partial to cheese puffs and half-pound Hershey bars herself, will assail me the way some of the relatives have come to expect. "Look at *her,*" she's known to say in something between a whisper and an out-and-out bellow. "Didn't she get *fat?*" No thanks, I'll pass on the extra serving of cornies.

You can have your fancy chain store diets, however, plus weigh-ins, ketosis programs, and phony milkshakes for breakfast. My own self-designed plan—the eat-everything-you-want-minus-the-Honey-Smacks-before-bed diet—will serve me fine.

Just wait. My cronies at lunch, not to mention those pessimistic camp counselors, won't even know me.

—September 1989

After blossoming to a curvaceous hundred and twenty-one pounds, I cut down on fat and began a stringent exercise program of treadmill walking and weight training. I now weigh in at a more comfortable ninety-eight pounds, which better fits my five-foot frame. The customers at the Junior League Next-to-New Shop expressed gratitude for all the size six and eight clothes that suddenly appeared.

Grille of My Dreams

"THAT YOUR JAG?"

The two men stood over my car in the parking lot, stroking the hood as if it were the bare shoulder of a seductive woman. They were surprised to see me, I know, expecting instead Pierce Brosnan or Elizabeth Hurley: someone deserving of such a sleek, futuristic ride, but hardly a middle-aged woman emerging from LensCrafters with a new pair of bifocals in a bag.

In a moment of weakness, I leased a shiny silver 2000 Jaguar S-Type, a new model boasting the retro-cool design of the 1960 Mark 2 sedan. I am known to buy things when I am depressed, frustrated, neurotic, or semi-delusional, but I generally don't commit $43,095 over a three-year period. The distinctive oval grille and angled headlights spoke to me, however, as they burst forth from the center of the newspaper's stock page, and they didn't say, "Hi," like a Dodge Neon. They said, "We're hot. Are you?"

Well, not really, but tell that to the two guys in the parking lot who by now were shading their eyes against the late afternoon sun, peering intently into the car's interior. Men are attracted to this car, I have come to find out, like they are to barbecue grills and the remote control. My front end has commanded very little attention in the past, but in the six months I have driven the car, I have become a head-turner. Men in opposing lanes give me the thumbs-up. Men on sidewalks spin around in their tracks to get a second look. Two male pedestrians once dodged traffic to gawk, and even teenagers too cool to acknowledge anyone over eighteen now nod in approval as I pass them on the street. When we drove to Ritter's Frozen Custard for an after-dinner treat, I returned to find a crowd encircling my car as if it were a lion exhibit at the zoo when the feral cat finally awakens. If my windows are down, I hear low whistles as I drive past, and strangers (read: men) boldly approach me at gas pumps and in parking lots. This is what Dolly Parton must feel like, only without the car.

When asked by the two gentlemen at the strip mall if the car were mine,

I almost hated to say yes. I had a sudden flashback to a shower in the college dorm, my scalp covered with shampoo. "It's Eddie Berebitsky!" shrieked a dormmate over the sound of running water. "Eddie Berebitsky's on the phone!" I hadn't just fallen off the turnip truck and was aware of the college ploy, during which a naked girl streaks down the hall and careens into her room to the flash of Polaroid cameras. But this time it was true. The hottest Fonz-like creature on campus—having heard that two fraternity pledges each claimed to be my boyfriend—was asking me for a date, sight unseen. I'll never forget the look on his face as I emerged from the elevator, bedecked in my A-line skirt and matching cardigan sweater, knee socks and headband. Suffice it to say he was expecting Goldie Hawn, someone deserving of two boyfriends. But what he got was Ruth Buzzi, and he expressed his displeasure with a grunt, then waved his car keys before my face and commenced the date, which consisted of driving around for thirty minutes and finally hitting the drive-thru window of Frisch's Big Boy for strawberry pie, which we consumed on the way back. Sometimes expectation exceeds reality.

As luck would have it, I'm the one driving the car with the pouncing chrome Jaguar perched on the hood like a bare-breasted nymph on the bow of a ship. Like the way we dress, our cars tend to reflect who we are or wish we were. Consider Marie, a former art director who lived a hippie-like life on White River in a little green-painted shack that tilted ominously toward the water. When the river flooded, she mopped. She cooked in a toaster oven and rarely wore shoes. I remember her driving with all the windows open, wearing a gauzy, transparent dress that billowed between her legs as the wind whipped through the rusted-out car. The seats and floor were littered with soft drink cans, audio tapes, notebooks, magazines, and leftover lunch bags. The car was not just an extension of her house, it was an extension of her soul.

The most distinctive car I owned prior to this one was a used 1963 Ford Falcon convertible that had been dredged from the Indianapolis Water Company canal. Once I got past the smell of rotting carp, driving it made me feel as free as the hair blowing around my face. More up-to-date, my '64 Chevy Impala Super Sport featured trendsetting bucket seats that were stolen right out of the car as I sat in Mrs. Obenchain's English class and it sat in the Broad Ripple High School parking lot. My brother perched on a paint can as he drove home, his sorry passenger weeping and hiding her face in the backseat, the only one left. That time, I lost my seats and found fame on the front page of the school paper.

Much as we might like to deny it, our cars define us. That same brother, still macho at sixty-two, has always driven rugged SUVs and pickups, which identify him as much as his cowboy boots and T-shirt that says STILL PLAYS WITH TRUCKS. I dated Tommy Prager because he had a Triumph TR4 convertible, and something about his hand vibrating on the four-on-the-floor, in total control of that speeding, growling beast, made him cool, even though he wasn't. Nor would Donald Trump seem as powerful stepping out of a Buick Skylark as he does exiting a stretch limousine.

When I purchased the car, a salesman sagely advised that you buy a Jaguar with your heart, not your head. "Do you have romance in your soul?" he asked at the critical moment.

"No," I flatly replied, removing his unwanted hand from my shoulder. "Do you have gas in the tank?"

Maybe my practicality precludes such car ownership, but who cares? So I'm not full of spirited elegance, sensuality, and originality like the car they describe in the full-color brochure. I guess that's why I like it. We must constantly reinvent ourselves or stagnate in our complacency like lazy frogs in a bog. We have to try on someone else for size every once in a while to see if we like her better. Seated on the ivory leather seat, behind her bird's-eye maple steering wheel, looking out over the metallic molded hood, the new girl feels pretty good.

—February 2000

Because I am too short to see over the side mirrors, I'm somewhat dangerous at four-way stops. The mirrors are positioned perfectly, however, for effective makeup application.

Hair Today

I ACCIDENTALLY SET my hair on fire the other night while cooking marinated chicken breasts on the outdoor grill. Supercharged by great globs of oily Italian dressing, the flames rose up in a whoosh, sending me (and my smoking bangs) shrieking to the sink.

Save a few fried ends, nothing much happened, although totaling my entire three-pound mass of uncontrollable tresses probably would have been a blessing. See, right now I'm between a bad short haircut and a bad long one: that never-never land where every morning becomes a battlefield of blow dryer and brush.

Time moves slowly while hair grows, just as it did when you had an unwanted perm in grade school and walked around for six weeks looking like Little Orphant Annie. Naturally, I'm not blessed with shiny, straight hair or curls. What I have resembles wrinkles, and if not attacked promptly after shampooing, it looks creased—like a cotton shirt left in the dryer too long.

Frustrated and carried away by visions of Demi Moore or Julia Roberts or some trend I had read about in USA Today, I had myself shorn one evening after work. Actually, it looked spiffy at first, although as it grew out in front I began to sport a hank of hair that fell over my eyes without provocation, prompting onlookers to wonder if anyone was behind it. Funny thing, when Julia Roberts flops an unkempt piece across her forehead, she looks sexy and chic. The same look transforms me into Benji the Hunted.

So much for short hair, which, by the calendar, is a long way from long hair. The problem is compounded by the fact that anyone topped by thick, unruly hair knows that it grows out but rarely down: Gravity does not apply. Scorned by a gentleman in our office who regularly has neat rows of hairs (he counts them singularly) transplanted in vacant areas near his forehead, I maintain that too much hair is just as much a curse as not enough. While I maneuver a thick-toothed comb through my incessant tangle, he pats his wisp lightly into place. "Tumbleweed Head," we've come to call him, in honor of a terminally bald cartoon character awaiting a stiff breeze and an occasional tumbleweed to pass overhead. My son, who has inherited the immovable mass, wondered as a lad why, when hanging by his heels from the jungle gym, his hair did not join him in his upside-down state. Not sprayed or teased, our helmets of hair are naturally Scotchgarded, I tell him, keeping us neat in appearance even around helicopters or hurricanes.

Unfortunately, during its growing-out stage, an increasing number of gray hairs have become obvious. More like fishing line than hair, they obey no rules, poking their ugly selves in the wrong direction no matter the style.

Fearful of looking like Walter Matthau, I'll pass on a dye job—but I wonder if Grecian Formula 44 is everything it's cracked up to be.

What I really long for is a signature style, like that of Dorothy Hamill or Elvira: a hairdo everyone associates with me. I'd never have to hunt down new stylists, and I'd never cut it off or let it grow. To get to that point, however, I have only two choices: wait out this interminable in-between stage or, armed with a sixteen-ounce spray bottle of Pam, head for the grill.

—April 1991

Dress for Distress

IF I DON'T HAVE any new clothes this season, there's a darn good reason why. I'm boycotting linen, that permanently creased, stiff-but-sloppy fabric that never should have advanced beyond tablecloths and hankies.

I made the mistake last year, ordering a crisp blue linen skirt and blouse from a spring catalogue. When I wore it to the office for the first time, I was greeted by our art director (self-imposed head of our internal "style council"), who asked politely if I had slept in my car on the off-ramp of the interstate. Fact was, I really couldn't argue with him. Sporting a collection of horizontal and vertical lines in the front and a shirttail creased upward to resemble a duck's tail in back, I was a sorry sight. Stooped over the ironing board before every subsequent appearance, I finally gave up. It was a losing battle, and I hope whoever finds it at the Goodwill store looks better in it than I did.

The sorriest aspect of this whole linen craze is that for some un-explainable reason, the stores are proud of it. Rack after rack of bright linen blazers and walking shorts, natural color dresses and crisp white suits all sport the proclamation: 100 PERCENT LINEN! Is this a good thing? To this shopper, it means 100 percent wrinkles. For mass appeal, why not just advertise an entire display as EXPENSIVE! or CUTE, BUT NOT WORTH IT!

In my search for the proper slouchy look without the accompanying disarray I weed out the 100 percent linen in favor of blends. Give me a little rayon mixed in for neatness, or better yet, acrylic. Some fabrics, undoubtedly petroleum-based, throw me. Take ramie, for example. Is it better than linen, like spandex, or worse, like burlap? Cruising a display of summer outfits the other day, I happened upon one bearing the tag, 100 percent Algodon. Although it looked and felt like cotton, it doubtless doesn't breathe, trapping its wearer like a Ziploc bag on a sweltering July day.

Aside from not buying linen, I'm not sure I trust anyone else who wears it, either. If they're not as crumpled as me, they must lean up against a wall all day, like Bette Davis before an appearance in a tight evening gown. And if a man wears it, I have even less patience. A close friend who lives in L.A. recently introduced me to her new significant other, a man some thirty years her senior who was dressed in a purple linen shirt (with open collar to expose the gold chain and medallion), off-white linen slacks, and matching linen slip-on shoes. He talked with a heavy New York accent and kept taking our picture with a fancy Nikon camera. For some reason, all I could envision were linen underwear and socks.

Our managing editor, who admits that he doesn't know linen from Lenin, reports rising from his chair with a map of Asia imprinted on the back of his sport coat, reason enough to bag the natural look in favor of polyester.

Those in the clothing industry try to convince us that linen is *supposed* to look wrinkled; it adds to the charm. Gatsbylike, we're supposed to sit on wrought-iron furniture out on a rolling lawn, fanning ourselves gently and wilting ever so slightly as the humidity rises. That's the same pitch used to sell soft, beautiful Coach bags and wallets. Vulnerable to the elements, the supple, uncoated leather improves as it weathers, they claim. As luck would have it, I spilled salad dressing on mine in 1988 and it's still spreading.

A Buckingham Palace spokesman recently stated that Elizabeth II, by virtue of her position, simply must be exempted from England's mandatory seat belt law. "The Queen," the quote read, "really cannot arrive at a public function in a crumpled outfit." We don't want to arrive at work looking like we spent the night at Motel 6, either. Seat belt-crunched or not, we're not giving in to linen. I suspect that if I dig far enough back in my closet I might even be able to find my first double-knit polyester pantsuit that probably looks as good now as it did in 1969. Sure, it won't break down in a landfill, but who cares? Looks, as our style council dictates, are everything.

—June 1993

Lady MacBath

*Warning: The following column contains brief
nudity and adult content.*

AS LEISURE ACTIVITY goes, I knew I had reached rock bottom as I stood
with a woven basket over my arm, picking through piles of juniper berry-
scented soaps, lotions, and body scrubs at the gingham-themed bath store at
the mall. The retailing ploy had worked, the fake fragrances and little-girl
colors beckoning me like the sirens calling to Odysseus. And so I shopped,
shoulder-to-shoulder with all the giddy fourteen-year-olds whose mothers
promised to pick them up before dinner, falling for the buy-one-get-one-
free gimmick. On a day when I was feeling particularly vulnerable, I spent
sixty-five dollars and required a valet to squire my bags to the car.

I don't know if my new addiction to the bath store—but more
importantly, the bath itself—is because of the recent spate of retailing or in
spite of it. I don't generally embrace fads, especially those not aimed at my
demographic. You won't catch me in capri pants or black sandals with
rubber platforms the size of tractor tires. But a time-honored bath removes
you from the grind that makes you hunch up your shoulders around your
ears and fret. A shower is certainly serviceable enough, but it is a symphony
played without violins.

Even though my husband doesn't share my enthusiasm for the tub,
he—a non-shopper of the first order—can be found at the mall dangling a
mini-shopping bag from his own fingertips. Buried in a nest of pastel tissue
paper will lie one bar of soap, always manly, never with frou-frou names like
Passion Fruit or Pear Glace. The ones he buys are usually transparent and
amber in color, with no fragrance at all, or brown and studded with
particulate matter. If you use this variety without a washcloth, you will look
like you have been flogged in an Indonesian prison. Once he brought home
a black bar that more resembled driveway sealer than mystery mud from the
Dead Sea, as its packaging promised. I didn't chance it.

In our master bathroom, I am fortunate enough to have a whirlpool
tub; however, because of my size-two frame, it mostly goes unused, lest I be
buffeted about like a bluegill. I prefer the old-fashioned bath, the kind
where you squeeze the last blob out of your plastic bottle of bubble bath,

step into the steaming water, and ease down like batter poured into a cake pan. The water need not cause a Fred Sanford-style heart attack, and there should be sufficient bubbles to perform imaginary breast augmentation, leaving a few to cling when you emerge.

As you recline in the silky water, you can think, but it's better not to. It's most therapeutic to let your arms bob to the surface and float, still and limp. You should descend just until you can blow a thin stream of bubbles from your lips, but no deeper, lest relaxation turn to drowning, at which point the entire exercise will have been in vain. It is important not to worry in the bathtub, about work or kids or that funny pain you should probably tell somebody about. To reach its full potential, a bath must be reserved for vacating the brain of trouble, much as you would separate an egg yolk from a white when baking a cake. I had a friend who, after suffering a miscarriage, climbed into her bed and retreated under the covers for a week. Once, when I was delivered some bad news while in the tub, I held my nose and submerged myself temporarily to find the proper aloneness. I didn't stay under for a week, but the solitude—however brief—was comforting.

A really good bath requires no outside diversion, least of all a magazine or book. I long ago abandoned the reading policy in the bathtub, mainly because it interrupted the peace process, but also because turning pages with wet hands makes one's paperback novel swell up like Liz Taylor after detox. Just lately I stopped thinking altogether in there, although I am responsible for a little bad poetry, and, on a melancholy day, one line of a country song that goes, "When you cry in the bathtub, your tears wash away." The rest of the lyrics escape me, but I have hope.

Characters like *Dennis the Menace* have given the bath a bad name. I can remember liking it even as a kid, when I would stare up at the glass-block wall that separated the tub from the commode, imagining goldfish in every block, baby sisters that didn't come, stories I thought of but never wrote. In general, too many moms make baths a punishment for all the wrongs that little boys commit in dirty backyards, scrubbing behind ears until the skin shines angry red, muttering and mopping their own sweaty brows, using long nails to lather tender scalps. Luckily, I was trusted to the task myself, allowing me to discover the magic and luxury of fifteen minutes submerged.

Now that I'm an adult with an earthier side, I'd like to try a claw-footed tub with a rubber stopper, the kind Julia Roberts used in Hugh Grant's Notting Hill flat. Either that or a washtub like in a James Garner Western, where a barmaid heats up water on a wood stove and pours it over my head.

I don't expect anything to happen in the tub, I might add, and harbor no fantasies of *The English Patient* or Robert Kincaid driving up the gravel road in his pickup truck. My husband has been getting a little suspicious, however, and has taken to tapping lightly on the bathroom door and asking with more curiosity than concern, "What exactly are you *doing* in there?" Thirty years of marriage or no, we both know that this time belongs to me, and I can stay until I look like Hume Cronyn if I want.

And that's the point. For less than an hour each day, I've found a place where there's no world outside the porcelain walls, no order to the universe. It is a thirty-minute frontal lobotomy, without the badge of infamy. I can use up all the hot water in the tank, admire the polish on my toenails, and consider absolutely nothing but the stress flooding from my pores like so much water down the drain. I can lather and de-lather, loofah and moisturize, all in the name of this new sport with no scorecard, spectators, or sprains. I can line up all the foolish potions I want, and light candles that smell like acorn squash if I feel like it. I can turn up my favorite CD and turn down the lights. I stop short of drinking champagne in a crystal flute, but one of those inflatable bath pillows that looks like a seashell is starting to sound like a good idea.

I only wish those who know of my newest predilection would stop calling me Tubby. In my present dignified and respectable state, I much prefer Prunehilda.

—August 1999

My addiction to the tub has grown to include candles, which I own in every scent from whispering pine to buttercream.

Self-Discovery

My irrational and immense fear of horses, I have masterfully convinced myself and others, stems from having been thrown from a particularly nervy one on a trail at summer camp some thirty-five years ago. Now that I look back on it, however, I think I may have jumped.

What Price Glory?

WE HUDDLED ON the beach that bright, chilly morning fighting the snap of cold wind that rose up and caught the hoods of our sweatshirts. The deep blue sky fooled us into thinking Florida warmth would soak into our faces, upturned to scan the cloudless sky for a sign of the space shuttle, which was to lift off within minutes. We shivered aloud and stamped about, clapping our hands on opposite arms, trying to busy ourselves with conversation and speculation. The launch was delayed because of icicles, or sharp sudden winds, or doors that wouldn't latch. We would wait it out, cold or no.

A collection of tiny sand birds caught our eye. Braving the cold, they broke free from their tight gathering, darted in unison to the approaching foam, then turned together and ran silently back when the water crept over their spindly feet. Baby sandpipers they were, taking miniature risks for a nibble of fresh ocean vegetation, chancing the pounding surf like a pack of eager toddlers braving a knee-high splash and then dashing back rather than dare a choking gulp of saltwater.

The major event of that morning is already chronicled in the history books. Witnessing the shuttle explosion firsthand was unforgettable—a shocking memory that did not dim as the eerily twisted cloud faded off into an unnatural white smear in the blue sky, like a child's finger painting hung to dry.

The professional crew, we rationalized, understood the risks and gambled accordingly.

The unparalleled thrill of being jettisoned into space has its price—a price the astronauts obviously had weighed and accepted. The fact that an ebullient high school teacher from New Hampshire was also a risk taker made the outcome a little easier to swallow.

I am not a risk taker and would not have considered applying to become the first journalist in space. The prospect skipped across my mind occasionally but was never more than an instant, mad daydream. Risk takers probably get more out of life, but one never knows whether the gamble will pay off, making the risk that much more tantalizing.

When a group of friends chartered a deep-sea fishing boat to bob about a choppy ocean, I waved from shore—unwilling to risk a bout of nausea just to send a glistening mackerel aflop on deck. A sweaty, laughing group returned, with raucous tales of exotic poisonous fish, last-second catches, and vomiting over the side. The one who played it safe has no yardstick as to whether the thrill was worth the anguish, but my own pleasant sunny day was uninterrupted by adventure or doom.

As a teenager, a flirtatious friendship with a hopeful young pilot who wore a ruddy complexion and a thatch of straw-blond hair led to an experience that bit my better judgment to the core. Just one short flight on his Piper Cherokee, and I would have the rest of my life to reflect on that exciting interlude, he pleaded. I caved in.

Buffeting about the sky like a box kite in March, that flimsy aircraft provided a gut-wrenching hour. With each air pocket, my fingernails dug deeper into the arms of the shabby vinyl seat, and the pilot—who later admitted that he didn't have a license but was only logging air time—flashed white teeth in a full smile, yelling "Having fun?" against the roar of the engine. A thumping landing and a cloud of gritty brown dust signaled my survival, but the risk I took that day had not made me happier or more satisfied.

Many years later, a European trip was not deemed complete without an expedition into the majestic Alps. A tiny blue used VW was our magic carpet as we set off onto the narrow winding roads whose 360-degree turns made it impossible to see more than ten feet ahead. No guard rails provided a buffer from the unbelievable drop, and with stomach in throat, I anguished that a view of the Matterhorn and shopping for a few thick wool sweaters could not possibly be worth the sickening danger. The tiny village of Zermatt, nestled in a valley amid the splendor of those magnificent peaks, was memorable, but I'd never risk it again.

Before leaving Florida after the historic tragedy had occurred, I happened upon a bleached wood box in a gift-shop window. Its enameled top was painted with a cluster of tiny sandpipers chancing toward the sea. I bought the souvenir—a reminder of risk and all its outgrowths—and each time I look at it, I shall remember a perky schoolteacher who nuzzled her little girl and then proceeded to chart the unknown. For her, the risk was too great. For fat-bellied birds lunching on succulent seafood, a bit of a launch to the sea wasn't. To me, the day-to-day risks seem chancy enough, their rewards tasty and dear.

—March 1986

We found ourselves on the beach once again in February 2001, witnessing another shuttle launch. As the rocket blazed its way across the sky, I held my breath, awaiting catastrophe. This time, the stream of smoke left an indelible, unending trail. Lessons learned in the space program no doubt paved the way for ultimate success. I was grateful to have been there to see it.

Disease Control

YOU CAN TELL A hypochondriac by the size of his luggage. A well-adjusted traveler checks in a hanging bag and a regulation duffel. A hypochondriac, however, requires a metal cart to transport his carry-on bag to the gate. In all likelihood, the contents of this carry-on include at least two antibiotics—one for upper respiratory infections, one for gastrointestinal—cough syrup with codeine, ear drops, anti-nausea suppositories, and various over-the-counter analgesics.

I know, because I am a certified hypochondriac. Selected members of our staff will soon journey to Mexico for an upcoming photo shoot, and no one's particularly worried about the possibility of abdominal distress. But aha! I am prepared. Along with antibiotics, my homemade medical kit includes an antibacterial stomach medicine as well as a prescription-only, controlled substance to arrest stomach discomfort. You never know.

I have reason to worry. One family trip to Florida found three out of four bedridden with a severe flu, causing us to haul sick babies to an unknown pediatrician who had moths flying around his examining room.

On another trip, a Christmas eve ear infection found a father and son in the condominium complex elevator on the way to the hospital emergency room. Okay, so the elevator got stuck between floors and they pounded for hours (one holding his ear), and no one heard. If only I'd been prepared.

When you're a hypochondriac it pays not only to be alert, but to be educated. If you bone up with a home health care volume, you can identify Rocky Mountain spotted fever and encephalitis, and you won't be caught off guard thinking it's a swollen mosquito bite or a stress-induced headache. They'll appreciate that at the emergency room.

It also helps to assign made-up diseases to common symptoms, thus avoiding a trip to the doctor, where you might really find out what's wrong, which, God forbid, might be something awful. For example, a toothache, which will require a foot-long needle and a drill, is probably just a virus below the tooth surface which, if left alone, will certainly dissipate. By the same token, if you practice having a stroke by going limp on one side, or a heart attack by careening to the carpet Fred Sanford-style, you won't be surprised when it really happens.

To prevent unwanted catastrophes, some activities are best avoided altogether. I never take my outdoor evening walk, for example, if no one's home. What if I suffered an irregular heartbeat and passed out? I'd no doubt lie there unnoticed, like so much road kill, until a family member returned home. It's just not worth the risk.

While some maintain their dignity when ill, I moan, scream, and demand someone tell me immediately how long it will last. My husband has learned to respond by advising me to rest my vocal cords and go to sleep. Only then, he assures me, will the malady subside. But he's not fooling me. If I suffer, everyone suffers.

It's gratifying to know I'm not alone. Some years back, I found a coworker studying a freckle on his forearm with the help of a hand-held magnifier used to examine photo transparencies. There we were, the two of us crouched over his arm staring into an eyeglass, trying to determine if the aberration looked suspicious.

This year, making it to February without contracting the flu is a victory. This is best accomplished by waving your hand furiously in front of your face when confronted with a stricken individual, disinfecting the grocery cart handle with baby wipes, and entering a public place wearing a mask as if you were expecting an Iraqi Scud attack.

It would probably be best to adopt the attitude that what you expect to happen never does anyway. In all probability, that means stomach cramps won't be a problem at all in Mexico. Ohmygosh. That leaves type B hepatitis. Do they have a preventative drug for that?

—February 1992

Get Lost

IT WAS STRAIGHT OUT of a Laurel and Hardy movie. The gentleman who drove us from the restaurant back to the hotel had just moved to the new city himself, and boasted of his quick acclimation. Unconvinced, we asked the curbside bellman for directions back to his apartment. The driver waved us off, sped around the circular drive, and peeled down the ramp, where he promptly turned the wrong way onto a busy one-way street.

Even though we could see only his profile by then, we could easily imagine the temperature inside his collar. While he may be too proud to admit it, I share this affliction: My name is Debbie and I am directionally challenged.

And I'm not alone. A recent *USA Today* article on this problem quotes a psychologist who says that animals migrate using tiny particles of iron embedded in their brains that orient them magnetically, like tiny compasses. Birds can navigate by the position of the sun, he continues, and some can hear the sound of the surf from hundreds of miles away. When God passed out those microns of metal, I must have been at the end of the line.

From my twelfth-floor office window I can see where 1-70 and 1-65 split, but that has never helped me find an Eastside hotel where we frequently conduct lunch meetings. On a particularly bad day, I called my associate from my car just as I approached the split. "Which way do I go?" I bellowed into the phone, confident that he would understand and react within an acceptable time frame.

This is nothing new. I've spent the better part of my life writing down elaborate directions with personal notes like, "Go by the big white church. Keep going. Get in the left-hand lane. Turn left." Inevitably accompanying this verbiage is a hand-scrawled map, which I turn upside down to find my way home. I once drove more than sixty-five miles on 1-74 toward Greencastle before I realized that (1) I was heading for Crawfordsville, and (2) 1-70, not 1-74, leads into Greencastle.

From Here to Maturity

Because I could sooner navigate my way out of Jerusalem's old city than any American airport, I take taxis, not rental cars, when I travel alone. And when my husband and I travel together, I pretend to have forgotten my glasses, forcing him to spread the map over the steering wheel while he drives (and curses) to see whether we're headed north or south.

This malady is surely genetic, like whether or not one understands algebra. When all else fails I can blame my mother, who once drove the wrong direction through a bank drive-thru lane and then complained to the management that the terminal would have been more convenient were it located on the driver's side. "It's no accident that Mozart's father was a musician," says a neurologist in the same *USA Today* article.

But I'm learning to live with my dysfunction. If I must visit a patient or doctor at the labyrinth they call Methodist Hospital, for example, I record landmarks on the way. Pass the cafeteria, then the gift shop, then turn right at the elevators, I admonish myself, knowing full well I'll probably have to hop on a gurney to get out before the sun sets.

It's comforting to know I'm not alone in my disorientation. When I was a preteen, my best girlfriend, Jackie, and I would spend our Saturdays buying matching purses at Joan Bari Bag & Gem at Glendale Mall. Under no circumstances could Jackie determine which of the two flagship department stores she was in, nor could she find her way from one to the other. With our twin totes dangling from our wrists, I'd drag her down the mall, thrilled that I'd found someone worse off than I.

On a recent business trip to Kansas City, I occupied the passenger seat of a cohort's rental car and stared in numb disbelief as he glided on and off interstates without an ounce of concern in a city he'd never visited before. I sat quietly, never alluding to the fact that I had no idea whether we were east or west of St. Louis. While the same psychologist quoted earlier would credit this to the fact that "Men don't get lost. They're just late," I'd rather assume he could simply hear the pounding of the surf.

—November 1994

The worst navigational experience I have suffered occurred in Phoenix, where I drove around Camelback Mountain for two hours and ten minutes before finding my way back to the hotel. My mother was right: Always top off the tank.

April Scours

PACK RATS SAVE everything. I, on the other hand, save only shopping bags—the handled kind retail stores distribute if you buy more than can fit in a flimsy paper sack. If you go all out and buy mattress pads or lamps, you get really big shopping bags, which makes me happy.

I fold them neatly and stack them on my closet floor, where they occasionally spring back to their upright state, creating more clutter than I like. Unlike stamps, ships in a bottle, or coins, my collection serves a useful, environmentally conscious purpose, especially in April, which I deem spring cleaning month.

Because we plan to move, this spring I am a woman possessed. Every evening I plant a shopping bag by my side and dig through closets like a pup in a posy patch. There is really only one way to clean effectively, I've found, and that's by throwing away everything. I mean *everything,* an appalling thought to my family, which for some reason wants to keep particular items of personal value.

The obsession must stem from a local newspaper campaign I remember as a schoolgirl, wherein Herman Hoglebogle gave everyone a green triangular-shaped flag that read, "Clean up, paint up, fix up." The goofy fictional character shaped my life.

Last weekend, for example, I started at the bottom, rooting through the basement storeroom where items I had moved from my last house still sat on shelves. *Use it or lose it,* I muttered, discarding daisy-patterned towels from my first apartment, every notebook from college, assorted moon boots, old-fashioned clock radios, and computer boxes we were saving in case the computers went bad.

Add to that kids' camp trunks and assorted collapsible cups, insulated canteens, and basic metal dinnerware. Their like-new condition didn't surprise me; if the kid brings his toothbrush home unopened after a month, what would make me think he'd eat s'mores on an army plate I went to four stores to find?

While the good stuff goes to various thrift and second-hand shops, the junk gets left for the trash, which happened the Monday after basement day. Sure, my driveway looked like Jed Clampett just moved in, but who cares? Gone is gone.

From closet to driveway, I occasionally get caught by a family member who usually overreacts thusly: "Hey, where're you goin' with those shoes? That's my favorite shirt! I might need those bookends someday!" A good cleaner ignores such admonitions, and tries to be sneakier the next time. Chances are, if you haven't hung that picture of an owl in a knotty pine frame by now, you probably never will.

Unfortunately, they usually spot me by my signature shopping bag, a sure sign they can kiss their belongings goodbye. Nobody admitted wanting that ratty Snoopy blanket on the closet shelf, but it somehow made it back from the curb before trash day. And I'm certain I've thrown away a particular pair of Hush Puppies at least two times before. Not only do they retrieve items from my sacred bags, but they know when to barricade themselves at their doors, arms spread like an eagle across their property, and shout, "*Enough!*" No matter. I'll get 'em next time. My goal, should I live long enough to accomplish it, is not to have to hire a mover at all. The way I figure it, we can each put the few possessions we have left in a shopping bag or two and tote them to the new house ourselves.

Besides, I never miss anything I give away, and that's all that really matters. That Tupperware celery crisper took up half the refrigerator anyway, and something tells me my days as a size four are over for good. The other day, however, I did find myself wondering about the editing rules I learned in college regarding split infinitives. Let's see, that notebook would have been in the broken-down box on basement shelf Number 2—the one my son delighted in informing me now resides in a J. C. Penney bag at the city dump.

—April 1992

Happy Trails

MY IRRATIONAL AND immense fear of horses, I have masterfully convinced myself and others, stems from having been thrown from a particularly nervy one on a trail at summer camp some thirty-five years ago. Now that I look back on it, however, I think I may have jumped.

The memories are vague, but somewhere in the mist I see a horse hungry for a nibble of nearby vegetation, a horse tired of the humdrum life, a horse looking to pick up the pace. Rather than practice the fine equestrian techniques I had been taught, I believe now that as that horse took flight, so did I, of my own volition. Wherever that horse had decided to go, I wasn't going with him.

I have managed to avoid close contact with these beasts of burden ever since. But I knew my number was up when the sign-up form landed on my desk. The company management retreat to be held in Arizona included horseback riding as an optional afternoon activity, and *everyone* had said yes. Like a preteen at a make-out party, I succumbed to peer pressure and, with shaking hand, checked off the box.

It was time to look fear in the eye and conquer it. After all, hadn't I done just that a few summers ago when I hopped aboard that ski lift for the second time? The first time, I reminded myself, a thunderstorm had forced the lift to stop, and there we sat, swinging what seemed like miles above the mountain, as lightning streaked across the darkening sky. Panicked, I turned to my teenage son and wailed, "Do you think we should jump?"

"Sure, Mom," he answered. "You go first."

This time, getting past other people's fears proved just as daunting. One told the story of a friend who was thrown and trampled, another the grisly tale of a rider whose neck was sliced with a clothesline as she galloped in a suburban neighborhood. I didn't stand a chance.

Having never considered approaching anything larger than a standard poodle, I was surprised at the number of folks who shared my fear. One of my comrades, a hulking fellow, asked sheepishly if he could just run along behind. Since we were doomed to progress, however, I did what all good trauma victims should do: went shopping.

How you look is more important than how you feel, I muttered to myself as I clicked through the rack of Western wear. Figuring if I was eventually going to be laid flat out on some dirt path I might as well be well dressed, I selected a cute denim vest, a little ribbed turtleneck, and some nice, soft jeans. This brought to mind my tennis days, another sport whose attire interested me more than the actual game. I was wearing a better-than-average short white skirt and matching tennis top when the ball hit me squarely in the eye, displacing my contact lens and forcing me to wear my Coke-bottle glasses for the better part of a week.

As the day of the ride approached, I began to mull matters of more serious concern. How would I get on and—worse yet—get off the horse and maintain my dignity? For the latter, my plan was simply to release one foot and then slide down the other side, landing like a sack of rocks in the dirt. How bad could it be?

Then came the mane event. The horse, the trail hands assured me, was the gentlest of the herd. Patches' sturdy back had held the bravest of eight-year-olds, which was little consolation to someone who has seen her share of eight-year-olds take their lives in their hands on daredevil amusement park rides. What I wanted to hear was that some poor eighty-year-old had survived the ride. But I was prepared, having tucked my health insurance card in my vest pocket and, in the absence of Prozac, gulped down two extra-strength Tylenol in anticipation of the worst.

Gritting my teeth in an attempt to suppress the dreaded scent of fear, I patted Patches gingerly on the neck, noticing immediately that the only thing we had in common was the condition of her mane, which somewhat resembled my hair on humid days. Correctly interpreting my twisted expression as pure terror, two cowboys accompanied me up the trail. My horse stopped to eat only once, and rather than jump off, which seems to be my pattern, I pulled the rein sharply to one side, causing her to turn around slowly in a circle and return to the same patch of grass.

It is safe to say I spent the first half of the ride worrying about bucking, kicking, and stomping, and the second half worrying about how I was going to get off. As time progressed, however, I found myself falling into the plodding rhythm, fantasizing about Antonio Banderas sweeping me from my perch, or simply tying up my steed at nightfall and making camp, heating beans, and using my saddle for a pillow. By the end of the trail I was joking with the cowboy in front, who fell somewhat short of Antonio in the looks department, and making cavalier banter about the bruised condition of my backside.

Actually, gravity pretty much took care of the dismount, and as I ambled off, looking like I just got off a horse, I felt downright proud. But even with victory in hand, I can't say that I'd ride again, unless I chance it on a pony wheel on the lawn of the nursing home someday. After my historic ride, I declined an invitation to go hot-air ballooning (too high to jump), but climbing atop that sure-footed stallion was a start. I faced down my fearsome enemy, and she was Patches. The sky, however, really is the limit.

—November 1995

House and Home

The youngest of four children and decidedly the most hell-bent on modern gadgets, I was eventually indulged with the family's first window air conditioner. It went in my bedroom, where I spent so much time my parents feared I'd grow mold or explode like Count Dracula when I finally did go outdoors.

On the House

AFTER SIX MONTHS of plucking cobwebs from corners, making sure no one eats over the sink, and running around screaming, "Quick! They're showing the house in twenty minutes! Throw the cat's litter box out the laundry room window!" I give up. Selling a house makes major surgery sound appealing.

They've come in droves, and one by one. They've complimented, swooned, criticized, whined, griped, and fled. Prior to listing the house with a real estate agent, we attempted the sale ourselves—a humbling experience. As I led one smiling wife from room to room, her husband growled like a mountain lion, headed for the driveway, and sped off. Apologizing, she slunk out after him, leaving me alone with my polished hardwood floors, gleaming porcelain sinks, and evenly spaced hangers in the closets.

They've come with their kids, who leave fingerprints on my son's prized computer screen and mementos in the bathrooms. They've come with their mothers, who want the armoire but not the house. And worst of all, they've come four times, lolling on my screened porch while my cat curls up on their laps. (That couple bought a house elsewhere but made an offer on the cat.)

Uncle, I say. *Uncle!* Not only have I scrubbed such unspeakable places as the basement water heater closet, I've suffered one family member's primary contribution, grabbing the soaps from all the sinks and showers in marathon time, as if that makes any difference. Three years worth of garden hoses lay tangled in the garage like so many dead rattlesnakes, and the cat leaves daily appetizers of filet au mouse on the doorstep, but at least all the soap's gone: no slimy puddles, no scent of Irish Spring, no sign of human habitation.

If nothing else, it's made me organize. In anticipation of the move, we've gone through every drawer, stacking paper clips, categorizing rubber bands by width and color, throwing out grocery store coupons with expiration dates prior to 1984. Mystery items, like tiny metal keys, must remain, however, because you never know. If we hadn't kept them all these years, what would have happened when a mischievous tyke closed the cat in a camp trunk, trapping her like a feline Houdini? With hands shaking, we tried every key until the latch fell open, sparing us from trying the next step: revving up the chain saw.

We've come close to closing a deal a couple of times, or at least so my spies tell me. While showings take place—lights aglow, spirits high—we head for cover, again, lest one suspect human habitation. We twiddle our thumbs at Pizza Hut, stroll the aisles at Target, or sit in our car at the end of the street, praying the couple in the Lexus turns into our driveway. Once our son (who sat on the curb in disgust) reported a Japanese family arrived in two Mercedes, leading me to believe they could swing the deal with enough left over to buy a professional football franchise.

You can't help but hate some people during the process, especially folks who insist on telling you about their niece, neighbor, or best friend who sold her house five minutes after it was listed, with buyers no doubt running up the driveway, hundred dollar bills flying out of their pants pockets. Worse yet are tales of unsolicited prospects offering to buy a house when and if the owner decides to sell. People who spread such lies rank right up there with men who tug on their trouser waistbands, complaining that they've lost so much weight just laying off Thousand Island dressing that all their clothes are too large. Add to that vacationers who explain that the weather in Florida had been clear, hot, and sunny for two straight weeks before you arrived and can't imagine why it's raining now.

No matter what anyone says, my house looks great. As a matter of fact, in its present painted, spit-shined, and shipshape state, I can't remember why I ever wanted to sell it in the first place. It must have been those bars of soap melting away in the shower.

—October 1992

Splendor in the Grass

BEFORE MOVING INTO a new, lush suburban neighborhood, keeping up with the Joneses was pretty simple. It entailed protecting your car from unsightly rust, maintaining only a modest amount of three-foot grass in the myrtle beds, and occasionally repairing the mailbox so it didn't hang open like a mutt's mouth on a dry summer day.

As luck would have it, we have moved next door to a lawn manicurist, a doctor in his off-yard hours, who has his grass leveled like a plush carpet. And that's just the beginning. I never knew the true meaning of humiliation until I found myself crawling around on the wet grass one morning after a storm, picking up sticks—hundreds of them—that had fallen from the many trees in the densely wooded setting. There is no adroit way in which to pick up sticks—no tools can accomplish the task, no modern convenience can quicken the pace. You must simply stoop, pick up, drop in a grocery bag, stoop, pick up, and so on. If you run extremely fast while bent over, however, you can get a momentum going, thereby getting a bounty of sticks before stuffing them in the bag. It is not, however, a pretty sight.

The neighbor, on the other hand, had no sticks. They had already been retrieved, silently, as I slept. Au contraire, he was using the moist earth as an opportunity to nudge out the three or four weeds that had pushed their near-invisible heads forth in his mulch beds. And what mulch beds they are—gently curving islands in a great sea of green, with each tiny shredded piece of bark in place.

Differing forms of vegetation form perfect terraced layers, separated by artistically placed limestone. Shrubs are china cups set just so in round saucers. Flowering trees are soft puff balls of pink and white, with no twisted branches that dare die.

To make matters worse, the fellow is a fine chap—a friendly, well-meaning sort who on occasion ventures over to where the grass yellows. "My, your grass is doing well," he encourages, or "Look how healthy your trees are." I think he feels sorry for us, but he does not disdain our efforts.

We are, after all, the same family who at our previous house "cut" our grass for two weeks without realizing there was no blade on the riding mower. And it was we who dared try to rid an oak tree of tent caterpillars by standing on a step stool and spraying an eight-ounce can of insecticide directly into the wind. When we once tried to fertilize the grass, we didn't keep the rows even, and had the only lawn in the neighborhood with dark green and light green stripes.

We know when we're licked. But it doesn't make us feel any less guilty. As I recently dragged a lawn chair onto the driveway and dropped down lazily to read a stack of magazines and enjoy a very large glass of iced tea, there he was, quick-stepping around in his mulch beds with a hand-held fertilizer tank, like an organ grinder with his instrument, feeding and cranking, feeding and cranking, as I looked on in horror.

But he smiled and waved, as always, while I sat amid all sorts of curious brown debris—pods and propellers—that falls from the thicket each day like rain. He has no such debris, however. Not because his trees are better behaved, but because he has the proper tools, while we do not. He has a blower and an air pump, and with goggles in place, he sets across the driveway like Bill Murray in *Ghostbusters*, eliminating all such foreign matter from each crevice, all unsightly leaves from the premises.

How hard can it be to prune the top branches from a forty-year-old sycamore tree when you have a sixteen-foot stepladder and twelve-foot shears? I could do that too, I rationalize, just as I could edge and trim around each tree if I had a gas-powered grass trimmer that sounds like a chain saw, and an automatic sprinkling system that introduces each new day with a gentle spray.

No, we prefer to prune our shrubs with pliers and spend the better part of each evening wrestling with a two-ton garden hose and sprinkler that makes all the appropriate chuk-chuk noises but does a better job soaking down the asphalt and splattering the window than it does moistening the grass.

We'll continue to pay the guy who cuts the grass—when he shows up—rather than try to compete with that gorgeous twice-a-week diagonal pattern, and I'll continue to respect the daddy long legs that live on my flowers, for they were there first, and I shan't disturb them by nipping, pinching, or fertilizing. That is surely, I reason, the way He intended it.

—July 1985

Chill Seekers

ON BRUTALLY HOT summer days, around dinnertime, I can't help remembering how life was before air conditioning locked us up in its cold, silent world. Even with windows positioned on all four sides, our house offered few cooling breezes, and although most family members could abide the sweltering conditions, I became Sarah Bernhardt, throwing myself on the kitchen linoleum floor, where I would stare at the ceiling in a mock death scene, or dash from room to room frantically waving an accordion-folded paper fan in front of my face.

The youngest of four children and decidedly the most hell-bent on modern gadgets, I was eventually indulged with our family's first window air conditioner. It went in my bedroom, where I spent so much time that my parents feared I'd grow mold or explode like Count Dracula when I finally did go outdoors. On one particularly stifling day, we gathered in my room for dinner, all six of us crowded around my student desk, gnawing on our barbecued steaks and homemade french fries while surrounded by two-tiered cafe curtains and flouncy dust ruffles, a pink princess phone, and picks and brush rollers strewn on my mirrored vanity table. While it is doubtful that chasing up and down the stairs with plates and serving bowls was worth the respite, the memory returns any evening that the temperature tops eighty degrees.

An avid worrier, my father didn't believe in window air conditioners for the simple reason that having one would require the closing of his and my mother's bedroom door. This would mean that if one of their brood should call for help in the wee hours, he wouldn't hear the desperate cry. Therefore, my mother, decidedly more relaxed in her approach to child rearing, spent twenty-some years flapping her arms in front of a window fan that probably made as much noise as any air conditioner but merely sucked in the hot air from outside and moved it around. Nevertheless, they remained accessible to the needs of their children, one of whom shut herself up in an igloo every night while everyone else tossed and turned in damp beds, flipping their pillows in search of a cool spot, splayed on top of thin sheets, praying for a breeze.

I kept my coveted window air conditioner set at Dyna-Cool, Number 5, which provided an icy blast akin to what one might find in Alaska in mid-January. Every night, my father would creep in, pile covers on top of me, click the window unit to Nite-Cool, Number 1, and retreat. And every night after the door closed behind him, I would leap from my bed, reset the fixture to Dyna-Cool and slip back between my cool sheets, pulling the comforter around my chin like an Eskimo parka.

Before my introduction to air conditioning, I remember how it was in my prior bedroom in the back of the house, directly across from the neighbors, whose late-night altercations became almost unbearable through our opposing open windows. I would slam down my window repeatedly in disgust, never quite getting their attention. Now that I look back on it, the couple undoubtedly had bigger problems than the bratty ten-year-old next door who couldn't sleep amid the racket.

For all the comfort it provided, the window air conditioner in my subsequent room eliminated not only the neighbors' loud squabbling, but all other natural sounds as well. It made me grow used to white noise instead of those mesmerizing sounds of summer nights: crickets chirping, the rustle of leaves, the occasional hoot of an owl. After years of living behind closed windows, I was struck recently by a scene in the movie *Michael,* wherein the angel played by John Travolta, on earth briefly and finally, stands silently in a farm field, arms outstretched, soaking in what he calls the "earth sounds" he will miss most. A climate-controlled kind of gal, I have lost touch with those sounds and smells, and even without sweat stains or frizzy hair, I'm probably poorer because of it.

Living in the suburbs doesn't help. There, houses are airtight, and one doesn't often find cooling breezes wafting through open kitchen windows. Central air conditioning units growl twenty-four hours a day in a society more partial to compressors than picnics under a tree. We unknowingly inhale Freon instead of the fragrance of freshly mowed grass, and worry that if we open our windows at night, burglar alarms will blare or, worse yet, intruders will invade our first-floor master suites as we sleep. For some reason, houses in older neighborhoods closer to the city's core remain open, allowing occupants to mingle their outside and inside lives more naturally.

It is possible, I suppose, to be so wrapped up in artificial climate as to avoid the out-of-doors entirely. Within two years, this magazine will relocate to a new seven-story building with its own attached garage. At that time, I can see myself entering my car in one garage and exiting it in another, never suffering windblown hair or the ravages of humidity, such as bangs that spring like question marks above my forehead. I know I'll never be a Jeep Wrangler type of auto traveler with khaki shorts and legs that are tan in back. I'm a perfume-and-pantyhose kind of girl, which probably better suits me for a Lexus that eliminates wind noise but offers a twelve-disc CD changer. I do, however, find myself yearning for those days before my window air conditioner, for a little dust on the floor and warped windowsills from an errant rainstorm. Mosquitoes buzzing around your ear in the night might have been annoying, but at least they reminded you that you were alive.

—August 1997

Is Anybody Home?

NOBODY'S CRAZIER ABOUT houses—especially new ones—than I. The Sunday real estate section gets more attention than a Ludlum novel, I'm attracted to "open" houses like a pack rat to garage sales, and I never stay in a place long enough to use all my personalized envelopes.

Luckily, my husband shares my enthusiasm for greener pastures, and like the Bremen town musicians, we can frequently be found peering in the windows of houses for sale, hoping no one is home. When we built our present house, we found it wasn't so much a better home we were after, but the entertainment value of traipsing out to the lot each evening, surveying the day's progress, and taking great, long, cleansing sniffs of unboxed cedar.

We've been in our present house nearly five years now, and I'm still not cured. I'm the one you see hanging out of the car window along Meridian Street, squinting to see inside the windows of the stately mansions, or mucking about in muddy cornfields sizing up prospective neighborhoods. As I get older, however, it is easier to see the tragic flaws in such an obsession: First, since some builder can always install Palladian windows, mauve tile, or a side-by-side refrigerator unlike any you've ever seen, you'll live in a state of constant jealousy, coveting the belongings that nobody as yet even owns. Second, and more telling, you're placing too much importance on something that in reality gets very little use.

Unlike our parents, who bought a home and *stayed* there, cooking meatloaf on Tuesdays and wearing pleasant paths in the carpet, we pass through on our way from work to dinner, like frantic travelers jumping from subway to stop. On weekday evenings we're too busy with full briefcases, social studies projects, and laundry to sit still and absorb our surroundings, and while neighbors spend sunny Saturdays planting spring flowers and mulching their beds, we're whizzing from mall to mall on errands we didn't have time to complete from Monday to Friday. Considering that home is only a stopping-off place anyway, constantly shopping for a new one is no better than spending a hundred dollars for groceries and at the end of the week finding nothing but spoons and cereal bowls in the dishwasher.

The revelation that we weren't spending near enough time there came during a stubborn ear infection, which, penicillin and all, humbled me to a quivering lump of self-pity and two days at home—which, I discovered, looks entirely different in daylight. Sure, the rain-splotched windows are more apparent, but so is the peace, the quiet, the opportunity to think. As a youngster, I couldn't fathom how in her last years my graceful, intelligent grandmother could sit for hours in a chair by the window, overlooking her perfectly tended flowers and saying nothing. Long after her death, I think I understand.

On my two-day stint I learned not only that birds—real birds—nest in our clump of woods and that a fat groundhog forages about each day, but that one neighbor built an entire garage onto his home without my notice, and that another's jolly golden retriever amuses herself by running around in circles with her dinner dish in her mouth. An occasional intrusion of daytime-TV provided food for thought: Tiny Tim is back, incontinence can strike the middle-aged, and they're making a movie of the *Jetsons*.

And forgive the grease stains on this page, but I tossed out the three-minute microwave popcorn and drizzled real butter on an authentic, home-cooked batch. I may not be over my yearnings to house hunt, and I can't make meatloaf worth a darn, but I think my grandma would be proud.

—June 1989

Where the Wild Things Are

NO ONE SEEMS PARTICULARLY worried that an unwelcome visitor will return this summer. The seventeen-year locust, it appears, is back. Where are the emergency fallout shelters? Where are the provisions? Where are the drums of malathion?

If nobody else is fearful of this hoard of vengeful cicadas, I am. The woods, where I live, will suffer most from the attack, horticulturists predict. There the ruthless bloodsuckers will drain our maples of their sap, gnaw our precious bark, and then burrow away, like fat, lazy pilgrims after a Thanksgiving feast, to procreate and plan the attack of 2004.

I've not been particularly well-adjusted to the rustic forest environment since the move there three years ago, anyway. Back then, when the worst predator was an indolent raccoon caught chomping potato chips on the deck, I didn't fit in. I came from a grassy past—homes with neat, square yards and skinny saplings held up with stakes. There, inflatable wading pools sat on hot driveways, and backyard picnics were uninterrupted by breezes or shade.

Thrust into the world of May apples and poison oak, carpenter ants and propelling seed pods, I had no frame of reference. Unlike me, woods people had wind chimes but no grass, spiderwebs on the windows, rusty wheelbarrows, and moldy basements that smelled like wet socks. And suddenly, I was one of them.

From the inside, the woods looked great. In spring, a lush green curtain provided a picturesque and peaceful view. But there were inhabitants of this serene landscape who wanted to be with us, to watch TV and eat at our table, take showers and read our library books. The first home wrecker we met was a yard-long, gray-green garden snake that slithered up the bathtub drain and, wrinkled and dehydrated from its perilous journey, flopped over the edge of the tub and died, hanging there like stockings left to dry. It was then that we awoke to life as it would be—rife with horror-movie mosquitoes and spiders as big as frying pans that fastened themselves to basement walls like so much grotesque artwork.

I became accustomed to the neighbor's constantly sparking bug zapper that every once in a while choked on something the size of a buzzard, and the inch of May "snow" that my children identify as "flying fuzz balls." I know there is no place to get a tan, and a seat on the deck produces a lapful of sweat bees, stickers, and assorted poisonous berries.

We learned to accept wood roaches that lumbered down the hallway like army tanks and the scampering of little feet in a home where the youngest child wears size-five shoes. I even adjusted to the nervy varmints who ventured onto my wood deck to suck out the remains of a whisky barrel planter and then tear up the flowers inside like a tomcat in a sandbox. But things became critical when I was torpedoed by an enraged honeybee while in the sanctity of my own *kitchen*. Rather than search for a passage to the outdoor flower box where most of its friends were congregated, it dive-bombed—stinger first—into my forearm, forcing a delirious homemaker to seek aid at an all-night emergicenter and pop Benadryl and wear ice packs for a full week. Not even a dozen sizzling bug zappers could help—the woods had won.

I remembered a childhood friend—a jet-black-haired girl with thin lips and sharp, pretty features who always had burrs in her clothes and scabby bites about her legs. She lived in the woods and relished the natural state. She made pottery at a basement wheel and wove thick fibers into nubby scatter rugs. There were always five or more kittens affixed to various tree limbs and screen doors, and shovels grew upright out of mounds of peat and compost. It was a foreign but heavenly haven for a pale city girl—and our dark, shady hideouts and trails of snapping twigs never left me.

Who would dream I would become her—without the artistic bent and outdoor flair—a misfit destined to sneeze twelve consecutive times each time I ventured out, and more often than not walk headfirst into an invisible swarm of thousands of tiny flying things. And then, slowly, I grew to like it—to relish the dappled design the myriad of leaves painted on my kitchen floor, to drift asleep with the constant, gentle rustle outside my back porch.

But it was not to last. Alas, the locusts were to abound, striking fear in the hearts of countrymen and suburbanites, who will hole up inside their cedar-sided abodes and watch their little forests topple before them.

I've withstood the rest, I maintain, so this will not daunt me. I've endured three seasons of strange and mysterious life forms—not to mention a peculiar staccato snap-snapping sound each summer that is either a rhythmic woodpecker with a microphone or a short in the farmer's electric fence behind me. I can face up to the unknown seventeen-year locust with the knowledge that he cannot destroy my spirit, and the promise that when he returns once more I will be too old to care.

—June 1987

In 2004, I will be fifty-six—not too old to care.

Strangers in the Night

THE FIRST TIME I heard the distant clomping, scratching, and scurrying, I thought it must have been a dream. I opened my eyes against the blackness, worried that my husband had, in a somnambulistic stupor, gotten lost in his closet again. Or perhaps I was back in my childhood home on that awful night my older brother dreamed he was captured by Indians and held captive in the center of a deadly campfire. The next morning we all ran to his room to see how he had scratched the cowboy wallpaper clean off the wall. But this time, no one moved. Loath to awaken my husband, I groggily processed the information and prepared myself for combat. The noise was coming from the attic above our bedroom: critters, I decided, and big ones at that.

Could whatever manner of wildlife that had invaded the upper reaches of our home crash through the ceiling and attack us in our most vulnerable state? And if they did, what would the headlines read? "Couple Viciously Mauled by Squirrels"? How would we live it down, even posthumously?

The activity continued until just before dawn, fueling the fire of my already rampant and increasing insomnia. My age and the hours I can sleep are now directly disproportionate to one another, and each advancing year obliterates at least one more hour of sleep, usually in four fifteen-minute segments, between two and six A.M. It is at such times that I relive events of the day, re-speak speeches I have made, re-eat meals that do not agree. Only at this age do I understand my father's response as I discovered him in the dark, standing beside his bed. "Daddy," this then-thirteen-year-old had prodded her sixty-year-old father, "what are you doing?" With his usual dry wit and practicality, he replied, "Letting the worry run down."

Now, not only are paths not taken, work undone, and opinions not proffered keeping me up, I've got damn rodents in the attic hosting an all-night party that I am forced to attend. And if that weren't bad enough, my husband's system of party crashing involves pounding on the wall behind the bed, as if the noisemakers were unruly conventioneers in an adjoining hotel room.

It was time to call in the professionals. Our trusty exterminator, averse to apprehending anything larger than a wood roach, recommended A Best Wildlife Removal, the name obviously more a nod to advantageous placement in the phone book than the elements of literary style. And it was necessary to leave this to the experts. My sister's beloved cat Daisy had, just a few years prior, lost a battle to a raccoon that had boldly entered the garage through her pet door and, after turning over trash cans and boxes, eaten her food and ultimately killed her. Now this enraged my brother-in-law, who, deciding to take matters into his own hands, caught the culprit in a trap, poured gasoline over it, and lit a match. Daisy's untimely death was thus avenged. Of course, the wildlife officer who visited him the next day did not sympathize, and although he was not hauled off to jail, he was sternly cited. How the raccoon police came to know of the incident remains a mystery.

Loss of sleep and possible destruction of our attic insulation was not worth the risk. A Best's representative, after advising us of the fee structure—eighty-five dollars for a house call and another eighty-five dollars for each raccoon apprehended and relocated to a wildlife preserve—set steel traps resembling macabre pet carriers at strategic locations amid our shrubbery. And thus night one was under way. Similar rattling and knocking from above interrupted our sleep as usual, but we rested better convinced that the nasty culprits would meet their just reward upon exiting. At dawn we ran to the bushes like kids on Christmas morning, gleefully discovering one occupied cage. In it sat a baby raccoon no bigger than a Smurf, its snout covered with red jelly from the iced doughnut positioned as bait. As wildlife goes, I hadn't seen anything sadder since Bambi.

And having lived in two houses near a patch of woods, we had witnessed our share of curiosities. I once discovered a rooster in my flower box, as well as two feral kittens and a snapping turtle (at the same time) in our basement window well. The kittens, too vicious to be stroked or fed, were carted to the animal shelter, and the turtle, which clamped its powerful jaw onto the end of a shovel, was deposited in a neighborhood lake.

On another occasion, the street was abuzz after an entire herd of cows from a farm that backed up to our property galloped down the cul-de-sac, a scene as colorful as a passage from *Lonesome Dove*. And on one of my recent nightly two-mile walks, I encountered either one mangy, wild-looking dog or a coyote. There we stood, eye to eye, while the one of us with a brain larger than a peach pit plotted her getaway, her casual lope turning into a dead run as she neared her driveway.

Far from providing comic relief, however, this was getting serious. Down a hundred and seventy dollars, we could only hope that A Best wouldn't release the creature in the nearby woods, setting off a cartoon-show chain of events whereby we might catch the same animal for five subsequent days, setting us back an additional four hundred and twenty-five dollars and as many jelly doughnuts as the little fella could eat. Such a convenience store snack must have tempting powers, as the next day we discovered someone's decidedly peevish pet cat in the trap. In short, this wasn't going well.

Thereafter, the traps remained empty, while the raucous celebration overhead continued. Suspecting mice, we considered inspecting the attic ourselves but decided against it. One's attic, you see, is like the lower gastrointestinal tract. Every five years or so it's probably a good idea for someone to shine a light into it, but it's something we'd rather not see for ourselves. Thereafter, our original exterminator climbed up into the duskier regions, tossed out a few poison packets and hoped for the best. That night as silence fell over our house, I lay awake staring at the ceiling, imagining the killing fields just nine feet from my head. Genghis Khan couldn't have felt any worse.

Our nights still punctuated with the pitter-patter of little feet, we fired A Best Wildlife Removal, having renamed the company A Worst Wildlife Removal. We then contracted with Critter Control, a company whose business cards feature cute little animal tracks and a list of pests we'd rather not host, including woodchucks and muskrats, both of which I am hopeless to identify outside of nursery rhymes and love ballads. The contract, detailing a ninety-nine-dollar initial charge and sixty-five dollars per pest removed, also warned of our liability should a certified technician fall through the attic floor and hang there from his head.

This time an official progress report was left daily upon the inspection of the empty traps, which were placed on the roof. Robin, our service representative, finally called, overjoyed to report that she had located the source of our sleeplessness: mice, and a lot of them. They had chomped a path through the insulation and taken up residence directly on the ceiling drywall, resulting in the stereophonic sound. The poison packets remained untouched while the rodents cavorted in the rafters, dancing, reproducing like rabbits on fertility drugs, and burping up the insulation. Freaked out at the thought of an infestation, we were assured by Robin that it could have been worse, citing the bat colony of a hundred to a hundred and fifty of the creepy creatures found in one house alone.

The good news is all's quiet on the western front. The bad news is now I can't sleep from guilt over the dead mice that must be lying on the attic floor like soldiers on the beach at Normandy. I also feel terrible about that poor cat, who is probably flashing back to her day as a prisoner of war, and the baby raccoon, all alone at Fort Benjamin Harrison's nature preserve, foraging the forest floor for jelly doughnuts. And I can't even think about her mama, who has no doubt tacked up missing posters on the trunks of trees, alerted wildlife officers, and cried herself to sleep every night worrying that her baby is underdressed and missing her medication. Things could have been worse for all of them, I try to assure myself as I twist in the blankets and sheets. I could have turned the whole thing over to my brother-in-law.

—January 2001

By the volume of mail the magazine received concerning my brother-in-law's inhumane treatment of the raccoon who murdered his cat, you'd have thought he was Attila the Hun. I say, a) an eye for an eye, and b) don't shoot the messenger. Perhaps Lee Walburn, editor-in-chief of Atlanta *magazine, sized it up best. "Tell them in our next issue we're going to run a recipe for raccoon," he said. "At least in the South when we burn up our raccoons, we have the decency to eat them." He wasn't kidding. The February 2001 issue featured said recipe, which accompanied an article on traditional Southern cooking.*

Junk Bonds

EVERYTHING IN THEIR love nest was new, like their marriage. Middle-aged and divorced, they were lucky enough to find one another, and the chemistry was as obvious as the collection of folk art displayed in their sparkling second-floor condo. Impressive, brightly colored pieces covered every wall, and wood windmills and figurines adorned every tabletop. The couple exchanged furtive glances, and when their fingertips touched, a guest could almost see the tiny sparks.

As my husband and I toured their beautiful new home, I couldn't help but marvel at the art that they had collected together, as well as the new furnishings and rugs, dishes, and cookware. The one-bedroom apartment looked like a Pottery Barn catalog, but the lack of legacy spoke volumes.

Our own home is admirably decorated, but subtly appointed with stuff that I cannot bring myself to discard—like the brightly colored souvenir toucan my son brought home from a science expedition in Costa Rica or the unsophisticated little stuffed lamb that accompanied a Happy Meal and bleats, "Maa-a," when you turn it upside down. Even though most of the house is white, I still like our knotty pine secretary filled with out-of-style Hummel figurines, and though no one's home to play Ping-Pong anymore, I keep the table upright in the lower-level spare room.

I admit to envying our friends' new and unbridled passion, as well as their crisp belongings and fresh start. All those shiny things obviously signify a commitment to their new life and abandonment of the old. But little saplings held up by rope and stakes often offer less comfort than big, old shade trees. My own thirty-one-year marriage has spawned a conglomeration of personal effects that defy categorization but warm me like an embrace. The 1947 oil painting of a rural Indiana landscape that hangs in our den graced my parents' living room for as long as I can remember. The elaborate frame is chipped and the color scheme wrong, but when I look at it even in passing, I feel like I am home.

The stack of kelly-green and royal-blue washcloths in my linen closet are all that remain of our first set of towels. The rest were sent off to camp and used to cover dust mops, but these have been around as long as we have. And even though my old copper-bottomed Revere Ware pots and pans were replaced by a shinier, aluminum-clad set, they still sit packed away in a taped-up box in the basement. I'm not cooking in them anymore, but oddly, I don't want anyone else to, either. And while I'm about as likely to host a tea as I am to drive a big rig, I keep my mother's bright yellow dessert plates just in case.

Things passed down from one generation to the next often hold the most meaning, and although I rarely use my mother's set of silver flatware,

From Here to Maturity

I like knowing it's there, in its original, hinged wood box, velvet dividers neatly separating forks from spoons. I throw lavish dinner parties about as often as I cliff dive, but occasionally I open the heavy lid and lift out a piece to stroke and admire. To assuage homesickness while away at camp, we followed our mothers' instructions and stared at the moon at an agreed-upon time, to connect us in spirit. Holding the same intricately carved fork my mother set out at a formal family dinner is my way of looking at the moon.

As a child, I considered hand-me-downs as trash definitely not to be treasured. I had my eye on my cousins' matching stuffed toy lambs, but what I got were their cashmere sweaters, complete with multicolored floral appliques delicately hand-sewn to the neckline or hem. To me, the older girls had looked like Sophia Loren in them, and as I stared down at my own chest, only Maynard G. Krebs came to mind. Surely something new with a round collar and puffy sleeves would flatter me more and help me mature. If only I had kept them instead of dejectedly stuffing them into the trash, I'd have had custom vintage apparel not available in trendy shops or catalogs: something close to my skin that had history and meaning.

When I look at my treasures now, I think of the blue cut-glass lamp my mother always regretted giving to her niece. It helps me understand why she presented me with her mother's gorgeous strand of cultured pearls, then took it back when her neck and her memory were bare. It's why I keep my first Royal typewriter, the one with a combination red and black ribbon, upon which I hammered out the stories of a little girl. Sure, it signifies how far technology has come, but mostly it reminds me that I can't get something off my heart until I put it on paper.

My older brothers had twin beds with horses carved into the headboards, and a matching dresser with horseshoes for drawer pulls. Because I can see the furniture only in my mind, I have kept my own son's bedroom suite, its walnut headboards and stocky nightstand keepsakes of the boy who became a man. And even though my father could never understand how a girl could affix stiff brush rollers to her scalp and then sit deafly and mutely beneath a blast of hot air, the beauty treatment helped shape my femininity, making a woman out of a girl. And so my salon-style hair dryer with its plastic spaceman hood and dial heat-control settings stands erect on its wheeled base in the basement, a monument to grooming and growing up.

Aunt Mayme's oil painting of ducks in a marsh isn't gallery-worthy, but I like it. Two of seven children, she and my father struggled between keeping their creativity inside and allowing it out. He could write and she could draw, but Depression-era responsibility and lack of opportunity kept them from exhibiting their natural gifts. His stunning love letters to my mother remain bound by a ribbon on her shelf, and Aunt Mayme's artwork hangs on my wall, not so much for sentiment but as a source of inspiration. Talent is fully realized only when it's shared.

Someday we'll probably act like other empty-nesters-turned-senior-citizens and downsize to a condo. Then I'll be faced with how to dispose of my mantel clock that chimes twelve times no matter the hour, or our son Jonathan's first-grade watercolor of a lion on the outside of a cage looking in, rather than the other way around. An ornate silver lazy Susan and my mother-in-law's demitasse cups will no doubt wind up in some sorry garage sale, despised by a future daughter-in-law or, worse yet, at the bottom of a Goodwill collection bin. In the meantime, I'm hanging on for dear life.

—December 2000

I wish I had kept the ceramic beagle awarded to me for winning the School 84 fifth-grade spelling bee. The final word was "mortgage." I never told anyone, but I knew it because of the frequency with which I played Monopoly.

Prisoner in the Porch

THERE ARE TWO THINGS I'm gaga over: babies and cats. I'll hold anybody's baby, anytime, even if they urp or scream for their mamas. Likewise cats, which I cannot greet without scratching their ears or dangling bits of yarn, twigs, or car keys in their faces.

As luck and nature would have it, I've had two babies and approximately two dozen cats. A lifetime favorite in the latter category was Casper, a white renegade with whom I spent the better part of my girlhood and who, with particular feline finesse, probably fathered dozens of white cats whose successors still stalk my old neighborhood.

While away at summer camp, my mother wrote to advise that at long last, Casper had run away, and to be prepared when I came home. Just in time for my homecoming, however, Casper returned, greeting me in my mother's arms at the train station. With his usual pride and prowess, Casper spared me his demise years later by simply disappearing into the night like a sliver of moon behind a cloud.

Others, although equally loved, met sadder or more gruesome ends. Take Tuffy, a fuzzy orange rascal whose tangled, matted fur belied his feline heritage. Forced to undergo the degradation of a warm, soapy bath, Tuffy darted off into the brush, never to reappear. Or Benjamin, a stately black and white longhair who disappeared one afternoon, launching a fruitless search of our apartment community. Dejected, we let two weeks pass before adopting Horrible, a tortoise-colored runt of the litter who satisfied herself by watching the toilet flush and napping in the wine rack.

None met so tragic an end as Frank—"old blue eyes," as we dubbed him—who stuck his head beneath a descending garage door to see who was coming, with fatal results. My own suffering should have been so brief.

Or Doc, a darling calico who slept on the seat of the riding mower and shunned 9-Lives but delivered mouse skeletons to our back door each day. Ours for several years, she met her maker at the hands of a teenage driver who came sheepishly to our door to ask if I might like to keep her collar. I did not.

With such questionable luck as pet owners, it was with the utmost care that we selected Paddy-Cat, a glorious calico who hailed from the Humane Society and who grew so stout and lazy as to be unable to jump to a chair without an audible "umph." With Frank fresh in our minds, we did not allow Paddy-Cat outside—the resulting inactivity no doubt responsible for her girth. Too lazy to nose out individual morsels of dry food, she would flip them onto the floor with her paw, then nudge them to her mouth with the slightest of effort.

A family member's allergy sent Paddy to her next owner, an outgoing, pretty hairstylist, leaving me not only forever babyless but catless as well. It was too much to fathom, and after nearly three years, I caved in. A friend's cat had given birth under her bureau, and as one of the first humans to sprawl on the floor and examine her offspring, I spied Scooter, the one most eager to explore and the obvious pick of the litter. She'd live outside in our woods, I vowed, safe from garage doors, cars, poachers, or dogs.

Only I couldn't do it, which has placed Scooter in a sort of cat limbo, having taken up permanent residence on our enclosed back porch. Allowed neither in nor out, she is a prisoner of sorts—privileged only by material things and her choice of cuisine. One meow and Scooter gets warm milk and chicken breast morsels, solid white tuna, or sizzled ground beef. She's had all her shots, a hundred and thirty dollars; been dipped and de-fleaed, sixty-five dollars; and sleeps on a corduroy pet bed, eighty dollars, that heats when plugged in. She has her own carpeted kitty condo, forty-five dollars; and a ceramic heater, a hundred thirty-nine on sale, which blows a blast of warm air directly into the corner she favors. Though it adds a dollar-fifty a day to our heating bill, it's cheaper than leaving her in the car with the heater running all winter.

In fits of boredom she'll race about the twelve-foot room in frenzied circles, now and then throwing herself up against the sliding glass door in glorious finale. For variety she will greet her approaching dinner bowl on her hind legs alone, needing only a tiara and tutu to resemble those silly lapdogs that prance behind the elephants at the circus.

On her few escorted visits outside she has behaved poorly, once jumping fifteen feet from an elevated wood deck to a nearby tree, shinnying to the top in seconds while we stood wailing below. She races for a wooded patch, disappearing under a blanket of dried leaves, her gray coat blending into the winter landscape and making her impossible to locate.

Except for the sub-zero days she spent atop the clothes dryer, inside is off limits, her attempts to slither in via a three-inch crack in the door foiled by whomever enters or exits. She exists as a sort of video pet, providing joy and entertainment behind an eight-foot sliding glass door.

Come spaying and spring, however, the world is her oyster. When the porch's glass panels are traded for screens, she'll get the run of the yard. Then the decision is hers—whether to venture to the hinterlands, the wind in her fur, or dabble about in nearby reaches, joining us when chicken is served.

—February 1990

Scooter, who has since been nicknamed "Woody" due to her rapid acclimation to the out-of-doors, spent approximately six years relishing the fresh air, flora, and fertile hunting grounds of suburbia. Advancing years, a kidney disorder, and damaged retinas have forced her back indoors, where at age twelve, she eats a vet-prescribed diet, naps, and gazes with limited vision out the window in an obvious attempt to recapture her youth.

Age
Before Beauty

My mother was right: Youth is wasted on the young.

Cruel Shoes

I WANT MY OLD feet back, the pretty slender ones with no sore spots, the ones I was proud of at the beach, Now, it seems, I hobble around on aching, ill-formed ones; I'm surly newspaper columnist Bob Collins with a better disposition.

I was just getting used to the two other post-forty maladies, far-sightedness and abhorrence of loud music, when the foot thing struck. It wasn't pretty, but I had learned to navigate in trifocals without throwing up or falling down the basement stairs, and at Deer Creek Music Center I knew to avoid the seats two rows from the bank of speakers. (That lesson came the hard way, after a loud concert in which the sound waves rocked me from the inside out, leaving me to question whether I was feeling the beat of the music or the garlic cream linguine I'd had for dinner.)

But the foot pain caught me off guard. What were those bony protrusions at the base of my big toes? The result of something acceptable, like too many fruitless hours on the stair-climbing machine? Or something more probable, like too many days cramming my big feet into little pointy shoes? Whatever the cause, the painful lumps could mean only one thing: I had officially turned into Miss Coffing, my sixth-grade teacher.

As grade school students, we shared plenty of laughs at that particular teacher's expense. But who knew? Perhaps she wore those black lace-ups we called "old lady shoes" because her feet hurt. And now, there I was, scouring the ads in *Parade* magazine, where mail-order shoes are called by name, like houses in a tract-home subdivision. The "Shannon" might do, or the "Verdi," man-made leather behemoths with wedged soles and four-inch pleated vamps. Disguised in my son's ski hat and Ray-Bans, I shopped the foot care aisle in the drugstore, thinking the flesh-colored adhesive pads might feel pretty darned good. And worst of all, after an office lunch at Downtown's Bazbeaux, I cupped my hands over my eyes and peered in the window of nearby Stout's Shoes, pretending to admire their historic basket retrieval system but secretly scoping out the fall line of Rockports and Easy Spirits.

From Here to Maturity

I didn't see this coming. One day I'm Imelda Marcos, stacking up boxes of Ferragamos and Nine Wests on my closet shelves, and the next I'm an eight wide, flopping around in gunboats with crepe soles and considering wearing my bedroom slippers to work. So I did what any responsible baby boomer would do: I sought professional help. Alone in the podiatrist's examining room, lost amidst a wall-length mural of the Alps, I noticed a twist-top room freshener (occupational hazard), and a compact vacuum (don't ask). As the blood rushed out of my clammy feet into my brain, I thought I saw Miss Coffing chasing me with a ruler for not carrying my library books in a plastic bag, toes cracking relentlessly in her hideous witch's shoes.

After an exam by a first-rate practitioner, a set of x-rays and twenty minutes face-down on a table while an orthotics assistant wrapped my feet in warm, wet plaster, I was ready for the verdict. Bunions. Five more degrees and I'd require surgery, after which I'd no doubt clomp around on those flat snow shoes they make you wear while you recuperate, like the ones worn by dogsled racers in northern Minnesota. I'd fight it every step, even if it cost two hundred and seventy dollars for custom-made arch supports to wear in my running shoes, regardless of the fact that I run only if someone's chasing me in a parking garage.

I don't know why I'm so surprised. My feet have always been my nemesis. Like a German shepherd puppy, mine outgrew the rest of me, and in my third-grade picture I sported legs like coat hangers, anchored by size seven battleships. My dad consoled me with the corny joke that, unlike my girlfriends, I had "good understanding."

These days I'd give anything for a laugh. Coupled with the fact that I can no longer see the prices on the grocery store shelves, my feet hurt. These factors limit my mobility somewhat, and pretty soon I'll probably need one of those motorized scooters to go out and get the mail. Until then, though, I'll amuse myself with catalogs advertising bra-strap pads and shower benches, awaiting the thirty-nine-ninety-five electronic shiatsu massage slippers I ordered from Hammacher-Schlemmer.

Hey, it beats the Alps.

—October 1993

Since I appear to be growing shorter, I have taken to wearing shoes with higher heels. After a particularly grueling trek through airports in three cities—clad in three-inch blocky heels—I stepped out of the offending footwear, threw them in the trash beside Indianapolis International Airport Gate B5, and walked barefoot and happy to the car.

My Generation

FOR ME, 1969 never happened. Searching my home for remembrances, photographs, newspaper clippings—anything—I came up dry. On a dusty bookshelf I discovered three Indiana University yearbooks—one from 1968 that barely survived a flood in my mother-in-law's basement and boasts 512 stuck-together pages, and two from 1966.

Still, in spite of the lack of physical evidence, the year that saw Woodstock—this month celebrating its twenty-fifth anniversary—holds many important memories for this former IU senior. On semester break, when others ran off to tropical climes for a little mid-year carousing, I got married. At the height of peace marches and hippie uprisings, we sublet an apartment for the summer and watched helplessly as the real tenant's aquarium sprang a slow leak. By fall the soggy wooden trunk upon which it sat had warped at the edges and the few surviving guppies that had not already hurled themselves out of the tank onto the harvest green shag carpet took their final gulps of oxygen and expired.

Intent on learning to cook, finish school, and live together, we were oblivious to 1969. I'm certain I must have read about Woodstock and looked on in disbelief at the TV images of the masses of humanity rocking on that New York farm, but the scene was as removed from my settled little life as the bombing missions into Cambodia. To me in the sixties, tie-dye was something worn by the aimless sorts who lounged on a wall on Bloomington's Kirkwood Avenue or tossed Frisbees at the nearby Dunn Meadow. Our sorority set of college coeds' greatest concern was whether our headbands matched our wool knee socks, and dope was the kid wearing his shirt buttoned all the way to the top who sat by us in English comp.

My only brush with alternative forms of consciousness involved not marijuana, but a very large punch bowl filled with "purple passion," a lethal mixture of grape juice and, I presume, vodka or rum. The concoction created the only moment in my life when I can remember laughing for such a sustained period in the absence of anything funny.

While the hippies that adorned the Bloomington campus served as a source of amazement and often-blatant entertainment, our lives did not intersect. On one occasion, in 1969 as a matter of fact, my young law school student husband and I were invited to the home of a close friend best known for his spectacles and scraggly beard, and for pontificating ceaselessly about matters of political or philosophical significance. Still, his bona fide hippie status did not fully register until we climbed the crumbling concrete steps of his white frame house set well into the shallow hillside of a dilapidated Bloomington neighborhood.

Once inside, neither the lack of furniture on the sagging hardwood floors nor the proliferation of cats nibbling at raggedly open cans of food startled me. What *did* was the claw-footed bathtub that stood in a nearby bathroom, unfettered by a door. In it sat a naked woman, long, wet hair matted onto her neck. She seemed, if not oblivious to her company, at least slightly amused by it. We stood wide-eyed, coffeecake in hand, as she splashed about, waving dinner instructions at her friend. Whether this was an open act of free love or simply a lack of desire to place the chicken on the rusted grate of the small barbecue grill herself still remains a mystery. My dinner of coffeecake was nonetheless the second most memorable event of the evening.

My bland answers must confound the members of Generation X who ask me what it was like to grow up in the late sixties. Hoping for tales of sit-ins and unwashed clothes, bra-burning and people with names like "Moonbeam," they instead hear tales of dinner with visiting parents at IU's Tudor Room and foursomes of young married women meeting for weekly games of mah-jongg. It stirs memories of a honeymoon in California, where we feigned joining a Berkeley protest march for the camera, giggling over the photos of each other carrying signs and offering the peace symbol. While many marked an uncertain time by living together in communes and bathing—however infrequently—in front of guests, reciting esoteric poetry and smoking weed, we lived life the way we had always lived it—within the rules, and within the privacy of our bathrooms.

—August 1994

The hippie in question ended up moving to Israel, where he married a French woman who translates movies into English. Two gorgeous child-

ren later, they divorced. I often wonder if he sees his free-spirited friends on his rare visits home.

Sight Gag

LIFE IS PRETTY EXACT. You are tall or short, skinny or fat, nearsighted or farsighted. I squinted my way through the first eight years of my life, sat in the front row to see the chalkboard, and generally perceived things in shades of fuzzy gray. Therefore, the diagnosis of extreme nearsightedness at age nine was no surprise. It was only yesterday that I exited Dr. Tavel's optometry clinic on Monument Circle in my first pair of glasses, shocked at how black, white, and utterly detailed the world could be.

Sensing that terminal nearsightedness was punishment enough for a self-conscious preteen, my mother saw glasses the way Christian Dior saw accessories. I was not saddled with some corny clear plastic frames like a few of my friends, but wore red ones that gracefully sloped up to a point at the corners. When we tired of those, we shopped for more: green ones with a flourish of rhinestones, Clark Kent frames like my dad's, white ones for before Labor Day, black ones for after. In my household, the means were definitely more important than the end, and I had more glasses clunking around in my dresser drawer than most other girls had combs and brushes.

Some forty years later, I find that life's definitive nature has eroded. My simple diagnosis has been aggravated with age, and I find myself both nearsighted and far, and like the boy who never knew whether to exit School 84 via the west door or east, I'm hopelessly disoriented. Unable to satisfactorily focus close or far, I'm like those contradictory road signs you see nailed to a post in old episodes of *M*A*S*H*.

In my sophisticated gas-permeable contact lenses, I can see grass grow in Wisconsin but can no longer see my speedometer, the date on my watch, or my TV remote control. Recipes are a blur (not that I had much use for them when I could see them), I can't discern pennies from nickels in my change purse, and the phone book has been rendered useless. Luckily, my age group was targeted by food manufacturers or at least half my calorie intake would result from fat, and to accurately decipher a restaurant menu I need to stand across the street.

I now know why my mother donated all her beautiful lapel pins to me, probably figuring that the forty-year difference in our ages would allow the younger of us to attach the clasp with some finality. Also, like her, I have begun to worry about the driver's eye test and am considering memorizing the chart while there's still time.

Unlike gray hair and a sagging face, however, this near-far affliction has no cure. My four-hundred-dollar trifocals allow me to read, watch TV, and examine my cuticles with a minimal degree of satisfaction, but navigating the stairs in them sets me reeling. And I don't admire those who wear bifocal contacts, tilting their heads upward like the queen of England, peering out the bottoms and down their noses at the same time.

Like so many other baby boomers, I wander through life with cheap drugstore magnifiers perched on the bridge of my nose, usually scowling over the top like a schoolmarm. Tempted to hang them around my neck with a cord, I resist for fear I'll resemble the salesladies who used to custom-fit brassieres in the foundations department at L. S. Ayres' old Downtown store. I wish to imitate the style to which I grew accustomed, so I possess more than a dozen pairs, which usually find themselves scattered like discarded tissues on various countertops, end tables, and nightstands around my house. The smartest ones, made from slick gray wire, cost eight dollars at Phar-Mor, and the worst, tortoiseshell wannabes from the spinning plastic rack at Kroger, went for twelve. In a desperate attempt to clone Murphy Brown, I splurged on a fifty-three-dollar pair at Neiman Marcus's accessory counter, which shed one nose pad before the bill had even arrived.

Everyone accepts my cheesy, old-lady assortment, and are no doubt relieved I haven't taken to sweater clips or plastic rain bonnets. All but my older brother, Fred, a rugged, good-looking devil who can't abide the half-glasses resting halfway down his baby sister's nose. If I'm caught looking over the tops at him, he pantomimes "No," and motions for me to take them off. If it's a draw between looking thirty again or the ability to read the back of the movie box at the video store, however, entertainment wins over vanity.

I accept my status as a 2.0 (moderate) lens wearer, and have tossed out all the 1.25 (weak) stepsisters. The single pair of 1.50 suffices for my computer screen and car radio dial, and the entire gamut of self-prescriptions seems to he working out all right. I was, however, appalled at the recent sight of an elderly woman at a nearby restaurant table. She carefully opened her menu, attached a miniature hook light to the top, pulled an oversized magnifying glass from her tote bag, and like Dick Tracy in a cardigan, proceeded to study the contents. *Oh great*, I muttered, thinking of Fred. *Something to look forward to.*

—February 1996

It's heartening to know that many of my contemporaries who have undergone LASIK surgery can now discern the individual body parts of ants thirty yards away but still need glasses to read The New York Times.

Gray Matters

ROMEO, WHOSE NAME appropriately reflects his clients' attachment to him, thinks I should color my hair. Most of the women who sit in his chair, you see, come in with roots that could anchor a sycamore; and with brushes and bowls and a glint in his eye, he makes them beautiful.

Nice, shiny, chocolate-brown hair, I figure, will make my wrinkles stand out even more, requiring plastic surgery which, because I cry in hospital operating rooms, I will avoid like the plague. This, however, is not a popular outlook. Most of my friends and acquaintances have sat in Romeo's or some other hair colorist's chair at one time or another, and they consider my opinion of gray hair about as modern as a poodle skirt. But I'm not budging. I see my encroaching gray as somewhat liberating, a visible symbol of acceptance, a vote for Mother Nature. Alone I will set the standard for women and men everywhere: Go forth in your pristine and Godlike splendor, invite the softening of Father Time, fight off the demons of No. 9A Pale Ash Blond.

But Romeo's not buying it. If you feel down, depressed, or old, he claims, hair color provides instant and dramatic gratification. He recounts the tale of one woman who, upon seeing her non-gray reflection for the first time, leaped from the chair, kissing and hugging him hard enough to knock the wind out of him. "I felt full," he says, "like I was really making a difference." Three weeks later, he recalls, she sent him a batch of cookies.

Falling short of directly insulting me, he advises that covering my gray will "calm down" some of my hair's coarseness, making it shinier and more manageable. I've learned to live with the gray traitors, however, even though they poke out like fishing line, defying the effects of conditioner, the blow dryer, and gravity.

Furthermore, I've had experience with hair color, albeit at the age of sixteen in the privacy of my bathroom. There I bleached my dark brown locks until they reached the near-platinum shade falsely depicted on the Clairol box. Thick white bangs covered my heavy brown eyebrows like a window shade, giving me the overall appearance of Twiggy on Ding Dongs. I might have felt sultry and ravishing, but let's just say no one mistook me for Sandra Dee.

And I can't help but remember the aftermath of a pre-midlife crisis by a prominent member of our magazine staff whose pixie-like hair turned a lustrous silver while she was still in her thirties. While she attracted (and continues to attract) attention for her majestic locks, which are now becoming white, she insisted on returning to the days of yesteryear. After her lunch hour one day, there she sat at her desk, her usual perky face topped with what looked like a black string mop turned upside-down on her head. What God had intended surely was preferable.

And I have seen old women, too, whose stiff, white pin curls look better than an auburn mane that frames their crinkly skin like a bad toupee. Over a six-month period a few years ago I observed a demented, sick, and elderly nursing home resident who sat in a wheelchair while clutching a pillow needlepointed with her name: Missy. Her youthful moniker seemed every bit as incongruous as her obviously dyed hair, which, when matched with the smudge of bright red lipstick and rouge the nurses applied, made her look like those poodles they dress up in tutus and toe shoes for calendar pictures. The comical garb does not make them ballerinas, just silly dogs. And all the paint in the world will not make us young again.

Counting down to a significant birthday myself, I plan a series of columns in observation of those landmarks that mark our descent, like why we say the Internet will never replace traditional communications (because we can't figure out how to access it) and why we are veering toward pants with elastic waists. Gray hair is just one pitfall all boomers face, along with crow's-feet, tired blood, male pattern baldness, reduced metabolism and increased appetite, and virtual blindness when trying to read a restaurant menu. A pair of magnifiers and a little alpha hydroxy I'll succumb to, but I'm holding firm when it comes to this hair.

Fearful I'll look like Walter Matthau in *Grumpy Old Men*, I'm shunning Romeo's advances, deciding that even if I grow into Bea Arthur, I'll be better off. But he nudges me forward, confiding his secret of using three colors on every head he transforms, to create a more natural, multi-hued look. But, he swears, "I don't push anyone who's not ready." Well, I'm not ready. Even if this gray matter is coming in in streaks and clumps, looking like something Tammy Faye Bakker might do on purpose, I'm still not ready. If I'm going to wind up in a nursing home hallway clutching a pillow someday, my hair might as well match my disposition.

—August 1996

Five years later, I now allow Romeo to make all the important decisions. Never say never.

Athlete's Foot

IF ANYBODY DOESN'T deserve a sports injury, it is I. Quite simply, I am not a jock. Period. I couldn't do a backward roll, I never played on any team, and in college golf class I never hit the ball off the tee once in eighteen weeks. Having no desire to see me again, the prof gave me a "D," and the next semester I opted for square dancing.

So being in therapy for what they call flexor hallucis brevis tendinitis (sore toe) must be somebody's idea of a joke. But first let's digress to the injury itself. About a year ago I invested in a good, springy pair of Reebok walking shoes and took to the streets every day, rain or shine—okay, shine—for a one-mile jaunt. Nothing serious: no equipment, no mileage, no hurry. Actually, it never really qualified as a walk; it was always more like an amble. Every evening after dinner I visited with the neighbors, petted the cute blond cocker spaniel across the street, sometimes even toted along some cookies or chips for the haul.

And then, inexplicably, I became the avenger in tennis shoes. Driven to succeed, I logged dark and snowy miles on a basement treadmill and took three fast laps around my neighborhood instead of my normal two slow ones. With perfect race-walking form, I was but a blur to passersby.

At about the time of my transformation, I nicked my ankle in three places with a two-bit Bic razor. Continuing my newfound athletic pursuit, I swiveled my foot ever so slightly to the right to avoid the angry spot. No big deal, right? Wrong. One internist (twenty-five dollars), a set of x-rays (seventy dollars), podiatrist (thirty-five), and twice-a-week therapy (fifty-four a shot) later, the injury lingers. I altered my gait, they said, and now I've joined the ranks of wounded jocks everywhere, reduced to sitting in a cellulite puddle on the sidelines, wearing an out-of-shape smirk and the same pair of ugly Rockport shoes my son's gym teacher wore her last year before retirement.

To add insult to injury, I was forced to describe the ridiculous act to two doctors, an x-ray technician, and at least two physical therapists, all of whom nodded with strained straight faces at the razor part. "How far do you walk a day?" they asked, to which my answer remained the same: "Unmm-phrrn." I might have boasted a daily five-mile run, but a lousy mile after a run-in with a twin-blade? Unspeakable.

I'd witnessed such profound accidents before, however, which made it easier. Didn't I hear a resounding clump in the next office just a few years before and find a coworker, who was known to rock endlessly in his desk chair, bottoms-up on the floor, two feet pointed skyward above his desktop? And didn't a fellow editor walk into a ditch on a nightly stroll and require arthroscopic knee surgery? And in a pickup tennis match with a neurologist, wasn't my face where my racquet should have been, causing a Wilsonlike imprint smack on my nose? (He was kind enough to forego the fee for subsequent headache visits.) And last but not least, didn't I require an emergency trip to the ophthalmologist after stabbing myself in the eye with a nylon-bristle brush while blow-drying my hair? I don't know why this latest accident should have come as any surprise.

Judging from the crowd in the sports medicine clinic—sort of a macho gym for klutzes—some entrepreneur had a pretty good handle on society's dexterity in the eighties. Propped up on a table with my aggravated toe at the mercy of a cheerful therapist in a warm-up suit, I searched out the room for entertainment. There, the injured enjoy a morose camaraderie, each wearing his affliction like a badge of courage: rugged jocks boasting of softball or parasailing injuries, and those who fell off kitchen bar stools or tangled with a razor remaining tight-lipped.

It could have been worse, I soon learned. The elderly gal across the way—fastened to a treadmill—stumbled over a speed bump (while not in her car) and paid the price with shattered kneecaps. And one overweight woman became fascinated with the way her toddler thumped down the stairs on his derriere and decided to try it herself (imagine fessing up to *that* in the emergency room). What resulted was a dislocated elbow and weeks on the same table where I now found myself twice a week. Add to that an emergency call from wrestler Andre the Giant, who had gouged himself in the neck with the shower nozzle at a downtown hotel.

Actually, for all the inconvenience and embarrassment, the regimen had its rewards, and the old *flexor hallucis brevis* steadily began to improve. Until, standing on the sidelines as my son and husband played tennis one hot afternoon, I couldn't resist. A ball bounced my way and this time I led with my racquet instead of my face. I lobbed it across the net, coming down squarely on my previously injured toe. The old pain seared through my foot and calf like lightning, and I was flat on my fanny once more.

I may have to re-enroll in the Academy of Athlete's After Effects, but at least I can hold my head high among the stumble-bunnies who bounce down stairs and trip over speed bumps. This time my sports injury's for real, which, if nothing else, should merit the only athletic scholarship I'm ever likely to see.

—July 1998

The Rules

BEFORE BOB KNIGHT threw me out of his office six years ago on the occasion of his fiftieth birthday interview, he offered his own pithy take on approaching life's sixth decade. "What the hell difference does it make?" he groused. "So I'm fifty. I could get hit by a bus this afternoon."

This month I face that same milestone—the birthday, not the bus— and rather than assume such a cavalier attitude, I prefer to think of myself as wise: a deep thinker and purveyor of basic truths, able to leap tall buildings in a single bound. Having lived a half-century and seen such things as x-ray machines at shoe stores and *My Little Margie*, I am nothing if not credible. This authorizes me to impart wisdom, sharing the following thoughtful nuggets—one for every year—that only come with age:

1. *Our Town* is the best play ever written.
2. When someone over fifty moans, it's usually because of a piece of flourless chocolate cake.
3. If people could unwind as well as cats, we'd be more content.
4. My mother was right: Youth is wasted on the young.
5. Hairpieces never look better than being bald.
6. Potato chips are better than pretzels.
7. Two of the most frustrating things to do are grow out your hair and lose ten pounds. It's never a good idea to try both at once.
8. If people were as quick to compliment as they are to criticize there would be fewer letters to the editor and we'd all be happier.
9. Things always look better in a catalog than they do in the box or on you.
10. White chocolate is an oxymoron.
11. The best place in which to read a book is a screened-in porch on a breezy day.
12. Tall is better than short.
13. Bathing suits don't look good on people over forty.
14. Ben Franklin was right: Early to bed and early to rise, makes a man healthy, wealthy, and wise.
15. Buying your first designer outfit is the hardest.
16. Apples from New Zealand are better than apples from the United States, except in October.
17. There are more good books than there is time to read them.
18. Even though experience is the best teacher, your kids don't want to hear about it.
19. One of the best things to eat is McDonald's french fries.
20. Turning your mattress periodically doesn't make it last any longer.
21. The best lunch is peanut butter and grape jelly on Wonder Bread, plus potato chips, chocolate milk, and two Oreos.

22. It doesn't matter who you hurt on the way up as long as you're not planning on coming back down.
23. Ice cream is better than frozen yogurt.
24. Our imperfections make us more interesting.
25. Everyone else on the airplane is just as scared as you.
26. Men can't do laundry as well as women. Men can't do most things as well as women, although they are usually more highly paid and better regarded.
27. Dark chocolate is better than light.
28. The most interesting and tender relationship is between a grandparent and grandchild.
29. The worst day to go to the grocery store is Sunday.
30. Everyone looks older than you at your high school reunion.
31. A manicure always makes you feel better.
32. You will spend many more years in the house without children than with.
33. Sixty-year-old women with dyed hair and face-lifts look like sixty-year-old women with dyed hair and face-lifts.
34. Macaroni and cheese never goes out of style.
35. You never forget the people who were nice to your children.
36. White carpet isn't worth it.
37. Gravity is not our friend.
38. People in nursing homes have wonderful stories to tell and no one to tell them to.
39. You can tell more about a person by the way he leaves a job than by the way he comes to it.
40. If men spent the same money and attention on their first wives as they do on their second, one marriage would suffice.
41. Going to a movie is better than renting a video. Going to a movie on a weekday afternoon is the best guilty pleasure.
42. Marilyn Monroe was right: Diamonds are a girl's best friend.
43. Nothing makes you feel more mortal or less significant than counting the rings on a tree.
44. Typewriters are better than computers because the printer and word processor are all-in-one.
45. Cosmetic surgery is like wallpapering one room in the house. It just makes the rest of it look worse.
46. Looking at old pictures only makes you sad.

47. If you haven't worn an article of clothing in a year, you won't wear it, and you'll never get thin enough to wear your tight clothes.
48. Angel food cake, pancake syrup, and marshmallows are the only good fat-free foods.
49. The conversation will be better if you wait for your kids to call you.
50. Carly Simon was right: These are the good old days.

—April 1997

Past Perfect

NOTHING STRIKES FEAR in the heart of an aging baby boomer like the prospect of a thirty-year class reunion, especially the gathering of a bunch of fraternity hotshots-cum-old men grasping at the straws of their youth. Nothing except being one of their wives, that is, grappling with the prospect of encountering an old boyfriend and former girlfriends who have probably defied their years with lasers and scalpels and tooth-bleaching kits.

I told myself that it didn't matter. What did I care how he looked now, or what he said, or if he remembered the tender promises we made? And if the girls whose shiny hair and perfect figures I admired showed up looking the same, so what? I was secure in my individuality, my intelligence, my experience.

Sure I was. And that's why I sat in the chair at the hairstyling salon giving orders to the colorist to make me young again. The gray had begun to leech into my thick hair like a toxic spill, making my admonition simple: Preserve who I was, naturally. Allow me to leave behind the years along with my roots. Choose any color you think appropriate, so long as I don't look like Judge Judy.

As I stared at my white face and dark hair in the mirror, all I could think was, *Cara mia—I have become Morticia.* Sensing my panic at the result, the hairdresser offered to soften things with highlighting, a technique requiring the amount of tinfoil necessary to roast a sixteen-pound turkey. "Leave well enough alone," warned the devil who sat on my shoulder and advised me to color my hair in the first place. He must have been the same buttinsky who thought permanent hair color would be a good alternative to semi-permanent, which fades to rust after exposure to the amount of sunlight necessary to absorb our thousand milligrams of calcium a day. Life is a series of trade-offs.

Outfit coordination was of course as important as the darkness of my hair, and on the morning of the reunion, I perched my magnifiers on the bridge of my nose and crawled around on my closet floor looking for my most fashionable purse. A mahogany one would have matched my hair, but I could not settle until I located the black microfiber shoulder bag nestled somewhere among my embarrassing display of black shoes.

Joyous upon its location, I leaped up, only to be whacked by the open cabinet door above, which drove the edge of my glasses into my nose and cheekbones with the force of a Mack truck in a head-on collision. I reeled to the floor, clutched my face in disbelief, and counted the stars that circled over my head, feeling like Daffy Duck in a Saturday morning cartoon. Icepacks or no, my bright crimson nose swelled ominously, deep blue circles rising beneath my eyes. But my hair was still brown! I had the right purse! I could still accompany my husband to the reunion, perhaps slinking away from the party room in pursuit of a convention of drunk brunette raccoons, where I could better assimilate.

Most people who look poorly opt not to attend reunions; it is a scientific fact. Only those proud of their hairlines, flat bellies, and wallets agree to parade around searching for compliments. This was proven by the first gentleman I encountered: a hunky doctor with jet black hair slicked back like Al Pacino in *The Godfather*. Gray was the order of the day, however, topping all but the women, who were as chemically enhanced as I, and one short, red-faced man in a toupee, which sat on his head at an odd angle, like a furry animal that had died there. (At a previous high school reunion, he had hurled it triumphantly into the air like a giddy graduate, but it was back.) Another good natured but potbellied man confessed to gaining forty pounds just to make everyone else look good and ensure his enduring popularity.

The former boyfriend was immediately spied, his bald head in no way detracting from his cute face, now set off with tiny wire-framed glasses. We had an uncomfortable jog down memory lane, our recollections of dates, dances, and lines in school plays alarmingly clear.

Even though we surveyed each other with the same eyes, the same hearts beating inside our chests, it was impossible to conjure up the same feelings. As we joked and bantered, another angel, this time bearing a striking resemblance to John Mellencamp, advised, "Your life is now," freeing me from torturous thoughts of paths not taken and what-might-have-beens. Memories make us who we are but cannot be recreated, any more than brown hair can make us young. Even though trainers, stylists, and surgeons can alter us superficially, the years add up and layer our souls, thickening us against the uncomplicated passions of youth.

After the band members packed up their instruments, revelers filed into a nearby hospitality room, greedily occupying every available chair. Where we once could have danced till dawn, the hours of standing had taken their toll, and a roomful of fifty-two-year-olds reminisced quietly with whoever we landed beside. Lots of choices make it possible for us to look like sitcom stars as we age, but in this group of contemporaries, no amount of brown hair or botox, liposuction, or sclerotherapy was going to change the truth. We wear our age in our eyes, whether or not their lids are allowed to droop.

A recent newspaper story proclaims "the new old," a term coined by gerentologist Dr. Ken Dychtwald, as those over fifty who are jumping out of airplanes, starring in movies, and having great sex (often with a new partner) at least once a week. Now, Sophia Loren's not a close friend of mine, but my guess is that underneath all that raw, animal sexuality is one pretty tired sixty-five-year-old. I can lift leg weights with the best of them, and I've got some darned impressive quadriceps to show for it. But the closest I want to get to the door of a plane is a seat in the emergency exit row (better legroom), and the last movie I starred in was eight millimeter, shown on my mother-in-law's living room wall. To preserve privacy and respectability, let's just say that it's tough enough to stay awake for the ten P.M. installment of *Ally McBeal.*

If age teaches us anything, it's that old boyfriends belong in the past, making us who we are today but presenting no new opportunities. Husbands of three decades understand this, which is why they don't skid across the party room floor like the Road Runner, knocking down chairs to protect what is theirs. And folks dangerously past middle age have gray hair, whether they decide to wear it like a badge of honor or cover it in embarrassment. While those of us attending the reunion painted our faces and selected our costumes, the others stayed home, aging honestly. Maybe they're the bravest ones of all.

—November 1999

The best part of the reunion was seeing my old friend, Cherie, whose hair is frosted blond.

Club Med

WE HAPPENED TO walk in on their St. Patrick's Day party. There in the Independent Living wing of Marquette Manor, old folks were festive indeed. An accordionist played a bright jig, and residents wore green plastic top hats. One lady who pushed a rolling walker proudly displayed a full head of green hair, which I hoped she had tinted on purpose. I hadn't seen so much socializing since my junior prom, as the happy crowd spilled over into the lobby and the dining room, where at five P.M., dinner service was well under way. No one, it seemed, was depressed but me.

We visited the facility as a possible future home for my husband's elderly parents, who are too ill to live alone and too well for a nursing home, sending us in pursuit of the newest form of senior care: "assisted living." The euphemisms alone boggle the mind, as institutions compete for the gentlest way to describe their services. Morningside of College Park, which offers individual apartments with no on-staff nursing, refers to itself as "Resort-style Retirement Living," a come-on probably not unlike one that convinced Jerry Seinfeld's sitcom parents to move from New York to Florida's stereotypical "Del Boca Vista."

At Sunrise's Willow Lake location, a "Reminiscences" floor houses Alzheimer's and dementia patients who aren't, I suspect, reminiscing about anything, from Count Basie to what they had for lunch. And Carmel's Windsor Court calls itself a "Personal Care Residence," which had me searching for the manicurist and masseuse. On the drive up Keystone Avenue to the house we lived in for more than a decade, we would pass Lakeview Health Care Center and wonder what lake the residents might be viewing, unless it was the adjacent low-lying farmland after a heavy rain. I always shut my eyes tightly on the way by, hoping not to see the seniors sitting dourly on the porch. Worse yet, I feared they would see me, one of the generation that put them there, with nary a shoreline in sight.

Regardless of what they call these chain-operated Olive Gardens of elder care, the facts don't lie. Such places are home when home no longer works. Folks who have spent lifetimes building families and generations are suddenly crammed into tiny living spaces where they proudly showcase photographs of children and grandchildren who are too busy to care for them themselves. On every bureau sits an ornately framed black-and-white photo of a husband and wife, though only one partner remains to remember the day it was taken. Old furniture crowds tiny rooms, like the grandfather clock I saw that nearly touched the ceiling and overtook the wall. It looked big and wrong and out-of-place, calling to mind a parent sitting in his kid's desk at Back-to-School Night.

Like the familiar smell of an elementary school corridor or a hospital ward, all these facilities smell the same: pungent, sickeningly sweet, at once medicinal and antiseptic. It was an odor that seemed to penetrate my nostrils hours after I left the premises, and visiting several in a weekend threatened to destroy forever my appreciation for flowers or fragrant bath oils or cookies baking in the oven. No amount of sniffing, blowing, or wiping could rid me of the smell of not just chemicals but of forgotten people left to disappear, little by little.

That said, I am no saint myself. My job and frantic lifestyle leave little time for housework, cooking, or even a movie, let alone the responsibility for two people in their declining and neediest years. Frequent travel and long hours knock my husband and me out of the running: We cannot care for his parents in our home or theirs. And judging by the waiting lists at such popular, highly serviced facilities as Marquette Manor, many other middle-aged children suffer a similar plight. If we wanted to badly enough, we could quit our jobs and streamline our lives to be of service. Obviously, we don't want to badly enough.

I often think of my maternal grandmother, who lived out her ninety-four years with dignity and strength, sharing her home with her daughter's family: three generations who grew up together. Now that I look back on it, I don't even know whose house it was: hers or theirs. I just know that when I came to visit, she shepherded me into her beautiful kitchen, pulled a tall bottle of ginger ale from the icebox, and sat down with me to take a long, cold drink herself. She ambled in her garden, not in a wide hallway with handrails, and her lovely rooms were as full of memories as her heart. In those days, assisted living came with love.

In professional facilities, the dining room is the focal point. Inevitably it's lighted with sparkling chandeliers; tables are set with heavy linens and lovely china; and waiters stand by with menus in one hand and, in the case of our St. Patrick's Day visit, green Jell-O in the other. This is where people age on the American Plan. In one facility's dining room, bustling with groups of four and six conversing and eating, I was struck by the sight of one old woman sitting alone. Having completed her soup course, she had piled up packets of crackers in a neat stack, presumably to take back to her room for a snack. It wasn't so much the thought of her nibbling like a little bird later that brought tears to my eyes; it was her lack of dining companions. As we age and are forced to face life alone, I think it is more natural to listen to the quiet than it is to become social again, to try to work our way into a group, to be as "popular" as we wished for in high school. Communal living must have its pressures, none of which I ever care to face myself. By then, it will be too late to worry if the ladies at Table Number Three like me or not.

Even with their "upscale" decorating schemes of pretty florals and plaids, well-situated silk plants, and the obligatory open books of poetry set atop mahogany hall tables, these places are as sad to me as the green hats worn by the partiers on St. Patrick's Day. Winding staircases and co-ordinated furnishings do not make an institution a home, and there's something comical about old people in silly costumes. Shiny brochures, chauffeured limo service to the mall, and perky young marketing directors in smart black suits tempt us but do not fool us. It's better to be in the arms of our families than in the lap of luxury. Unfortunately, our society has created the demand for the institutionalization of our beloved parents and grandparents; the facilities weren't built in a vacuum.

For her sake, I hope the woman on whose wall hung a pen-and-ink sketch of her home—with its clapboard exterior and pretty shingled roof, snow lying softly on shrubbery out front, smoke swirling delicately from the chimney—can't remember it all that well.

—June 2000

My husband's parents now live in Morningside, where they enjoy the dining room most of all.

Recall Notice

THE TWO GENTLEMEN at the restaurant were counting on me for advice. After all my years at this magazine, nine spent reviewing restaurants, surely I would know where else they should dine. After rattling off a few old favorites, I focused on downtown. I wanted desperately to recommend Bertolini's, but the name "Bertolini's" would not come.

I could see the angel hair pasta pomodoro on the plate, the crisp romaine leaves tossed with creamy Caesar dressing. The bright menu came alive before my eyes, and I swear I could even identify a server. What I could not do was conjure up the name. As I stood with my forefinger resting contemplatively on my chin, they looked at me like pigs were flying overhead. Of course, I thought of it later, slamming my fist on my table in mental victory. When it counted, however, my aging brain simply froze.

This is happening with greater frequency. Now, not only have the lenses of my eyes stiffened up, requiring that I wear magnifying glasses to see my dinner plate, I can no longer command my brain to serve me in an emergency. In detailing this story to a comrade, he asked if I started going through the alphabet: his personal trick. No, I prefer to let nature take its course, even if frustration and embarrassment will undoubtedly result. My mother, who used to employ the memory technique of association, often told the story of a former acquaintance by the name of Mrs. Applebaum. "Applebaum, Applebaum," she had instructed herself, hoping to lock the name into memory. And then, the trick. "Apples are goody." Of course, the next time she saw the woman, the greeting was automatic: "How nice to see you, Mrs. Goody."

The fact that my mother raised me to address others by name, shunning the shy, "Hi," and then *nothing*, makes this memory fade even harder to take. At the office, for example, two young women by the names of Lindy and Laurie have recently joined the staff, occupying an office for two across the hall. They are basically the same age, both perky and *Friends*-like in their look and demeanor. In short, I am helpless to remember which is which, and after nearly a month, time and patience are wearing out. The statute of limitations only runs for so long in such matters, eventually disallowing the perpetrator a new introduction.

For some reason, when I meet someone, the name slides off as if my brain were made of Teflon. It's like geometry theorems or chemistry formulas: there are no nooks and crannies into which they can burrow. Now, lest I be construed as a complete, raving idiot, I should explain that I can remember what I wore on a date to the Tee Pee restaurant in 1962, when I told them to hold the beets on my salad. I can recite complete passages from books I cherish and remember in detail every kiss ever bestowed on me. The harder I try to remember someone's name, however, the worse it gets.

Take the other day in the ladies' room. Rather than looking at the floor, I stared straight at the person standing at the other sink and bravely said, "Hi, *Julie!*" as proud of my breakthrough as an acrophobe on the observation deck of the Empire State Building. "Hey!" she said cheerily in return. "But I'm Mary."

I thought of this when I was staring incomprehensibly into the linen closet at home, having absolutely no idea why I was there. Then I realized the disability had spread, like a behavioral virus gone awry. There is no way to describe that feeling, like when you write a check and have no idea what month it is, or call someone and blank out when he answers the phone. Those moments are like waking up after a night in the drunk tank, with no memory, grateful you haven't married someone you didn't know. I console myself that if you think you have Alzheimer's disease, you probably don't, relieved that I'm not out walking around in traffic in my pajamas.

It does seem odd, though, that a person can recall every color and seam in her prom dress but nothing about an HBO movie seen hours before. Consider the following conversation with an associate whose gray matter is petrifying at the same rate as mine:

ME: I love the movie about that young doctor who moves to a small town.

HIM: Uh-huh.

ME: You know, the guy from that TV show, with a sister named Mallory?

HIM: Hmmm. Gotcha.

HIM (*thirty seconds later*): Doc Holliday!

BOTH OF US: That's it! Doc Holliday!

Of course the movie is *Doc Hollywood,* but we were satisfied we got as far as we did.

Experts warn that the average person over forty loses a thousand neurons a day, causing us to clutch our heads in a panic, hoping to retain all that we can. New prevailing wisdom is that certain portions of our brains shrink due to stress, which is no greater comfort. Either way, I need what has vanished, and it's getting harder to compensate. I fear that by the time I'm sixty, I'll be staring into the mirror at a stranger, scratching my head.

You see, a few weeks ago, I answered the phone to hear my mother-in-law on the other end. "Katie?" she said. "Is that you?" For just a fleeting moment, I had to wonder.

—June 1998

Kids Growing Up

I was the preschool cupcake-baker, the kindergarten room-mother, the first-grade lunchbox packer. That was I standing by the barber's chair to make sure he didn't look like Bud on FATHER KNOWS BEST with his freshly cut hair, and the one who pushed green beans through a grinder with butter and salt because they tasted better than the ones in the jar.

Cabin Fever

As THE END OF summer rolls around, it comes time for yet another finale: the wrap-up of summer camp. Such blissful memories the thought evokes: humid nights under a mosquito net at Girl Scout camp, where I—one who preferred Jackie Gleason and ironed sheets to campfires and daddy long-legs—endured the wilds for just five days before begging for home.

Slinging arms over shoulders and singing "Kum Ba Ya" might have proved entertaining to my tentmates, but alas, I yearned for my loved ones. It was the ghost stories in the cemetery at dark, I think, that prompted my fateful letter home. "Come get me," I sobbed, "or I'll surely die."

Heeding not the psychology textbooks but only their hearts, my parents sent my older brother to rescue me. He scooped up the bony mass of a failed camper into his arms, kicked my duffle bag along the gravel road to the car, and returned me to civilization. It was the only time I remember him carrying me, but it was a sweet enough memory to last a lifetime.

It was with that background that I launched a child of my own into the uncharted wilderness to spend a month under the stars, and as his return approaches, I'm not sure who has suffered more. The week before his departure was filled with all the usual anticipation and preparations. He hid his trusty possessions from the sticky fingers of a younger brother, and I shopped daily, marveling that anyone who stored dirty laundry under his bed could possibly require sixteen pairs of socks, eight pairs of shorts, and fourteen T-shirts.

The stacks in his footlocker grew higher as each day passed, the felt-tip laundry marker growing more fibrous with each addition. I was exhausted, and he was bored. I knew he was desperate for pre-camp entertainment when he thumped the cat into the trunk and slammed the lid. What he didn't count on, however, was the latch swinging shut. After ten horrifying minutes, he located the key and managed to jiggle open the trunk. The cat, I think, still does not miss him. At least she looked relatively nonplussed when she finally emerged from under the bed three days after his departure.

Dropping him off was as agonizing an experience as I care to remember. The car ride was silent except for his inventory of each passing piece of modern civilization and his last-will-and-testament requests. The cabin proved shocking—half an A-frame with splintery, dusty shelves; sagging bunks on which were strewn all manner of sleeping bags; and graffiti on the wall marking time as if chronicled by so many convicts on death row.

To add insult to injury, only one bottom bunk remained, and our downtrodden lad meekly staked his claim on the unpopular berth nearest the counselors at the rear of cabin Number 13. It was a rare, sixty-five-degree, sprinkly, dark, summer day, and I left him clinging to the chain-link fence at the pool like a kitten on a screen door, goose-bumped and forlorn.

The letters home, however, have been encouraging. A parent learns to discount such things as, "Only twenty-seven more days and I'll be home," and "On pick-up day you can come between ten and four. Come at ten." Pleas for a stamped envelope to someone unreadably named "Gix" go necessarily unheeded, as do requests for *Mad* magazines, invisible ink pens, and rubber feet for the talent show.

Only such messages as, "I'm better now," are cause for alarm, as are those requests for hard-soled shoes for cliff jump (cliff jump?) and notification that he had to spend only two hours on the work wheel. The what? Is he chained to crudely fashioned spokes like a mule in Mexico? Is this what cost nine hundred dollars? I suddenly remember his fear as we drove him to his destination. "What if," he shivered, "there is a murderer on the camp grounds?"

"Nonsense," we replied. "Too much HBO." I will, I think, be anxious to learn the definition of the work wheel.

The one letter that remains the classic, however, details Melinda, the dancing partner of the all-camp Saturday night party. "She is beautiful," he writes. "Should I ask her to the weekend walk? Write and tell me what to do in your next letter." Old enough to be in love, I muse, young enough to seek advice from another generation.

He will come home, I'm sure, with just short of five unmatched dirty socks and somewhere less than seven of the fourteen T-shirts, three of which will say "Sam" or "Brian." A pasty blob of something that was once soap will have slimed up the other clothing in the trunk, there curiously will be sand in everything, and I won't know until his film is developed what really happened.

Two things of which I am sure, however: The cat won't be anywhere near the scene of unpacking, and someone named Melinda will be but a distant memory.

—August 1985

Our older son, Gabe, never returned to camp. His younger brother, Jonathan, however, tried it three times before declaring himself a failure. When his best friend Michael's mother and I retrieved them after a week at basketball camp, we were horrified to discover that all of Michael's underpants remained stacked in a neat pile in his duffel bag. We didn't ask any questions.

Fair Game

TO SOME, FEBRUARY may mean heart-shaped cookies with red sprinkles and George Washington cherry pie, but to any central Indiana parent of school-age children, it means something not nearly as cute: the science fair, hall after hall of father-crafted projects destined to make a fool out of anyone with the nerve to stick celery in blue ink and watch the color crawl up the stalk.

Children are expected to undertake thought-provoking, important experiments alone, but the best my children have been able to master without assistance is to drop a nail into a bottle of Coke and watch it wretchedly disintegrate like the Wicked Witch of the West after an uprising of Dorothy and the guards. Show me a third grader who can rig an electric doorbell that chimes "Hey, Look Me Over," and I'll show you a kid whose father has a workbench the size of New Hampshire. The only projects a kid can pull off alone are making a lima bean grow toward the light, cultivating mold on the inside of an orange peel in a Baggie, or watching an aspirin boil up in a glass of baking soda and water.

Society has forced me to get involved—begrudgingly—but that doesn't mean I have to like it. The rules are simple: no live animals, and that goes for slimy chamelions who slink from a brown shoe box to a green one, and no torture, including seeing how long it takes a grasshopper to die without flies, or vice versa.

One year I coerced a first grader into discovering what makes a popcorn kernel explode when it gets hot, a nifty experiment complete with such visuals as a glass of kernels (before) and a matching glass of popped corn (after). Unfortunately, some kid who forgot breakfast got to the "after" jar before the judges, and all that remained was an irate principal, who made a plea on the P.A. not to consume the contents of anyone's experiment, a crying first grader, and a mother who had stretched her creativity to the limits and didn't even get an honorable mention.

Another year, when a fifth-grader demanded a socially significant project—the only ones that ever win—I masterminded discovering the effects of toxic waste. Because my own self-inflicted rules eliminated animals and torture, plant life was all that remained. We concocted the poisonous brew and fed it to a healthy schefflera, at the same time administering fresh water to its flora friend. For two solid weeks, both plants fared exactly the same and, in desperation the night before the fair, I stuck the supposed loser into the microwave on reheat for six minutes. I got a green ribbon.

That was the year before I crawled around central Indiana lake beds to obtain water samples to test for levels of hardness. In addition, I knocked on strange doors in Carmel, Beech Grove, and Greenwood asking for a few drips from the faucet, which we, and I use the pronoun loosely, lined up in baby-food jars into which we dripped a testing chemical gleaned from a forty-dollar chemistry set. They all turned the same shade of blue, and I got a B-minus for the six weeks.

Last year, examining how a solar collector worked seemed simple but thrilling enough, with a plastic kit from the toy and hobby shop providing the framework. Since it rained for five straight days and there was no sunshine to store, we resorted to a desk lamp and a sixty-watt bulb.

We ventured into the school on a Saturday morning—you could cut the excitement with a knife—carrying a Ziploc storage bag with an eight-inch plastic tub that didn't work and a list of hypotheses and observations on a single sheet of limp poster board that batted about in the February wind like a wraparound skirt on the golf course. Imagine our dismay upon seeing multilevel pegboard displays with boat engines, and glass enclosures populated with white mice imbibing differing levels of caffeine. I abandoned the horrified twelve-year-old, who spent his required three hours catching the chart in his lap each time the Scotch tape gave way and incurring the wrath of compatriots who had brought bacteria-laden petri dishes and ant farms, automatic volcanoes, and electronic air purifiers.

He said that by his shift's end, the solar collector had become a dumpster for apple cores and candy wrappers, and the judges just shook their heads and suggested he take up the violin.

There are professional services for everything from party givers to errand runners, personal shoppers to centerpiece designers. Why, then, can't I hire a science fair coordinator to cheerfully assemble the latest in technology and give my kid the credit? Better yet, why don't I open a store where a yearly list of five hundred or so ideas is available, as well as instructions, all materials, and to-your-door service at twenty-five dollars if required? I could become rich, specializing in blue ribbons and proud parents.

For this year, however, timeliness and creativity are out, and I'm planning a comparative survey of the absorbency of paper towels. I can't wait to see the competition.

—February 1986

In Jon's final year, we compared the effects of second-hand smoke by placing squares of unbleached muslin in smoking and non-smoking sections of various restaurants. We returned a week later to find them identically free of discoloration that results from tar and nicotine. It was worth it to lock myself in our powder room and smoke a pack of Lucky Strikes, exhaling directly onto the fabric squares that had hung in the smoking section. We received a blue ribbon and made it to regionals.

Slam Punks

I'VE NEVER BEEN much of a kids' sports fan. During Little League baseball, I was the only mother who sat at the end of the team bench because I forgot my lawn chair, and while everyone else jumped to his feet to cheer on his offspring, I crouched in tornado-drill position, certain that a stray baseball would bop me on the head, detaching both retinas and rendering me unconscious.

Though mothering a peewee basketball player provides fewer obstacles, I still find it difficult to master a graceful perch on the metal bleachers, and there's simply no place to situate one's purse without the fear of quarters and lemon drops raining to the hardwood like so much ammo over Guam.

Other than that, though, I've memorized the game rules and am proud to say I now fit in. Those rules—the real hard-knock-life lessons—aren't taught, even at Bob Knight Basketball Camp. They come from five years of Sunday afternoons spent in damp, smelly gyms, kissing bruised, sweaty foreheads and rummaging through piles of coats and warm-up suits on the gym floor, searching for a boy's gray fleece sweat pants that are exactly the same as everyone else's.

These rules—or better yet, eventualities—follow:

- The uniform is everything. You simply can't expect precision, diplomacy, courage, and skill from five boys whose shorts don't match. It is also easier to win when the back of your shirt reads Melvin Simon & Associates than when it says Roto Rooter Service. You don't identify the opposing team by its sponsor, i.e. "We're gonna bust Reliable Motors today." You name players only by their relative size and the color of their jerseys, i.e. "Did you see that fat kid on orange?" or "That small kid on purple is going to be dead meat." It is unacceptable to let your shirt hang out, but cool to cut off the sleeves.

- Time-outs to have your mom tie your shoes are embarrassing, emasculating, and thus discouraged. Listening to your father, who is writhing in red-faced rage on the bench, is also unadvisable. If the coach is nudging you in the direction of the player you are to guard, and your father is unintelligibly hollering, "Mmmph, smyr—*wake up, sonny, and stay on your man!*"—listen to the coach. You are permitted, however, to glance at Dad after you've scored a basket to get a two-fisted thumbs up and watch him clap a fellow fan on the back and boom, "That's my boy!"

- A score of 2–0 at the half is acceptable and should be applauded, especially if the kid who scored the single swish is yours. It is not necessary for players to watch the clock or the scoreboard, but it is necessary to listen for the halftime buzzer or the ref's whistle. Players should not screech to a halt when the buzzer sounds on another court. That requires a lengthy explanation from the ref and more screaming from Dad.

- You cannot dribble on your knees, leap over the line during a free throw, or choke the kid you are guarding. When you crack heads with the red-haired kid on blue, it is frowned upon to cry, feign death, or feebly ask the coach if it's time to go back to Kansas yet. It is also impossible to guard with one hand and chew the fingernails on the other, even if you're clutched.

- You can run up and down court only so many times without attempting a shot. After six or seven scurries up and back, put it up, even if it doesn't stand a chance. When you and an opponent both have hold of the ball, someone eventually must let go. Pulling it to and fro and yelling "Mine!" is fruitless.

- If all else fails, and you don't know what you should be doing (or what "DEE-fense" from the crowd means), put up your arms and flail them back and forth like a traffic cop signaling a semitrailer to stop. It makes you look competent and involved. When play resumes after a time-out, don't join the other nine players milling around center court as if it were intermission at a Broadway play. Find someone appropriate to guard and begin to run in place.

- Video cameras on tripods and baby sisters are not allowed on court. Both provide unreasonable distraction and considerable danger, particularly if the baby's soft spot is still intact.

- Shake the hands of the opposing players after you lose. Do not pout, cry, refuse to do so, or squeeze their hands like lemons. This is poor sportsmanship.

- As a parent, don't gloat or accept congratulations when your son is high scorer with eight points. One man's pride will surely be next week's lemon-squeezer.

—February 1987

The Good Earth

TO MY MOTHER-IN-LAW, it is inconceivable that anyone wouldn't want a garden—wouldn't positively rejoice at the prospect of kneeling in the mud, glorify the sun rising over the crops, show off cracked fingernails caked with potting soil and Rapid-Gro. For years, she sprinkled and sprayed, clawed her way up one row and down another, and joyously compared the height of her corn to her sister's next door.

Never could I retrieve my kids without at least a fifteen-minute tour of the vegetation: Did you ever *see* such perfect cucumbers? And just *look* at the size of these tomatoes. Tired and uninterested, I'd nod my way from patch to patch, mumbling my mm-hmmms while consulting my watch.

Until harvest time, when I'd arrive with bushel basket in tow to collect the booty—my just reward for withstanding the daily lectures and displays. Our summer overflowed with fresh, tender green beans and crisp, narrow cucumbers. We munched on sweet baby carrots and the heartiest tomatoes. Unlike her succulent bounty, spoiled rotten were we—unwilling not only to imitate her miraculous methods but to hear of them as well. Like the Little Red Hen's unscrupulous neighbors, we would only help her eat her grain.

And then genetics played a curious trick on us. At eleven, our younger son proclaimed that he wished to continue the tradition—that in our yard a garden would arise, a harvest of riches to be enjoyed by all but tended by one. With plastic-handled spade in hand, he attacked the earth with grit and determination, tossing clumps of sod over his shoulder in ritualistic revelry.

A diehard saver, he blew two weeks' allowance on seeds, and with blueprint in mind sowed them in perfect rows, at perfect distances and depths, to grow perfect produce which he agreed to sell us at the perfect going price. A faultless plan was his, made even more credible by a white wire fence and two plastic windmills. His would be the Rambo of gardens, where vegetables would grow to the sun and thwart their predators, where circular fences would hold up weighty tomatoes, and green peppers would sprout just days after planting. Both the gift and the burden were his, and the rest of us supermarket heathens stood back in awe.

Sensing the significance, we did not interfere, even though I questioned the placement of the slightly irregular plot. On the side of a hill (as local hills go), it sits at a slant. Envisioning robust radishes tumbling into the tender leaf lettuce, I said nothing. Imagining rivulets of eroding water rushing downstream, I stood silently by. Realizing that it had been placed at least one-fourth acre from the nearest outdoor spigot, I watched as he wrestled a full five-gallon watering can down an embankment and across a field to his thirsty charges.

I sought hints from well-meaning friends and passed on the advice. He lined the patch with marigolds to ward off critters and set mothballs around all four sides like dominoes to further discourage uninvited guests and causing the surrounding acre to smell like my great aunt's mink coat.

And then we would wait—just water and wait—to see if warm days and good intentions were enough to ensure us our crop. I remembered my grandmother standing small but erect in her showplace of green, where a shiny fence surrounded towering rows of tomatoes, and nightly salads were picked on the spot. I saw my own mother's picturesque garden of heavy tomatoes tied to stakes with discarded stockings, a weedless wonder edged with chicken wire, where my father would pluck a red beauty and eat it like an apple, straight from the vine. Nothing like *homegrown* tomatoes, he would say, in a house where unripe specimens lined the windowsills like soldiers protecting their fort.

I thought of a childhood neighbor, a nasty-tempered old woman who plucked and snipped at her garden from daybreak till dusk, hissing at us as we came near, and of my own paltry attempts some twenty years later, when I carved a three-foot patch of gloom and despair. In it I grew sixteen green beans (four for each of us one momentous dinner) and tomatoes that were black on the bottoms from their non-fertilized stems.

Sick with the flu for one day, today's young gardener banished me to his labor and, cursing the earth, I lugged the leaden, sloshing watering can down the hill and over the scratchy field of weeds to his heavenly patch. Coming back into sight, I saw him at the window, hands cupping an ashen face, awaiting the report. Just inside the door, he met me with a look of dread. "They're dead, all dead—I just know it," he moaned, eyes lifted slowly to carefully read my expression.

It's too soon to tell whether we'll invite in-laws over with open Baggies, but things are proceeding by plan. We may not sample morsels straight from the vine, or reap enough for a party of produce, but if all else fails, I know one brave young man who will be able to boast a bumper crop of mothballs and marigolds.

—June 1998

Bad news: One sultry night a predator—raccoon, rabbit, we don't know which—gnawed the garden to the ground. It looked like the field after the Battle of Lexington and Concord. My son's greatest green-thumb victory since then has been a four-foot hemp plant, which I tend, unsure if it is legal or not.

Driving Ambition

I CAN TELL BY the jangling of car keys that destruction is near. The only thought that enters my mind when a certain sixteen-year-old flashes this noisy symbol of independence is a mythical newspaper headline: TAIL-GATING TEEN AWAITS FOREHEAD TRANSPLANT.

Heaven forbid. But what possible good can come out of the fact that while counting the days until his driver's license was issued, his greatest goal was picking up his best friend and going—alone and unencumbered—to a Northside restaurant offering more than fifteen varieties of chicken wings? These are not the aspirations of a man in charge of his destiny, let alone his vehicle.

Which brings me to my major argument with legislators who made it legal for sixteen-year-olds to drive in the first place. *What were they thinking?* Such "adults" can't rent R-rated videos, vote, or buy a pack of cigarettes, but they can get behind the wheel of a car and accidentally take out a sidewalk's worth of pedestrians while fiddling with the radio. Does this make sense? Don't get me wrong: A straight-A student, my kid's darned responsible. But I'd just as soon have him perform brain surgery on me than take me to the dry cleaner three blocks away.

The good news is that since this month marks his solo driving debut, I won't have to go with him anymore—something that will eliminate numerous screaming matches and no-win arguments. Take the time he waited dutifully at what he assumed was a four-way stop (it wasn't), and then entered the intersection straight into oncoming traffic. As cars approached at full speed I literally leaped across the console, jammed my foot onto the brake and veered into a nearby parking lot. Since this did little to convince him that he possessed the defensive driving skills of Evel Knievel, he promptly exited the car (a good move) and walked home.

My impromptu driving tips fall on deaf ears, as usual. I, like most parents of teenagers, am always wrong. You really don't have to stop before you turn right on red, and you *can* enter an intersection if the light has already turned yellow. You *do* use your turn signal when entering a space in a supermarket parking lot, and it *doesn't* matter which way the arrows painted on the pavement point. On the driver's test, you only have to parallel park behind one car, not between two, so you really *don't* need to learn how. And you *should* speed up when you approach a red light, and slow down when merging onto the interstate.

He learned these rules at driving school, a place that gives you an "A" if you pay the tuition, show up at class, wear your cap backward, and look cool. This is the same place where you learn that when turning left at an intersection, you allow the approaching left-turning car to position itself behind you, not in front of you.

Sure, in my day we stuck our hands out the window to signal a turn, but we took the responsibility more seriously. I started to learn at fourteen in what is now Butler University's Hinkle Fieldhouse parking lot. Perched atop three phone books, I experienced the subtle sounds and feel of first, second, third, and reverse as I slowly made my way around the asphalt. Now, a friend reports, her fifteen-year-old got behind the wheel the first time in a school parking lot with only one concern: "Do you think I can make it from zero to thirty before I get to the other side?" Another friend—this time my son's—reports two violations the first weekend he drove: speeding and reckless driving. If my son did that, I'd kill him before the traffic did.

Since this is not my first child to reach this milestone, I don't know why any of this surprises me. In the older boy's first licensed month, he veered into another lane, sideswiped a minivan, and then maintained it wasn't his fault. Later he coasted through a stop sign, only to meet another young driver—head on—who was also gliding through. (Her front teeth are healing nicely.) When I am a passenger in his car, I groan, cover my eyes, make whistling sounds through my teeth, and generally become catatonic as he follows three to six inches behind the car in front. The bottom line is, we may not be able to get auto insurance from anyone short of Lloyd's of London, but maybe we'll get a group rate at traffic school.

—March 1993

Spoiling him rotten, we presented Jonathan with a new Toyota Celica for his sixteenth birthday. It took only a few hours for him to call crying that he had been rear-ended in, of all places, the car wash.

College Boys

LITTLE DID I KNOW ten months ago when I wrote a weepy column about sending a kid off to college that I'd have an equally hard time adjusting to his return. I was warned, sure, but I scoffed at such doomsayers: bad parents, I rationalized.

Then, I wrote of sitting on the edge of his bed staring vacantly at his lava lamp, of remembering the posters that occupied his now-barren walls. The problem is, when he came back, he didn't bring with him tidings of joy and gratitude; he brought with him a computer printer filled with Oreo crumbs (or dried ants, I can't decide), fourteen pairs of black socks that were once white, and a toaster oven that produced not only hot Pop Tarts but a layer of green fur on its lower casing.

Somehow things seemed less threatening when I visited his dorm room. Sure he had collected enough pizza boxes to build a makeshift bookcase, but they were in his house, not mine. A new rule now applies: Whatever you take to college, you leave there.

College men not only behave like slobs, they also get their days and nights mixed up. I first discovered this when, observing the young lad approaching his car at eleven P.M., I asked just where he thought he was going. "Out" is of course the expected answer; I just didn't expect it at eleven o'clock. Judging from other parents of college-age students, there must be hordes of them roaming the streets after midnight. And I guess I should consider myself lucky for getting an answer at all. Oddly enough, college students who tested out of an entire year of foreign language often forget how to speak at all, answering such questions as, "Where were you last night? When did you get home?" with something resembling, "Rthr. Nderr," or better yet, an exaggerated shrug.

This select subset of society also travels in herds, like antelope. Instead of dates, like the ones my generation recalls where we got dressed up and went to the Uptown to see *Under the Yum Yum Tree*, they crash Mexican restaurants in gangs of ten, rent videos, and pretty much "hang out" until at least three A.M. I'm getting accustomed to the timetable, however, and tried not to act surprised when I apprehended my college returnee in the garage at four A.M., where, for some reason that made sense to him, he was changing the motor oil in his car.

For all the independence, however, money remains a sticking point. We put money in the checking account, he charges on a credit card, then writes a check and thinks he's paid us back. Something's wrong with the system. We got over one hurdle by insisting that the two hundred and fifty dollars he earned selling 500 Mile Race souvenirs be spent to cover the insurance deductible for a car wreck and not for a down payment on a stereo system with each speaker the size of an upright freezer. Never mind that after the accident, no insurance company in North America will cover us; his two hundred and fifty dollars was at stake.

Besides money, entertainment seems to rank high on the importance meter. Movies, videos, CDs, and, above all, live concerts, matter most, with no thought to proximity. So what if Nirvana is performing in Cincinnati? The herd can stay in a hotel and go to King's Island while they're there—perhaps on a credit card with us as the addressee. (No problem, he'll pay us back with a check.)

Luckily, we can concentrate on another teenage child at the same time, this one a fifteen-year-old with a new driver's license learner's permit. Never mind that he thinks he should speed up when he enters a turn and hugs the right shoulder unmercifully, barely missing mailboxes and kicking up clouds of dust like the Road Runner on a chase. He's licensed now, and I fear nothing short of a Ford-Cosworth engine will do come sixteen.

It's going to be a long, hot summer.

—July 1992

Home Alone

MY FAVORITE MOVIE scene—one that continues to fascinate and haunt me—comes from *Grand Canyon*, a story of miracles and self-discovery. In it, the mother, out on a jog, happens upon an infant in the bushes. Sweeping the tiny baby into her arms, she proceeds to swaddle her with leftover clothes from her own grown son, fall wildly in love with her, and ultimately adopt her. I've watched the movie a dozen times.

As my youngest prepares to leave for college this month and I confront the empty nest, I'm pretty sure—like her—that I have enough mothering left for at least one more. Unlike Roseanne or Bill Cosby's Cliff Huxtable, moving the kids out has not been a high priority. I prefer to think of myself more as Mrs. Cleaver, endlessly clucking over the Beave. Lucky for June, however, that she never had to let him go.

My own performance in this arena, unfortunately, has been less than stellar. As I anticipated my older son's departure to college, I was certain I had enough career flowing through my veins to fill the void. But just as a new puppy never takes away the ache of the dog you lost, no job on the planet can fill that empty bedroom. Instead of facing the transition with intelligence and maturity, I sat on the end of his bed and wept, and journeyed down to IU every Saturday morning for a month to do his laundry in the dormitory basement. When his contemporaries started asking me when to add the fabric softener and began calling me Mom, I realized the error of my ways and left him to fumble on his own.

Life surely won't be the same without the only family member who can operate the VCR and access the Internet. Always ashamed of my dysfunctional behavior, I console myself that I wasn't even in the same league as the human snooze alarm, a mother who called her daughter's dorm room every morning at seven to awaken her, and then again twenty minutes later to make sure she was up.

The term "empty nest" is usually followed by "syndrome," which, I suppose, officially makes it a condition or disease, like toxic shock or carpal tunnel syndrome. No wonder I feel so sick. As much as the disorder bothers me, the empty nest itself worries me even more. The term brings to mind that one house on the home tour with a sign out front proclaiming it the EMPTY NESTER. Invariably a ranch-style (we couldn't possibly make it up the stairs), it features such optional amenities as a wheelchair ramp, outdoor lap pool for arthritic bones, and Pullman kitchen with a miniature refrigerator in which to store our fiber supplements. I see it as sort of a halfway house between Walton's Mountain and Miller's Merry Manor.

After spending the last twenty-two years concentrating on the comings and goings of two children, what the remaining two inhabitants will talk about is yet to be seen. Will we sit across from each other at a lonely kitchen table—just us and our fat-free salad dressing—mooning about what used to be, or will we eagerly plan our retirement home in a little Florida trailer park, cruises aboard the Love Boat, early-bird dining? I'm practicing by watching selected episodes of *Mad About You* to see how two people function with no outside life, and by learning to utter such phrases as, "How 'bout those Pacers?"

While my husband and I will doubtless endure, I'm less sure how I'll get along without that special someone who sees Disney movies with me ("One adult and one child," he tells the ticket taker), and who body-slams the couch and demands, "Don't we have any real food around here?" Where will I be without someone who knows how to set the clocks after a thunderstorm and protects me from neighborhood dogs on my evening walks? How will I live without the one who gingerly deposits the cat's dead mouse filets in the woods rather than leaving me to stack up the carcasses on a snow shovel and then run across the yard shrieking like Pee-Wee Herman with a fistful of snakes?

I don't think I can survive without the kid who helped me select a cool new bike upon which I look as little like Arte Johnson as possible, and who can tell me for the hundredth time what an illegal defense is, as well as a sack and a pick-and-roll. It will be more than lonely without someone to summon me from his bedroom to show me all the Simpsons characters he has downloaded onto his new five-thousand-dollar notebook computer that we bought to ensure a minimum GPA of 3.5.

It was just weeks ago that I watched him shine in his cap and gown, full of wit and intellect, charm and good looks. With my graying hair and lonely heart, I find it hard to face the fact that as families go, I probably have more to look back on than look forward to. Not allowing myself to ruin this passage for him, I laughed with everyone else when he displayed a map of his new campus, outlining each path with his finger. "Here," he announced, pointing out a short drive outside the dorm, "is where Mom starts to cry."

Well, I won't cry, at least where he can see me. I'll leave him happily unpacked, surrounded by his beloved compact microwave, refrigerator, twenty-dollar director's chair, and telephone answering machine. I'll pull away biting my lip as hard as I can, and when I get home I'll journey out into the yard, beating the bushes with everything that's in me.

—August 1995

Family Practice

IT WAS PROBABLY poetic justice that as I lay in the emergency room suffering excruciating, unexplainable stomach pains, my son was receiving notification that he had been accepted to medical school. At the same time I writhed and cried and begged for mercy from anyone wearing a lab coat and a name badge, he was about to begin the journey himself.

At the end of the day I walked gingerly from the hospital with a diagnosis of irritable bowel syndrome, while on his apartment doorstep sat seventy-five-dollars-worth of congratulatory balloons. In the most helpless of states, on that gurney in that sterile cubicle, I realized the awesome power of doctors and came to grips with the fact that my son might actually become one.

I have always been able to picture him in blue scrubs, the drawstring pants tied around his narrow waist, a stethoscope slung importantly around his neck. Some spiritualists report the act of rising out of their bodies and witnessing the activities below them. This is the ethereal way I see him practicing medicine, his words at a premium, using a well-placed joke, making the right decision. After four years of relentless studying and a perfect grade point average, he has earned the privilege. As his mother, it is a bonus I couldn't possibly deserve.

Having children is not an unselfish act. No one thinks about bringing a child into the world for the sake of population growth or furthering the species. We have children because we want them: to hold a baby in our arms, to nurture someone dependent on us, to create a family for comfort and company. We are curious as to how we will duplicate, and watch our swelling bellies with pride and expectation. If we can kiss their petal-soft skin and curl our fingers in their tiny fists, that's thanks enough. After we reward ourselves by giving them life, we don't expect they pay us back in act and deed.

In most children's growing vocabulary, "no" comes shortly after "mama." They embarrass us in restaurants, stomp out of shoe stores, turn to rubber as we drag them through supermarket parking lots. When we stand over their homework, they become zombies, staring into our pores but avoiding our eyes. We sit upright in bed awaiting their tardy returns and pray we won't hear the dreaded words each time a siren wails or the telephone rings. When they present us with a Mother's Day bouquet or a crumpled honor roll certificate, we reel from the shock. We expect the abuse, which helps us to better appreciate the unlikely payback.

"My son the doctor's" older brother has a wonderfully offbeat sense of humor. The first time I realized that a child might, without provocation, thrill us, occurred as he sat on the floor in an infant seat at eight months of age, watching me wrap holiday gifts. He wore a one-piece suit decorated with dachshunds, and something struck him as funny. I don't know if it was his upside-down view of the dogs, the shiny ribbons, or the way I sheared and taped, but he began to laugh. Not a funny half-giggle, the kind proud mamas mistake for gas, but a raucous laugh, a gut-busting, infectious, hyena-pitched howl. I could do nothing but roar in return, and there we sat, the two of us, one rolling out of his miniature chair, the other doubled over on the bedroom floor. I can't remember ever laughing so hard before or since, and it was joyous to learn that a parent could be rewarded in mundane but monumental ways.

When his little brother was on the way, I sat in a rocker in his empty nursery, a musical lamb on my lap. It played "Thank Heaven for Little Girls," and I was sure my wishes would be granted. To my protruding tummy I sang "Jennie Rebecca, five years old . . . ," the lyrics to a popular TV commercial in the late seventies. Jennie was the name I had chosen, after my grandmother, who had crossed through Ellis Island some eighty years before. Jonathan was born a half-year later, his bright pink face and thatch of unruly blond hair a shock to his brunette parents. I believe he was as surprised to see me as I him, and any thoughts of frilly frocks and dollhouses vanished in an instant. As they wheeled me to my room, my sister hollered from the hospital nursery, "He's a doozy!" He has turned out that way indeed.

Through the years, I did little to advance his dream to become a doctor. Inspired by his best friend's older brother, he followed the path unaided, studying, achieving, burying himself in laboratories and learning. We rehearsed for his interview before the admissions committee, although only one of us did so with a straight face. "And what is your opinion of the health care industry?" I asked seriously. "While I know nothing about the health care system, my mother believes I look like Fred Savage," he deadpanned. (He does.) Knowing now that he must have answered the questions impressively, I feel the way a parent does when he sees his kindergartner on stage doing the Hokey Pokey, singing a Christmas carol before a crowd, wearing his cap and gown.

Parents must also face the time when their children know more than they do, at least academically. I could no more understand his coauthored report, "Analysis of the Interaction of Viral RNA Replication Proteins by Using the Yeast Two-Hybrid Assay," in the *Journal of Virology* than I could speak Swahili. His parents, who taught him colors and the letters of the alphabet, stared stupidly at the publication, proud but outclassed. The eventual shifting of roles results, when ultimately parent becomes child, child becomes parent. Though still a comfortable distance from a nursing home, I have had a taste of that dependence, made obvious when I suffered a panic attack in the crushing, sweltering crowd that surrounded the Planet Hollywood opening downtown. "You'll be fine," he assured me, shouldering his way through the throng, steering me hand-in-hand.

I admit to having doodled "Dr." before his name the way an infatuation-struck teenager writes her prospective married name in the margin of her algebra book. This time, the dream has come true. I believe I could die tomorrow and feel fulfilled. Well, not before I actually see him in that getup, and he beams down at me, all tall and strong and full of good intentions.

—January 1999

Beginning his third year of medical school at Emory University, Jonathan is considering a specialty in cardiology or neurology, but that changes with every fascinating course, each miraculous hospital rotation.

Miles to Go

EVEN THOUGH MY contact lens specialist informs me that I have fewer tears than I used to, I'm putting the ones I have left to very good use. This, I tell my son who has moved more than five hundred miles away, is his fault. I have lectured myself before my magnifying makeup mirror, justified the truth in the theory of roots and wings, and celebrated his success at being accepted into a prestigious medical school in the South. Gone is gone, however, and no amount of practice at summer camp, college sixty miles from home, or school trips abroad prepares a mother for the separation she fears will be permanent. Even when her child is an adult, being forced apart feels like ripping a scab from a sore that is still festering: too soon, too sudden, too raw.

"I'm not dead," he proclaims when he hears the quiver in my voice over the phone, and I'm grateful he can't see me staring at his neatly made bed, the down comforter puffed up to showroom perfection. This is a child who followed me wherever I went, and I grew happily accustomed to his lean body just inches from my hip. If I sank into a chair, he fell to the floor at my feet like a contented cat in a shaft of sunlight. When I climbed into the car, he was there beside me, just for the ride. But he grew up, and took with him the company I came to expect and adore. The one who is embarking on a new journey, a street map dog-eared and torn on the floor of his car, surely looks at the experience more optimistically than the one who has nurtured him and feels only the loss.

In the famous Norman Rockwell painting, *Christmas Homecoming*, which graced the cover of the legendary *Saturday Evening Post* on December 25, 1948, Rockwell poignantly captured his wife, Mary Rockwell, welcoming their son Jarvis home from school. The young man clutches Christmas packages under one arm and dangles a sloppily packed valise from his free hand, prohibiting him from returning his mother's exuberant embrace. We see him from behind, offering us a clear perspective of the rapture in his mother's eyes. More than fifty years later, I know how she felt.

I never thought I'd be one of those mothers waving her hankie as her kid boards the plane. We are a tight family of homebodies, born and raised here, who stayed put here. Parents and siblings of three generations join up for holidays and on Sundays, where we share lunch and have since I was a little girl in search of corn fritters at Russet Cafeteria. If anyone can be heard over the din of gossip and crying babies, they are usually elderly folks who stop by our table and comment how lucky we are to have each other so close. I imagine them sitting in easy chairs with doilies on the armrests, waiting for the phone to ring.

There is now a hole in our ranks, and I can satisfy my hunger for him only by dragging myself through airports, wrapping my arms around his sturdy shoulders, and squeezing his handsome face between my palms. I am the mother at Hartsfield Atlanta International Airport's Gate B15, straining her eyes to see if he is there—and then, two days later, hugging him until he is breathless when I leave, swallowing sobs as the car pulls away.

We rush everything into an infrequent Saturday and Sunday these days, making it difficult to enjoy the time. We know how fast the minutes tick away, how soon we will be back in our seats on the plane, savoring the memories. When I'm there, I want to run from store to store buying him shoes and socks and thicker sweaters, ordering him more than he wants to eat at a restaurant, replenishing the paltry stash in his pantry. It is difficult to limit mothering to a weekend.

My mother was born and raised in Cincinnati, and I vividly remember the frequent train trips on the *James Whitcomb Riley* to visit her family. When we returned, I was never sure which place was really home to her. Dad's sisters were not Rose and Ann, the beautiful girls who made up her trio as she grew up. A second home, I learned, is never as good as the first. My father, who lived his ninety-four years here, spent the last six months of his life in a nursing home, struggling against the dementia that robbed him of his stellar sense of humor and razor-sharp mind. Even in the depths of it, when he could no longer recognize his wife of sixty years or his children, his flashes of lucidity would shock us. Horrified, we heard from the nurses how he would call out his address into the night; he needed them to know where he lived: in his home on Meridian Street, where he belonged.

A friend sent me a funny *The Far Side* cartoon of a mother cow, upright in a frilly apron, watching out the front door at a herd piling out of a taxi. "Look," she declares to her husband, "the cows have come home." The penciled inscription beneath it read, "And yours will, too." I don't know whether that is loving insight or hopeless naivete, whether he who grows accustomed to a big city with its sparkling skyscrapers and trendy restaurants, hordes of stylish young people, and ten lanes of traffic ever comes back to what he left behind. Will a simple circle in the center of town suffice? If not, maybe he will come to appreciate his hometown for its accessibility, its beauty and size, its cherished residents.

I am thinking about the logistics involved in sending a tuna-noodle casserole packed in dry ice, and wonder if botulism will be the unfortunate result. When he performs his duty to call and advise me that he has returned from a trip, you see, he proclaims that he is "home." Are there enough dinners in the world to send, or will his good upbringing subconsciously deliver the message that there will never be another place like this, another support system so delicate but unbreakable?

If he decides to return after his medical training concludes, I plan to give the term "family practice" a whole new meaning. If not, I'll continue to scour the weather page in *USA Today*, imagining him in the sunshine or rain, and rely on e-mail and voice mail and UPS Ground as a link. Like Mrs. Rockwell, I'll do what I can to make up for how disconnected we are by miles by how connected we are in our hearts.

—January 2000

After reading this, an empathetic mother in Atlanta e-mailed me a request for my tuna-noodle casserole recipe, which she offered to make and deliver to Jonathan.

Mother Load

ON A SCALE OF one to ten, I got an 8.8. Any way you look at it, that's a good, strong B-plus: better than above average, worse than excellent. But for someone who always strove for A's, my score was a kick in the pants. Maybe asking my two adult sons (ages twenty-seven and twenty-three) to rank growing up with a mother who worked outside the home wasn't such a good idea. Even though I fell 1.2 points short of perfect, I always taught them to tell the truth. I guess I should have been careful what I wished for.

The exercise was part of an informal survey, something I'd been considering for some time. In a seventeen-question quiz, I asked them to transcend. Did having a mother who worked scar you for life? Will you spend years on a therapist's couch, blaming me while attempting to piece together the shards of your shattered psyches? As a sometime latchkey kid, were you frightened, insecure, the host of neighborhood gang fests? The cavalier way some of my questions were answered was a balm on the raw conscience of their mother, who by the nature of the job wears guilt like Joseph wore his multicolored coat. When asked what they thought I did all day, the younger of the two replied simply: "I knew that you went to the Broad Ripple office and got drunk at lunch at the local bars. And then there was the whole brothel thing."

But seriously, boys. One of the more telling answers concerns how they felt when I went to work in the first place. At the time, Gabriel, the older of the two, was seven, his younger brother Jonathan, three. For seven years of unrelenting shoe-tying, carpool-driving, and breakfast-, lunch- and dinner-feeding, I stayed by Gabe's side, or, more accurately, chased less than four inches behind him, including the time I ran after him in a shopping mall when he stood up in his canvas stroller and took off with the contraption strapped to his back like a hiker's backpack. I was there to apologize to the mother of the youngster whose fingers he smashed when he collided a row of chairs against one another at the shoe store, and I was the one he called a tarantula at ninety decibels when he objected to the punishment.

I was the preschool cupcake-baker, the kindergarten room mother, the first-grade lunchbox packer. That was I standing by the barber's chair to make sure he didn't look like Bud on *Father Knows Best* with his freshly cut hair, and the one who pushed fresh green beans through a grinder with butter and salt because they tasted better than the ones in the jar. Not surprisingly, his younger brother's response to the question was, "Honestly, I don't remember you first going to work. Life before that was just a lot of amniotic fluid." But his older brother's answer floored me. "As long as I can remember," he said, "you were always working." Somehow I don't think he meant washing dishes.

Neither of them objected to being left alone for two hours after school, although in their early years a housekeeper-cum-grandma figure was there, her wooden spoon tucked neatly into her waistband in case a little boy needed a reminder that his three warnings were up. Thankfully, Gabe never felt deserted or scared, though he reports wishing I had been there to hear about his day right after school—rather than two hours later at the dinner table. "By then," he said, "it had faded to the back of my mind." Jon, on the other hand, joyously remembered his after-school antics, the most vivid the day he and his buddy, Andy, lit a tennis ball on fire and rolled it down the hill, only to meet up with Andy's father at the bottom. The final score from the kid his mother abandoned for the workplace when he was just out of diapers was a nine and a half. The older one, the kid I stuck with like glue until school claimed him, brought down my average.

While Gabe named seventies TV icon Carol Brady as the ideal fantasy mom, his more jaded brother thought life was better without his own mother there every second of every day. "We had more interesting things to talk about at the dinner table than whether I had practiced my trombone," he reported. Oddly enough, it wasn't until about fifteen years' worth of dinners later that I found out about the time he chased a little neighbor girl around the block as she attempted to walk her 145-pound English Mastiff on a leash the length of a hangman's noose. High comedy, indeed, especially when the tiny girl's mother came to our door to complain, and I brushed her off with, "My kid? Impossible." A certain blindness accompanies adoration, although the perpetrators do have a tendency to come clean sooner or later.

What I did at the office all day when I wasn't tippling a few highballs at lunch and scheming with the madam was something of a mystery to them both. Because of the attention garnered by my nine years as a restaurant critic, it is not surprising that Gabe thought that was all I did. Jon, equally off base, believed I didn't edit but designed the pages of the magazine, probably due in part to the graphic presentation of photography, layouts, and film I gave to his second-grade class. I suppose I never really knew what my own father did as he trudged off to his auto parts store every morning and came home every evening to scrub the grease from the cracks in his thick fingers with a bar of Lava soap. "Out of sight, out of mind" applies to more than just romance.

In order not to bash myself unmercifully, I should note that both sons are proud of their mother's accomplishments, even if their memories are a little dim. I looked forward to the day mothers were invited to visit Jon's first-grade class, thinking how lovely he would feel as he described my career as a magazine editor. As I stood before his classmates, he spoke plainly and without hesitation. "This is my mom," he said. "She stands at the sink." Now, of course, he says he busted his buttons, especially at my financial independence. "I was proud when you drove a really nice car and picked me up at Sunday school," he said. It is humbling to know that a person's professional calling can be distilled into the automobile she drives. In concurrence, his brother stated that I did what I had to do to get ahead and enjoy the finer things in life, making me, I suppose, a latter-day, money-grubbing Joan of Arc. Nothing wrong with that, he now judges, adding shopping sprees.

I don't know whether to consider it a compliment or a criticism, but nobody mentioned food. I did my fair share of daily cooking, and either I made sure that something was simmering in the Crock-Pot before I left for work, or I wrestled with a couple of pounds of raw hamburger when I came home. It wasn't until their high-school years that we began to eat more often in restaurants, for which Jon, at least, is grateful. "How the hell else would I have known what caprese and polenta were?" he said in appreciation for his gustatory education.

I'm happy to say that neither of them seems ruined for eternity. They both report enthusiastically and without reservation that they would never marry a woman without a career of her own. All the things I worried about in those hours between two-thirty and five P.M. never transpired: no one was kidnapped, burned up in a house fire, poisoned, or confronted by an escaped killer at the front door. They didn't lie helpless on the living room rug, unable to crawl to the phone to dial 911. A gas leak did not silently steal them from me, and I never came home to a driveway filled with emergency vehicles and sealed off with crime scene tape, a person of the cloth standing at the doorstep ready to deliver the tragic news.

Happily intact, and even after delivering his eight point final ranking, Gabe closed his survey with what I'm sure he thought was a pat on the back. "I'm glad you were able to hold down a job, move up in the ranks, and still make time to raise two kids," he said. "Bravo and thanks for everything." After the nights I slept on the floor of their rooms waiting for their fevers to subside, and the mornings I sat in the car on a dark street corner watching them safely board the school bus, how could he have thought it was the two of them I was making time for, and not my career?

I don't know, but I suspect it accounts for my 8.8.

—May 2000

We Are Family

He would stand me in the yard trying to straighten my throwing arm, pitching me uncaught balls, and attempting to perfect my errant free throw, which never even grazed the net.

Sister Act

OUR ROOM WAS like any other girls' room of that era. Two twin beds of blond wood were separated by a squatty nightstand on which sat a Sylvania clock radio tuned to WIFE and a crooked metal lamp with a thick paper shade my brother had made in shop. Most activity centered around a luxurious, crescent-shaped dressing table, with mirrors on every surface, a single shallow drawer, and a gathered, floor-length skirt.

We didn't spend a lot of time together, my sister and I, but the memories are clear. I liked dolls, she did not, but the room was lined with miniature beds, inflatable mattresses, and all manner of Muffies, Ginnies, and Terri Lees, each snugly tucked in. She sang in school plays, and the house reverberated with her concertlike piano version of "Flight of the Bumblebee." I, on the other hand, plinked out an unspirited rendition of "Smoke Gets in Your Eyes," sang a flat accompaniment, and watched the metronome click out of sync. She laughed with her friends and danced to a rock 'n' roll beat while I wrote furiously in my diary with a gold Cross pen my grandma had sent.

When we crawled into bed, however, the nightly ritual began and the gap was bridged. Whoever was definitely awake began by thumping her hand on the mattress with a rhythmic, "dum-dum-dee-dum-dum." The other would quickly respond with a resounding "dum-dum," which meant we could giggle, talk, gossip, or scheme without fear of yelling out onto deaf ears.

I never thought of her as pretty—just five years older. One night, however, she donned a white piqué dress with a heart-shaped bodice, and in her clear plastic spring-o-lators clicked down the stairs to her date. I'd never seen a more perfect sight. It was only after she was married and came back to visit that I felt envious and abandoned. When she gazed into our vanity mirror with his admiring glance over her shoulder, I knew I would be doomed to the guest room forever.

If anyone had told me on that day that the ensuing years would bring us closer, I never would have believed him. True, we started out with only our midnight tapping to bond us, but we ended up inseparable friends. It is she and only she who tells me the truth in the fitting room, and she who tries out a prospective hair stylist first. We're the only two who would agree to buy our brother a ninety-pound cement birdbath for his fiftieth birthday and then lug it to his door alone. Only with her do I fall into fits of hysterical laughter, and only together do we cart tuna sandwiches and Pringles to the drive-thru, order Diet Cokes, and eat lunch in the car.

It was only natural that for the first time since we'd shared a room we would vacation together—with husbands, no kids—and revel in our sameness. In ten days together we discovered such eerie likenesses as identical waves in our hair and the fact that we both walk around while we brush our teeth. The differences are small: She can kill a moth with her bare hands while I run squealing from the scene, and she keeps her cereal in the freezer, while I—like most—do not.

Since the only thing we really disagreed on in the past few years was whether or not *Raising Arizona* was dumb (it was), we had no trouble planning our days. We'd sightsee and walk, sunbathe and shop, drink chichis and talk. For two unathletic souls, an undertaking more adventurous than a late lunch was unthinkable. Unless, just once, we'd douse our coifs and our pride and snorkel in public to the reef. To make it simpler, we'd rent two of a curious new invention called a See-Board, a surfboardlike contraption with a built-in mask into which you place your face, eliminating the need for even the most rudimentary equipment.

Once afloat I hung onto my raft with one hand, her arm with the other, and together we battled the waves to our destination: two salmon swimming upstream, one too frightened to even venture a look below. When I finally did, I caught a glimpse of the back of another diver's head and something orange with spines. With a shove or two from fellow snorklers eager to rid the surf of at least one panicked diver on a fluorescent board, I paddled breathlessly toward shore. She, however, continued to bob up and down on the horizon, admiring the deep-sea splendor and stopping only occasionally to massage her arm where I had left my mark.

When she finally realized I had disappeared, she jettisoned herself with uncanny speed and finesse to where I lay limp on the sand. Beaching herself like a harpooned whale, she flopped alongside, where we both lay silent and lifeless atop our aquatic vehicles. The memory we would later share was not of fear or abandonment but of matching bruises on our hipbones and raging sunburns on the backs of our calves, the only parts of our bodies that had remained above sea level. In the future we have vowed to view tropical fish only in the safety of the dentist's office.

We're content in our relationship—my sister and I—and only last week were we chuckling at the prospect of someday hobbling along together, wearing matching pocketbooks and black wool coats, and sporting look-alike blue hair. The vision continued to get funnier until we caught sight of ourselves in a storefront window. Arms linked, we took a good, long look. Same overfluffed hair, same diminutive stature, same nearly flat shoes, same bags slung over our shoulders, we realized we really didn't have far to go.

—May 1988

Here's what my hair colorist said: "You and your sister look exactly alike, except she's prettier."

Here's what I said: "Nuh-uh. Mom says I'm just as pretty, and I believe her."

So what? Judy doesn't color her hair, bleach her teeth, or even pierce her ears. And she is gorgeous. She also knows all my secrets and always will.

Hoop Dreams

THE VANTAGE POINT was familiar: my brother's second-floor bedroom window, his favorite spot to dangle me from my ankles while I howled in a mixture of sheer thrill and utter terror.

Instead of the usual upside-down view of the sprawling backyard dotted with shade trees and set off with all manner of playground paraphernalia, this time the view was right-side-up and steady. At least twenty teenage boys, including my brother, ten years my senior and a master of good-natured torment, populated the regulation-size basketball court with twin goals at the rear of the yard. Sure, other families on our Northside block had makeshift courts at the ends of their driveways, the less fortunate getting by with a backboard nailed above the garage door. With my chin resting on the windowsill of my brother's room, however, I could witness the basketball game to end all basketball games in our own backyard, where two opposing teams of five players each dribbled, drove the lane, and free threw their way into the annals of Hoosier Hysteria every summer evening.

Some disagreement continues as to who actually installed the magnificent court. I recall a disheveled and somewhat scary handyman-turned-concrete contractor by the name of Ditch Ditchner. No, insists my mother, whose razor-sharp memory belies her eighty-eight years, it was Beech Beech, another worker at my father's auto parts and salvage yard. Regardless, someone with the same first name as last busied himself for weeks one summer under my father's direction creating one Indiana neighborhood's finest bastion of statehood: a relatively level concrete court with matching goals, bounded on three sides by trees. This left one side open to the gaze of a grade-school girl and her older sister, whose heart beat so uncontrollably at the sight of the swarthy nightly visitors that she had to lie down merely to catch her breath.

Word spread quickly, and the crowd grew to such dimension that either Ditch or Beech was forced to return to install "benches" (a log on each side of the court) to hold players doomed to second string. Cars lined the driveway two deep as afternoon turned to evening, forcing my father, returning home after a long day at work, to park a block away. Official "no parking" signs were immediately posted in the driveway, and those who heeded the silent warning as well as that of my mother, who monitored the driveway with all the precision and grace of a traffic cop on Times Square, parked up and down North Pennsylvania Street. This, of course, resulted in the players' unfortunate habit of cutting through the house from front door to back on the way to the court, some stopping off at the refrigerator for a one-handed snack.

This did not last long, with my brother in charge of the rules of play: no double dribbling, elbowing, or traveling; no spitting; and no sweating, food, or drinks in the house. The outside spigot ran constantly as muscular, shirtless lads in their late teens and early twenties trotted back and forth to the grassy patch under my brother's window for a long, sloppy drink from the garden hose, thrilling me to a close-up look at the star players and sending my sister for her smelling salts. In short, everyone was happy: most of all my brother, a small but natural athlete who could master any sport without the benefit of lessons; every Hoosier boy within shouting distance; my parents, content to know where their spirited son spent his evenings;

and me, a girl without athletic prowess who learned the art of spectating at an early age.

Not that my brother didn't encourage me to become a player myself—if not to become a winner, at least to "get tough." When darkness forced the crowd to disperse each evening, he would stand me in the yard trying to straighten my throwing arm, pitching me uncaught balls, and attempting to perfect my errant free throw, which never even grazed the net. We had a bad history, however, as his years-earlier attempt to attach my stroller to his bicycle by a rope and play Indianapolis 500 ended in a bloody nose (mine) and a chase scene with my mother, wielding a spatula, as the undisputed victor. None of his lessons in coordination proved fruitful, and a recent bout at our own driveway basketball goal left my twenty-year-old son shaking his head in dismay and stating flatly that, backyard instruction or no, I shot a basketball like Mr. Burns on *The Simpsons*.

Uninterested in watching any sport from the sidelines, my brother has continued his athletic pursuits well into his fifties. Everyone has long since given up on me, although he'll still thump me in the stomach with a ball or remind me of the time I swung a golf club and struck a neighbor girl in the mouth, forcing her to miss school for an entire semester. What he didn't know, however, was that the example set by the horde of hooligans in our yard every evening some forty years ago prepared me perfectly for adult life in the Hoosier state. Unlike most women, I can tell a man-to-man from a zone defense and know a pick-and-roll when I see one. And long after he married and moved out of the house, I stood alone on the crumbling court and learned how far away the goal can seem. Even with no one admiring you from the bedroom window, the pressure to perform can be too much.

Content to be a basketball watcher, I nonetheless revere today's female athletes, who not only have to make the grade, but must earn the respect of their judgment-passing male counterparts. My brother could never have turned me into one of them, but what he did teach me was that a girl with the guts to hang head-over-heels from a second-story window was probably tough enough.

—March 1997

Imagine my surprise when I received an invitation from the current owner of our family home to come see the new basketball court, which they had renovated for their own children. My mother, sister, and I toured "our house," which, although extensively remodeled, seemed smaller than I remember. As a keepsake, the owner gave me a brick from the original court. I use it as a bookend.

Child Support

THE CALL CAME just after midnight, wrenching me from sleep. My heart pounding, I commanded, "Answer the phone!" even though it sat less than a foot from my head. Disoriented, my husband bolted upright and ran around the bed, complying. By this time I had already knocked the phone to the floor and, with the cord stretched to its limit, pressed the receiver to my ear.

"Mom?" I heard my son's voice, thin but steady.

"Are you all right?" I asked automatically, the same way a mother instinctively feels her child's forehead for fever or chases after him with a hat and gloves. "I'm fine," he said, "but I was just assaulted in the law school parking lot." By this time I was on my feet, dragging the phone across the floor as I paced. He explained unemotionally, as only a man can, while his mother clasped a sweaty palm across her mouth. A thug had approached him as he was entering his car after a night in the library, asking, "You looking for trouble?"

"No," he answered innocently, then jumped in the car and, hands shaking, hit the automatic door locks.

In a split second, two other punks climbed out of their Ford Mustang, which had blocked him from behind, and began beating on his car with a tire iron. Just like that, they smashed his taillights and windows and beat in his doors while he sat inside, trapped. Why he didn't ram their car and run over them, I'll never know. It's what I would have done: Act now, think later—a way of life for one who is ruled by the logic of the heart. Lucky for me he has his father's more thoughtful approach.

Satisfied that their heinous act was complete, the perpetrators climbed back in their car and waited as their victim sped away. Then they gave chase as he tore through traffic toward the police station. Long story short: As he was recounting the experience to the officer on duty, another policeman brought them in—three dangerous juveniles in handcuffs, caught. High on drugs and found with illegal substances and stolen merchandise in their car, they didn't stand a chance. The fact that earlier that night they had pulled the same stunt on other unsuspecting students, one of whom didn't make it into his car before being beaten, hadn't helped. The APB had succeeded, and my son was the one to make the positive ID while one young criminal, full of hate and smirking, called the cop the "N" word.

I am satisfied that my son behaved perfectly, his wits about him. But a mother worries still: It is the initiation rite to our vaunted sisterhood. Did they see your face as you identified them, I asked, and what happens when they are released? Will they come looking for you? I spent the rest of the long night alternately crying and shaking, imagining all possible scenarios. What if he hadn't gotten into the car fast enough? What if he'd had to stretch across the front seat to lock the passenger-side door manually? What if they had beaten his head with the same tire iron that decimated his car? What if, God forbid, they had brandished a gun?

Of course, none of that happened, my husband reminded me as I fought sleep. And even my son, obviously shaken, seemed more worried about the condition of his car than his skull, still thankfully intact. I, however, twisted among the sheets, a victim of my own pessimistic ruminations. Our actions allow us to lay off our children as they become adults, but our minds and hearts betray us. "Little children, little problems; big children, big problems," my mother likes to say, and I wonder if I am still a problem to her. Her advice is spread thin now, like a fine layer of butter on toast. It is up to me whether to sample it; she doesn't push.

I push. "Did you report it to the dean?" I asked my son the next morning. "Why isn't the lot patrolled? Do the IU police know about this? Are you going back tonight? Alone?" At this, he breathed a deep sigh, accustomed to my relentless intervention. The difference between an overprotective mother and a rottweiler, the joke goes, is that a rottweiler eventually lets go.

Oddly enough, just the night before the incident, I had been consumed with worry about my younger son, suffering the ravages of the flu. By himself. In a dirty apartment with no food, let alone hot chicken soup. Drink fluids, I had advised on the phone, lots of them. See a doctor. Stay home from class. There was the usual silence on the other end. That night I dreamed I went into his room and found him asleep in a crib. Now, I'm no psychiatrist, but I believe I am getting closer to understanding why my mother still introduces me to her friends as "the baby."

My cousin lost her mother last year at the age of ninety. Now parentless, she can't get over the feeling of being orphaned—at sixty-one. As much as we resent it when we are young, each of us needs the steadying force of our mother, the person older and wiser, the one who teaches us values and answers our calls at midnight. In my job I travel frequently, and I always call my mother, ninety herself, when I land. It can be on a cell phone at baggage claim or in the backseat of a cab thousands of miles from home, but it's to her I report: I'm here, I'm fine, no need to worry anymore about wind shear or ice on the wings or midair collisions. She always acts relieved and says, "Thank God!" Actually, I think I need the reassurance as much as she does, like a child who will run for blocks with a skinned knee, holding back tears until she is met at the door by her mom.

I will try to let my sons grow up in peace, make their own way, fight off their own assailants. In addition, I vow not to need them more than they need me, and help them need me less and less. I wonder, though, if after your life is threatened, only your mother can register the proper shock, the requisite love, the undying gratitude that you are alive. And maybe you need that forever.

—May 1999

Forever Young

I LOST MY MOTHER at Bed Bath & Beyond. This is not as bad as it sounds. I misplaced her only temporarily, amid honorable intentions. Appreciating (and identifying with) her propensity for shopping and love of home supplies, I knew she would be amused by this mega-housewares store, to which I had promised a visit for many weeks. In an attempt to save her some steps, I dropped her off at the door and ventured into the busy parking lot to locate a space. When I returned, she was nowhere to be found.

Other eighty-seven-year-old mothers, I suspect, would forget who brought them in the first place, wobble toward the door to await their daughter's sturdy arms, or inch gingerly forward in their wheelchairs and then shake their heads in disbelief. Not mine. Apparently, charge card in hand, she had grabbed the first shopping cart in view and taken off at full speed down aisle one. The fact that we are both under five feet tall complicated the search somewhat, although I thought I spotted the top of her fluff of gray hair somewhere over the drying racks. After bellowing at each other like elephant seals in the wild, we hooked up by the bed pillows, where I commenced to follow her through the store like a schoolgirl.

I've always been aware that my mother isn't like most mothers. Never was. The mother of one of my best friends wore aprons most of the time, and her house smelled like boiling chickens. My mother made French pastries and bubbling cream sauces. When other mothers wore housecoats, mine wore Chanel, and she had an authentic Hermes Kelly bag years before the first knock-off hit the American market. In short, my mother was hip before it was hip to be hip.

It surprises some that at eighty-seven, my mother reads *The Wall Street Journal*, *Women's Wear Daily*, and the Sunday edition of *The New York Times*. In her home office a fax machine keeps her updated on stock trading and churns out correspondence from her host of grandchildren. The other day she confided that she wasn't sure *exactly* how an HMO worked, and that this appeared to be a good year for the BMW. Though she's in what some might consider not just the autumn but the winter of life, my mother nevertheless built and moved into a new house, and after my sister and I lamely organized her kitchen, she pulled everything out and did it again.

Mother's Day always presents a unique challenge. I look on jealously as some daughters shop for pink geraniums, pretty bathrobes, or lovely scallop-edged writing paper. I may be putting the cart before the horse, but if I'm not mistaken, my mother has been hinting around for a PC, complete with Pentium processor, external speakers, internal modem, and CD-ROM. I can't imagine what functions someone in her late eighties would perform on such a system, but she'd probably fool us all and stay up nights surfing the 'Net.

Our family physician recalls the advice of a one-hundred-year-old patient whom he treated through house calls. Every time he went, her tip to him was the same: Buy Exxon. "If only I had listened," he bemoans, "I could retire today." When people say you're as young as you feel, they are referring to this investment maven and my mother.

Sometimes, convinced she should relax, I try to make life easier for my mother. This never works out. Consider the time I suggested she try one of those electric carts at the supermarket. No chance of wearing out before you get to the dairy case, I told her, and besides, it might be fun. Always ready for something new, she complied. Let's just say if they employed old-people police at the grocery store, she'd have been picked up for wanton disregard of the law. Gunning the thing for all it was worth, she crashed into an unsuspecting shopper's cart in the cereal aisle. Apologizing profusely, she retired the vehicle to its stable at the front of the store, declaring that the daggone thing was just too slow. I admit to only my closest friends that on occasion my mother still picks out my clothes. There is no doubt that I was the best-dressed kid in school, and I can't remember ever shopping. Somehow articles in just the right style and size appeared in my closet, and while some kids whined that their mothers made them wear clothes painfully out of style, I was an eighth-grade woman ahead of her time. I boldly wore the first matching headband and knee socks, the first miniskirt, and the first hip-hugging, bell-bottom pants.

Everyone's proud of his or her mom for a different reason. A fellow editor likes to tell the story of how his mother knocked the screen door off the hinges and chased a rapist until she tackled the man at the end of a dirt road in the north Georgia mountains. Me, I'm proud of my thoroughly modern mother, who, while staring ninety in the face, still climbs into her car and looks for adventure every day. "I treasure the old memories," she'll say casually, "but I'd like to add a few new ones."

For all of us, the choice is pretty simple: Stay current, which takes considerable effort, or get lazy and cash it in. The way I see it, there's no time like the present to learn to program our VCRs, access the Internet, and order direct TV. If we don't, the world will skip right by, leaving us middle-agers to croak in front of our *Lucy* reruns.

In my case, however, there's a tough act to follow. Not many my age have someone an entire generation ahead who can figure a 15 percent tip in her head even faster than she can pump her own gas, show me up in her spiffy Fila warm-up suits, and grasp the index of economic indicators without needing an explanation. Even unpleasant medical procedures evoke an appropriate axiom made famous by my mother: "You pay to stay." The time and energy she has put into the process tells me something more: Both the price and the payoff are right.

So this Mother's Day won't find my mother adorned with a corsage, eating a cafeteria chicken dinner. We're planning to share a rack of lamb at someplace fancy, after which I'll dig through my car to locate her gift: a brand-spanking-new version of Windows 95. No doubt I'm the one, however, who'll need the instruction manual.

—May 1996

At age ninety-two, my mother had her driver's license renewed. We arrived at the license branch at seven-forty A.M., at which time I took my place in line outside, in nineteen-degree cold, awaiting the eight-thirty A.M. opening. I instructed her to wait in the car, however, after she popped out twice to see if I was warm enough, I gave up, whereupon she promptly cut in line. No one murdered her, although several shot her some pretty mean looks.

Soul Food

ON A RECENT SUNDAY I watched my three-old great-nephew Levi make his first purchase. This sweet little boy, with a precious disarray of blond curls, and eyes that turn chameleon-like if he is wearing blue or green, approached the fast-food restaurant cashier, the top of his head level with the counter, smacked down a dollar bill, and said softly but distinctly, "I want a chocolate chip cookie, please."

Now, because I have not yet earned the privilege of doting grandma, this cannot be construed as the kind of shameless bragging one witnesses at a mah-jongg table. The lump did not rise in my throat simply because of the boy's act of shy independence or the clerk's willingness to stoop down to meet him eye-to-eye. It was that it occurred at Sunday lunch, a fifty-year custom that has defined the very fabric of our family.

No matter the makeup, some group or another of us has observed the tradition of gathering at a restaurant on Sunday at noon. As a child I watched TV families pass platters of fried chicken around a table to observe this day of rest, and as much as I envied their conviviality, easy laughter, and endless chatter, I knew I had it better. Rain or shine, the people I loved journeyed to some choice restaurant, stood together in a cafeteria line or crowded around a table with too few chairs, made jokes nobody else understood, and grew a little closer without even realizing it.

In the early years we ventured to such historic haunts as the Hawthorne Room on Sixteenth and Meridian, where a busy McDonald's stands today. There my mother chased my unruly brothers as they climbed the namesake tree in the lobby, and there I tasted my first hamburger not made in a skillet at home. Topped with crunchy, hot onion rings, these "roto steaks" provided a glimpse of just how good restaurant food could taste. More often than not we found ourselves at Russet Cafeteria in Broad Ripple, where unfamiliar corn fritters tempted; or the Lantern Room on Thirty-eighth and Meridian, with its little metal bowl of Chinese noodles and dish of hard peppermint ice cream for dessert.

As memorable and delicious as some of those meals were, the food was hardly the main course. It was togetherness, the weekly time to let my mother dine instead of serve, a chance to laugh and not worry, an opportunity to plan the rest of the long Sunday afternoon ahead of us.

Even as some of us eventually married, the girls outnumbered the boys, and the lunch convention inevitably became a feminine gabfest. There my husband, a new initiate to the ritual, would talk to my father about finance and cars—something, anything, to disrupt the tittering about which nail polish was most stylish, whose purse held more, why one fat-free cookie was better than another. I can still see the look on other restaurant patrons' faces the day we compared new bras by peering down one another's blouses, or the time we exchanged shoes and hobbled across the room to determine whose were best. Our loving sisterhood, which included nieces needing no indoctrination, spanned three generations of outspoken, opinionated, type-A personalities who grew dependent on that Sunday book club/movie review/shopping extravaganza that transcended the square of fish and tartar sauce on our plates.

I am convinced that our weekly forays kept my parents young as well. Granted, my father always got stuck with the bill, and granted, we always responded when he tapped our knees under the table to proffer a tightly packed wad of cash, but I think he got something out of it as well. Not only could he and my mother proudly display their growing brood, but they could count noses and then compliment each other on the creation of such an august group. And who else's parents, already in their eighties, would try such newfangled food as bagel sandwiches and pizza, just to please the crowd that now included a fourth generation of babies?

We have always spurned the fancy places with their brunch buffets of

Belgian waffles and liver pate, favoring instead the popular joints where everyone is comfortable. Not long ago at Steak 'n Shake, I noticed a wool overcoat and hat draped over a chair, and had to shake myself out of believing that my father was back, to lead us again with his hand on his wallet, and his blue eyes twinkling.

In fact, when he was living his last six months at a nursing home, we followed Sunday lunch with a weekly group visit, where we surrounded his wheelchair, regaling him with kisses and hugs, and stories he could no longer understand. Once, we set a new great-grandson on his tray, and he feebly declared, "a king," quite a proclamation from a man in his nineties, old age having stolen his reason and his precious memories. And the Sunday he died, my sister and I removed his fleece warm-up suits and photographs from his room and met the rest of our family at MCL cafeteria, where we sat silently and picked at our food. To outsiders this must have appeared a macabre celebration—out to lunch just hours after losing the family's precious patriarch—but it was in fact a tribute of love and devotion most would be helpless to understand.

I watched the same great-nephew who made his landmark purchase drink from a straw for the first time, take his first reluctant steps, and call me "Great Debbie" for the first time at Sunday lunch. There I have held on my lap his wailing baby sister, named for my father, and squeezed hands with my own sister, knowing lunch doesn't last forever. Perhaps what we eat and where is not nearly as important as the people eating there.

—May 1998

There are now five children under the age of seven in our Sunday lunch club. The spaghetti strands and cracker wrappers on the floor are a sight to behold.

Family Affair

AUNT SARA IS PROBABLY approaching one hundred, but we're not really sure. When her grandchildren threw her last birthday party, the invitation read: 95! (WE THINK). Aunt Sara, you see, has earned the right to her vanity, and besides the smudge of red rouge and oversize faux pearl earrings she wears, concealing her age keeps her young and beautiful.

One of the four remaining siblings in my father's family of seven children, Aunt Sara is one of the lucky ones. Even though she resides at a nursing home, she makes her own fun. At mealtime, her wheelchair is the first to appear at the dining room doors; at lunchtime we've observed her there as early as ten A.M. In a gravely voice deepened by antiquity, she seems to growl, but to us, it remains friendly. "How old are those boys?" she asks me over and over, then turning to her seventy-five-year-old daughter and commenting in what she thinks are private tones, "You know, she's awfully pretty." I love Aunt Sara.

In a horrific move following a life-threatening condition, we rallied as a family to place my father, ninety-four and not quite as fortunate as Aunt Sara, in the same nursing home. Arm in arm, with sobs caught in our throats, my sister and I traversed the halls to observe the facility, filled with overworked nurses and wandering residents, sick people in wheelchairs, the old with no hope. Besides Aunt Sara, we could find nothing comforting here. Helpless to provide the constant care he needed, we acquiesced, wearing our guilt like a shroud. I was abandoning the man who had stopped Little America's kiddie roller coaster midway, climbed aboard, and lifted me out. I was turning over to complete strangers the man who walked me down the aisle, the good-humored soul who confided to my first-grade teacher that I'd called her a "babe." I often look heavenward, feeling instead that my place is reserved in hell.

To the nurses' surprise, my mother, sister, and I visit every day. Each lunch hour, the three of us—our shoulders sagging—climb aboard the elevator, afraid of what we'll see when we unload. Will we be lucky, and find him at a near run, pulling along the physical therapy aide like a lead dog, or, more likely, find him unattended in a wheelchair at the nurse's station, head drooping, surrounded by unfamiliar sounds and unfamiliar people?

Although the meals they prepare are surprisingly appetizing, the smell of the food and the place never escapes me. He is used to the aroma of my mother's baking, I think. Her gentle touch, the feel of his easy chair, dented in from years of use. I torture myself, but find myself helpless. Are his clothes clean enough, his face freshly shaven? Is his signature moustache—the one he twitched at his grandchildren's tight fists with the requisite

"Gobble, gobble, gobble" sound effect—trimmed neatly enough above his lip? More difficult to answer, has anyone talked to him today?

My evening visits leave me the most empty. He is tired, and tears well up in my eyes more readily. I help him with his meal, and although weakened by age, he remains a gentleman. Others on the unit scream and complain, their horrible sounds expressing the same displeasure they surely displayed when they were young. My tiny white-haired father is dignified, the same good-natured optimist he was as a youth. While his body has shriveled, his eyes still blaze bright blue, and when he searches my face, I'm not sure who needs whom more. For minutes he has an ally, someone to stand up for his rights and insist on his comforts. Then I retreat to the elevator and, unable to bear his disappointment, never look back.

On a good day, our band of three finds him alert and smiling. Characteristically unselfish, he asks how we feel, and we respond joyously. It is time to visit Aunt Sara. The wheels of their chairs entangled, they hold out their hands to each other, one studying the other's face. "Look, Aunt Sara, here's Daddy," I yell into her deafened ears. "He looks pretty great for ninety-four, don'cha think?" And then the unthinkable. "How old are you?" She looks at me in disbelief, hand still holding my father's. "Well," she huffs. "Let's not get into *that.*"

For my dad, the jokes and sarcastic quips are but a memory. That he will spend his final days in this place overwhelms me at night, when I am alone in the dark. At the nursing home, a team of aides helps him dress and bathe, eat and navigate his space. At home—that warm, fragrant place—the needs are too great. Although we will never grow accustomed to its lovelessness, the routine of the nursing home has grown on us. While most younger family members—afraid of their misshapen relatives and unintelligible language—stay away, we are compelled to go. Our photos are mounted on the bulletin board in his room and in frames on his window ledge. While we doubt that he recognizes them, we find comfort knowing that even when we are absent, we are always with him.

Others whose family members suffer a similar fate often observe, "You'll never catch me at some nursing home, drooling on myself and eating baby food. I'd rather be hit by a bus when I'm sixty-five." Fact is, however, none of us asks for what we get. And the closer we boomers get to old age, the less flip our comments become. Unless Dr. Kevorkian is driving the bus, it's pretty much out of our hands.

Aunt Sara, however, takes it in stride. Seeing her at her patrol post by the dining room doors, I step gingerly among the battalion of wheelchairs and approach her carefully, so as not to alarm. "Aunt Sara," I summon, my holler heard by all, "how's it going?"

She shrugs her century-old shoulders and then replies, "So far, so good."

—October 1994

Aunt Sara died at the age of ninety-five; my father on New Year's Day, 1995, at ninety-four.

Popular Culture

In our important notes, my best friend, Jackie, and I always included the crucial close: "SBBTTVVE," which—translated only to the two of us—meant "Scooby Booby Buddy To The Very Very End." Now, these were terms of endearment not to be taken lightly, and never to be issued face-to-face. When you want to profess your love and can't summon the courage, write it down.

Letter Perfect

IT STRUCK ME WHEN I was asked for my cellular phone number and I had no idea what it was. As a youngster I remember memorizing our phone number: Broadway 8571. Now, however, I lay claim to six numbers, if you include home, office, voice mail, e-mail, car phone, and portable. And I'm not even that darned important.

If your mental capacity allows you to convey such numbers to your friends and business associates, you can probably get used to a telephone ringing in your coat pocket. Otherwise, it's sometimes nice to communicate the old-fashioned way. While I don't pine for the good old days, I admit to a special attachment to letter writing, the only really personal way to reach someone's soul.

For most of my childhood I corresponded with my grandmother in Cincinnati, and a cherished gift was a gold Cross pen that she sent me for my birthday. I began each letter with, "How are you? I am fine," but if she tired of it she never let on. When she and my mother talked on the phone, I had no need to join in; our news was transmitted—and our relationship sealed—via the three-cent stamp on the envelope.

The communication between my best friend and me was no different. Granted, we spent many late hours on the phone, but our true souls were revealed in Study Hall 322, where our most poignant and important notes were passed. Along with the latest gossip—who liked whom, whose matching skirt and sweater was pretty, and which snob we hated—we always included the crucial close: "SBBTTVVE," which—translated only to the two of us—meant "Scooby Booby Buddy To The Very Very End." Now, these were terms of endearment not to be taken lightly, and never to be issued face-to-face. Through these notes I learned one of life's meaningful lessons: When you want to profess your love and can't summon the courage, write it down.

There's something about a piece of flowered stationery and someone's distinctive scrawl that's reassuring. I continue to receive a monthly letter from a hundred-year-old magazine fan who resides in a nursing home and likes me to know how she feels. While each letter undoubtedly contains a reference to something she read in the previous issue, the most important tidbits are that her nephew sometimes comes to take her to her favorite restaurant, The Tasty Spoon in Beech Grove, and did I know that her truest and oldest friend, with whom she lived and worked at Western Union, passed away some years ago? This same information is transmitted in every letter, but whether I care or not is immaterial; what matters is that the very act of writing it relieves her. This is not a message to be left on voice mail.

When my twenty-one-year-old son offhandedly mentioned a few valentines he transmitted and received over e-mail, I guarded my response. While it seems inconceivable that someone can pour out his heart via the Internet, I guess any communication is better than none at all. I can't help but flash back, however, to Valentine's Day 1958, when I was granted the honor of delivering the entire fifth grade's valentines to their respective classrooms at P.S. 84. As I stood at the doorway of Mrs. Shirley's room, one of her cuter student's ID bracelet heavy on my wrist, I could feel my heart pounding through my chest. "Your valentine mailman," I announced in a quivering voice, trying not to look at the ID bracelet's original owner. And as I turned on my heel and sped to the next classroom, I could only imagine his reaction as the card with my signature reached his desk. How can a computer message compare with i's dotted with a heart and a spray of Jean Nate?

A few years after the ID bracelet fell to the bottom of the drawer, I gleefully began a letter-writing campaign to every boy I liked who was away at summer camp. I preferred the comforts of home, and there was nothing like lying face-up on the floor in the foyer, waiting to hear the jangle of keys that signaled the mailman's arrival. This spot proved to be ideal for an upside-down view of the mail slot, with no more musical sound than the clang of the swinging metal door and the thunk of mail onto the foyer floor. I could make a day of writing, waiting, and reading, anticipating the word "Love" on the signature, or a "P.S.: I Miss You." I once met a fellow while on vacation in the Catskills, with whom I corresponded throughout college. Save the three days we spent together when I was seventeen, we never laid eyes on one another again, but by the tone of our mail you'd have sworn we were bound for the altar. As well as transmitting the truth, a letter allows you to hope.

While the information superhighway threatens to take over communications, I hold onto the hope that paper will survive. To me the smoothness and lusciousness of the page allow us a sensory pleasure not available through the clattering of keys. When my father passed away a few months ago, the most meaningful condolences came in letters, where senders felt free to share a poem, recount their own losses, offer hope, or remember my dad. I found myself reading and rereading their messages, finding comfort in a handwritten line here or there. Like a grieving relative running his hand over a lost soldier's name on the Vietnam Memorial, I found myself touching my father's name on the paper, bringing him closer to me again.

My niece, who married last month, saved a scrapbook of RSVP cards to her bridal showers and wedding. I like that, and think she'll enjoy rereading those personal inscriptions. Electronic memory will never replace our own, and a yellowed love note—or simply the letters SBBTTVVE—endures.

—April 1995

My name is Deborah and I am addicted to e-mail. When the little envelope appears on the bottom right-hand corner of my computer screen, I am once again at my old house, hearing the mailman's jingling footsteps. Writing is writing, I have concluded, whether via the clatter of a keyboard or the stroke of a pen. And I'm still better expressing myself with my fingertips than with my tongue. By the way, I met Mildred Riggs, my hundred-year-old pen pal, when I surprised her at her birthday party. Her letters stopped coming a few years ago.

Martha Mania

THIS WHOLE MARTHA STEWART phenomenon is beginning to annoy me. For the uninitiated, Martha is a down-home, food-, flower- and craft-meister who has, with her shaggy hair and J. Crew couture, captured the hearts and pocketbooks of millions. A TV show, countless books, guest appearances, and her own magazine featuring her face on every cover are just the start. To quote one of our own staff, "Martha makes the world a more beautiful place. I worship her."

I don't. I also don't yearn to make mocha shortbread, rhubarb iced tea, or pumpkin creme brulee. I don't buy into the art of hydrangeas and I doubt that I'd ever purchase five colors of green paint—from mossy to sage—to custom handcraft a verdigris concrete planter. Perhaps to a generation raised on fast food and cable TV, Martha represents the romance of staying home. "She's a goddess," proclaim fellow staffers. Maybe to some, but like a wedge of custard pie, Martha makes my teeth ache.

On a recent TV show, Martha demonstrated the nifty trick of making Halloween bats from coat hangers and black panty hose. They hung above her door to greet trick-or-treaters, accenting a row of black and gold luminaria that lined the walk. I prefer Erma Bombeck's long-ago Halloween admonition to her children to put a paper bag over their heads and tell everyone their mother just had a hysterectomy.

I could tolerate wrapping a lamp with hemp or making stuffed chicken Provençal, but this holiday decor, along with painting cabbage leaves with chocolate to make molds, sent me over the top. If Martha is a goddess, I'm Aphrodite.

While trying to convert me, one fan explained that in Martha's world, the pears are put up with ease, potatoes wrapped in cellophane serve as Christmas gifts, and the lighting is always perfect. I can't relate. The apple pie she featured on a recent show did look splendid, and I'd even consider emulating her method if only she'd send me the crust. But I don't want chickens in my yard (they didn't do the Clampetts any good), and I'd sooner pitch in at a barn-raising than attempt homemade, heart-shaped lollipops.

Admittedly, if I didn't have a full-time job, a family to nurture, and a house to clean, I might think Martha had some darn cool ideas. As it is now, I'm lucky if I have time to wait in line at the bank on my lunch hour, let alone dig for clams at three A.M. Perhaps these activities that absolutely nobody has time to do serve purely as an amusement. They're fun to imagine, but without her full-time housekeeper and staff, I doubt that even Martha has time to be Martha.

Count me out. I've already paid my dues cooking macaroni and cheese in a basement apartment when I was first married, and I have no desire to grind my own cinnamon. I'd rather read a menu than the instructions to a recipe for tomato and French bean salad, and I doubt that any kid of mine could ever have been captivated by birthday cupcakes topped with marzipan carrots and snips of chervil.

My monthly calendar includes waiting for the plumber and making spaghetti sauce, but does not include painting sixty-six storm windows, cleaning the canoe, or hand-dipping candles. Rather than providing me with a pleasant escape, Martha gives me 112 pages of things to feel guilty about each month.

Quite simply, I'm not looking for more work: We can live without lamb chops with prune chutney for now. I'll regard Martha as the Donna Reed of the mid-nineties, aglow in her shirtwaist, pumps, and pearls, frying veal chops. A source of amusement but not a role model, Martha can continue to act as a Mr. Wizard for Generation X. As for me, I'll set my sights on Generation Baby Boom, which probably could use a magazine of its own. Perhaps I'll be on the cover myself, running Saturday errands, the golden late afternoon sun fairly glinting off my dry cleaning bags.

—December 1994

Buy and Large

I CAN STILL REMEMBER the day it opened. Accustomed as I was to supervised visits at the corner drugstore, the advent of a major chain across the street heralded unheard-of consumer opportunities. Racks of garden hoses, every hair coloring agent imaginable (ash blond achieved the most comely results), and enough comic books to fill an entire summer beckoned like sirens on a Greek island. With five dollars in hand, I had infinite choices, and Mr. Schoener watched out his drugstore window as customers left behind his soda fountain and cellophane-wrapped greeting cards for greener pastures at Haag's Fifty-sixth Street.

Granted, no one at Haag's would ever take a quaking seven-year-old behind the pharmacy counter and patiently teach her how to swallow a Unicap vitamin by putting it back as far as possible on the tongue and chasing it down with a huge wash of water. No one else would overlook the dozen or so tiny, round pills, wearing slightly less of their red coating, that were spewed on the floor, or suggest that she practice with Le Sueur peas at home.

But when faced with such unbounded retail options as giant packages of brush rollers, tablets with matching envelopes, and fluorescent yo-yos, you could *keep* personal service. Mesmerized by the shopping possibilities,

I made the four-block walk each day, and spent all my disposable income there before I was ten.

In short, I became the brunt of many family jokes for my fixation not only with Haag's Fifty-sixth, but for my unquenchable desire for "supplies," as we liked to call them. With such a background, how could I contain myself when I got word of a new Meijer store nearby? I scanned the voluminous ads, viewed my promotional videotape, and prepared to consume.

But something stopped me. It isn't just that I've outgrown supply shopping as a sport. And it isn't that, right or wrong, I hate coupons and penny price comparisons. Maybe I've just gotten older, and I pride myself not only in avoiding crazed crowds where snipers might be present, but in avoiding retail establishments where searchlights grace the entrances.

Or perhaps it was that I had already paid my dues at Cub—another mega-shopping experience that didn't measure up to the thrill of Haag's Fifty-sixth. First off, I don't know what to do with three pounds of individually fresh-frozen sliced peaches once I lug them home, and I couldn't lift a 128-ounce box of Tide remotely near the washing machine even if I wanted to. And when I want three good, crisp apples, I don't need four thousand to choose from. No, I'd rather traverse the aisles of the nearest boutique grocery store, Joe O'Malia, where my greatest concern is whether my cart will jump an unexpected crease in the carpet, causing me to spill my sample-size cup of chocolate raspberry decaf.

On the rainy Friday evening I finally ventured to Meijer for the first time, I instantly faced my greatest fear: parking aisles identified by letter and no shuttle service to the door. Once inside—even facing thirty-eight checkout lanes and a display of twenty-inch fans as large as a bunker—the unexpected happened. I liked it. I was at Haag's Fifty-sixth again, only here I could browse an aisle of Mr. Coffees as far as the eye could see. I could buy cowboy hats or Naturalizer shoes, vinyl placemats or an above-ground pool. I could have my shoes repaired or buy red seedless grapes, visit guest services, or select from six varieties of low-fat frozen waffles. Rain clattered on the roof but I didn't care. I was like a scientist in Biosphere II—I could live here indefinitely, sustained by artificial forces and ultraviolet light, as oblivious to the passing of night into day as a drunken gambler in a Las Vegas casino.

Since I never seem to need anything at four A.M., I doubt I'll take advantage of the twenty-four-hour schedule, and since they have yet to open a cholesterol-screening clinic, I'll have to attend to my health-care needs elsewhere. But the very thought of the place, with its cereal aisle so long it forms a horizon line before you even get to the Lucky Charms, intoxicates.

Only two things worry me: Are there enough people in the world, let alone the city, to buy all that merchandise, and if I have a stroke in the potato chip aisle, will anyone find me in time? Other than that, I'm sold. Some may say the store's too big, but where else can I find chocolate-covered marshmallows and a Betty Rubble T-shirt all under one roof?

—July 1994

Party Line

IT WAS ONE OF THOSE miniscule episodes that sticks with you forever—flashing back every so often when you're not expecting it. At eight A.M. on a dreary pre-winter day, I drove along a main thoroughfare approaching our office. In front of me, a woman drove a station wagon with a couple of rowdy toddlers in the rear, socking each other on the head and generally challenging one another's right to live.

Suddenly, the rear door fell ajar, and one child, clothed in a fuzzy yellow footed sleeper, tumbled out onto the pavement. No crash, thud, horn blast, squealing brakes, or chase-scene background music accompanied the accident. Just quietly, swiftly, and without fanfare, the youngster thumped to the ground.

Incredibly, the woman kept driving, unaware that the backseat mayhem had spawned a near-tragedy. Instantly, I screeched to a halt, swerving into the opposite lane and leaning on my horn to capture her attention. At the same second—her car still moving—we leaped from our drivers' seats and rushed to the child, who was sitting disoriented but upright on the cold pavement. The mother gathered her up in her arms, and, embarrassed by her own neglect, hurried the baby back into the car. She then sank back into her seat to digest the ordeal.

It was then that I decided one mustn't be distracted in the car—one must concentrate only on passenger safety, defensive driving, and speed control. I have not forgotten the experience, but I have—knowingly and criminally—forsaken the oath.

I have juggled countless fast food lunches on the seat beside me, holding a drink and a fish sandwich in one hand and the steering wheel in the other. I have driven to the vet with a hissing cat standing on my shoulders and have held one arm across a dozen roses in a vase to keep them from toppling over. I have guarded a goldfish bowl (occupied) on the seat beside me, and have driven home from the plant store with a jungle of corn plants and ficus trees totally blocking every view. I have filled the seat and floor behind me so full of clay pots and bedding plants that I couldn't straighten up the driver's seat, which squished me into the steering wheel like an astronaut strapped in for lift-off.

I have spread road maps across the console, rehearsed speeches into the dashboard, and applied mascara in the rear-view mirror. I have hoisted myself into a standing position to grab the arm of a misbehaving child in the backseat, and given entire if-you-do-that-again-I'm-going-to-stop-this-car-and-let-you-out lectures while facing backward.

But now, I fear, I have committed the consummate atrocity, the most unspeakable act of our generation. I have accepted—and installed—the most obscene of eighties gifts: a cellular phone. When a generous relative presented the unexpected but lavish doodad, he squared up my shoulders and admonished me thusly: You'll love it. You'll take a stack of messages home from the office and use all your time to the fullest. You won't know how you ever lived without it. Don't drink coffee and talk on the phone at the same time.

At fifty cents a minute for peak air time, I ran up a ninety-dollar bill the first month alone. I called everybody I knew just to boast that I was at Thirty-eighth and Georgetown. I called my mother at seven A.M., my children at eight, and the dentist at nine. I called information, the operator, WTPI's traffic control center, and Bob and Tom's cash song line. I won't do it again.

The callee, however, pays even when it wasn't her idea, so I didn't appreciate the stranger who called and said, "Susan? Is that you?" or the one who simply asked, "Have you got the money?" And I'm still left with such nagging questions as, if I call someone else's car phone, who pays, and is there an information for car phone numbers?

Once only the plaything of those with more money than sense, the car phone seems to have invaded the real world. Squiggly black rear antennae have taken over the highways, multiplying like gerbils with each passing day. Didn't VCRs begin this way, with just a few idle rich taping and toying and making the rest of us green with envy? Wasn't there a time when only a few cars had stereo tape players with Dolby sound? Someday soon, I predict, phones will be standard equipment in cars, positioned somewhere between the CD player and the electronic map.

For me, it's already too late. I have shamelessly broken my own vows of safety and concentration and am nothing but a moving target. I've wrapped the spiral cord around both the steering wheel and my neck while turning the corner and have missed exits on the interstate. I have beeped callers into oblivion by resting the touch tone mechanism on my shoulder and have inched over into the wrong lane when engrossed in somebody's juicy story. For the sake of all my innocent passengers, thank goodness I don't drive a station wagon with a loose rear hatch.

—March 1987

Even though cell phones have become mainstream, I'm a proponent of banning their use in moving traffic. My associate, Jack Marsella, rear-ended another vehicle while immersed in conversation, and he's the best driver I know. Since car phones are no longer stationary in their dashboard holsters, I carry my mobile phone everywhere. If someone needs me badly enough, they can reach me in my purse.

Custard's Best Stand

ON THE HOTTEST of summer nights, when we peeled our shorts from our sticky legs and kicked off our shoes just for the cool of the grass on the soles of our feet, we saw their family of seven slowly pull out of the driveway next door, packed into a woody station wagon, on their way somewhere. We stood in the front yard and watched, my sister and I, ever jealous as they cupped their hands to their mouths and hooted, "Cool-off ride! We're going on a cool-off ride!"

We never discovered where they wound up with the windows rolled down and the nighttime breezes lifting their hair like an ocean gust under a sail. We just knew we wanted to go along. Cool-off rides were their rite of summer, one we were never invited to share. In time, our smaller family developed its own after-dinner custom, which led us on the long trek up North Meridian Street to Northwood, a drive-in restaurant famous for its waxy cups filled with creamy frozen custard, a salty pretzel hung on the plastic spoon to counteract the sweet. As we licked our spoons dry, we were convinced no one else's cool-off ride could possibly have led to such a heavenly destination. Even our older brother, in dread of being seen with his parents after nightfall, greedily sucked down the cool treat from his supine position on the floor of the backseat. Long after Northwood begat Frisch's Big Boy, Jolly Roger, the Reunion, and ultimately the bank building that resides on the spot today, we counted it as our most precious gift of summer.

The years in between then and now, filled with their own versions of Baskin-Robbins and Ben & Jerry's treats, satisfied our cravings but did little for our souls. Ice cream was ice cream and nothing more: better than what was dipped from a grocery-store carton but not what was joyously swirled into that cup at Northwood. And frozen yogurt: *feh!* Little fun is gleaned from deciding between fat-free and sugar-free, especially when the most tantalizing offering is a bland and gritty chocolate-and-vanilla dispensed side-by-side in a cup, hoping but failing to tempt us.

As parents of small children, my husband and I tried to revive the cool-off ride. Night after night we loaded up the car with neighborhood kids and headed for the Carmel Dairy Queen, this time air-conditioning forcing our car windows shut tight against the sweltering Indiana night. Once, as we backed out of the driveway, a tyke from two doors down banged on the rear window, tears leaving clean tracks down his face caked with dirt from a rousing game of after-dinner kickball. "What about me?" he wailed, waving a wadded dollar bill in his hand. "I've got money!" We had become the Pied Pipers of Peanut Buster Parfaits, and even our undistinguished destination could not sully our vaunted reputation as parents who knew that in whatever form, only ice cream could make a summer night complete.

It has taken the better part of a lifetime, but I honestly believe that our town has at long last topped Northwood. Ritter's Frozen Custard stands now grace our environs: places where we can breathe in the night air and feel glad to be alive, where we can watch the sun sink into our beloved flat Indiana landscape, where we line up shoulder-to-shoulder with the people we love, pondering which luscious treat will be ours. Of the ten area stands, I favor the suburban Fishers location, which distinguishes itself by its proximity to Metropolitan Airport. Here, we are distracted from our gustatory pleasures long enough to keep our eyes peeled for planes ascending and descending, so close we can see their steel underbellies as plainly as the butter-toasted pecans on our hot fudge sundaes. The heart of growing suburbia ensures a constant stream of toddlers hugging Styrofoam cups to their chests, digging the custard with the points of their spoons, and scraping the creamy mess along their shirts on the way to their mouths.

The mood is as casual as a picnic on a sunny day, and this is one of the few places I am not horrified to be spotted in my scrappiest jeans and ¡Yo Quiero Taco Bell! T-shirt. What matters is not pretense, but the puddle of smooth, sweet chocolate that seeps from the center of your tongue through your teeth until nothing remains but the memory. Ritter's is smart to close for the winter; this is a place equated with freedom, for Sunday nights not followed by school-day Monday mornings. A trip there is to summer what the first outdoor barbecue is to spring: a harbinger of better times to come.

If the night is hot enough, a sign in the little serving hut tells you what you already know: DRIP FACTOR HIGH. WE RECOMMEND CUPS. Part of the sport, though, rests in combating the cone, licking in circles faster than the kids racing around the concrete umbrella tables. Here, no silly malted-milk ball rests in the bottom of the cone to protect your shoes; only hand-mouth-eye coordination separates the men from the boys. And tempted as you might be by trendier Glaciers and multilayered sundaes named after Indiana sports teams, the most uncomplicated treat always prevails. Like a long kiss or warm bath on a Saturday afternoon, basic is best: plain chocolate and lots of it, pressed softly into an unadorned cone, with nothing on top but your tongue.

We've witnessed unusual sightings at Ritter's, such as a tornado whipping across a leveled cornfield on a perilous summer night when our cravings won out over good sense. That night we hurried home across a rain-swept interstate, juggling our cones and cups, trying not to wind up like the semi that had clunked over on its side just a few lanes away. And on another evening we watched as a pizza delivery boy pulled up to the side door, handing off a dozen flat boxes to the teenaged employees who surreptitiously offered round cartons of the fresh dairy treat in exchange. A drug deal in an urban alley couldn't have transpired more smoothly, and their secret was safe with us.

Unlike capri pants or seventies miniseries on TV, we don't love Ritter's because it hearkens us back to our past. We love it because it is simple. It is wonderful, homemade, high-calorie ice cream that snakes its way out of a stainless-steel tube on the other side of a glass window. We love it because it is rated G, and because we yearn to tear ourselves away from our e-purchases and DVD players to sit outside and eat something plain and delicious from a flat-bottomed cone. We love it because we know that only the basics can really satisfy, like a long ride on a two-lane road to an ice-cream stand by an airport, where kids stare up in the sky and watch for twin-engine Pipers to sputter and soar, forgetting about the dinosaurs in their Happy Meals. And we love it because you can't find true happiness in a corporate paycheck or a newly leased car but rather on a clear summer night, at the other end of a plastic spoon.

—July 2000

Ritter's Frozen Custard, which began with a family run store in Franklin, Indiana, in 1990, now has thirty-three locations nationwide, with plans to expand to one hundred more locations in Florida over the next ten years.

Danger Zone

THE AIRPORT GATE AREA was packed with people, all eyes fixed on the overhead TV. The screen flashed images of Janet Reno describing the FBI's search for the Oklahoma City bombers, along with intermittent sketches of John Doe Number 2 and video excerpts of the injured and grieving.

Unexpectedly, a loud alarm sounded—an intense, uninterrupted buzzing designed to capture one's attention in a millisecond, and hold it. Wary by nature, I am usually the only one to panic in such a situation, instantly sizing up the exits and proceeding at a dead run while everyone else shrugs and questions those next to them. This time, however, the alarm stilled the crowd, and faces became white and unexpressive. An obvious, irrational fear had gripped the passengers at Gate B7 in Atlanta's busy terminal, if just for a few seconds. An embarrassed attendant quickly shut a restricted door, instantly disengaging the alarm and signaling to the crowd that all was well.

While my natural sense of distrust and panic has been the source of jokes to my friends and family—I command an aisle seat at the movie theater (quicker getaway) and carefully spot exits wherever I go—the sickness has spread. It's no longer funny to feel squeamish on an airport people-mover crammed with unfamiliar bodies and suspicious luggage, and I'm sure I'm not the only one who surveyed possibly unsavory patrons at a crowded license branch on a recent visit. Mistrust now runs rampant: Unfortunately, in 1995 there is much more to fear than fear itself.

As a kid, we knew the threats, which did not come in the form of bombings. Taking candy from strangers was strongly discouraged, and any suspicious-looking men cruising the school grounds were to be reported immediately. We trooped outside without coats on cold winter days when the fire alarm sounded, and learned how to crouch in the corridor—heads between our knees, wrists clasped behind our necks—when dangerous weather threatened. Learning to heed warnings was the key, a luxury we are not afforded today.

Reacting to the unexpected has made us jumpy. In the magazine world, when we run a negative story or publicize questionable characters, an editor invariably warns that at any time someone wielding an assault rifle could invade our cozy midst, turning our desks into "death bunkers." What we realize, however, is that most malcontents vent verbally; it's the ones we *don't* hear from that worry us most.

At a recent showing of *The Shawshank Redemption,* the film was suddenly stopped, accompanied by the instantaneous lighting of the theater and a blaring siren. A warning to vacate immediately flashed onto the screen and resounded via a loud computer voice, met mostly by shocked viewers who, popcorn still in hand, remained affixed to their seats. At least I think they remained seated, as I didn't look behind as I instantly took off for the exit nearest my aisle seat. With everything from scud missiles to nerve gas to fear, I wasn't about to wait it out.

Catastrophes like the one in Oklahoma City haunt our calm moments as well. I worry more in my twelfth floor office than I used to, envisioning the pancake effect of a bombed multistoried building. When the fire alarm sounded some weeks ago, I was on the fifth floor by the time the rest of the staff decided whether or not it was a false alarm. The calf pain I experienced for days after, I am happy to report, was not thrombosis, but merely bruised muscles from the pounding of flesh against concrete. And another alarm that jarred me awake in a twenty-fourth floor hotel room the night of the Oklahoma City bombing caused my heart to pound with such intensity that I wasn't sure what would kill me first: a terrorist attack or cardiac arrest.

The trouble with irrational fear is that one never knows if it is rational until it's too late. When a Middle Eastern gentleman seated next to me on an airplane removed a copy of the Koran from his case, took off his shoes and, rolled-up rug under his arm, made his way to the lavatory in the rear of the plane, I struggled whether to report the incident or respect his religious freedoms and remain silent. Deciding that a bomb would reduce us to powder anyway, I kept quiet, avoiding his glance for the rest of the flight.

Like that incident, I'm rarely proud of my wariness. Unable to locate my teenage son at home while calling from work and from a dinner engagement one evening, I automatically assumed that he had been abducted (or worse) and, after making a hysterical fool of myself to his friends and their parents, I fled the restaurant before my food was delivered and lead-footed it home, sure I would find police cars in my driveway. What I found instead was the kid camped out on the back porch with the cat, where he had sat for nearly three hours after locking himself out, certain his conscientious parents would arrive home any minute.

Anticipating the worst is wearing. Living in Indiana or anywhere in the U.S. is beginning to feel like a night in the Gaza Strip, although I felt more secure on a recent trip to Israel than I do here. At least there citizens know what to expect, and the everpresent military has a way of making one feel protected. It takes some getting used to to reconcile that man can turn on you with all the ferocity of nature, and that crouching in a hallway listening for the rumble of an oncoming tornado probably won't help.

—June 1995

What with the recent spate of school shootings, I am grateful my children are no longer school-aged. Now all I have to worry about are drunk drivers, snipers, burglars, and drive-by shootings.

High and Mighty

IN THIS MATERIAL WORLD, some temptations are simply too great to resist. I've been considering an automatic bread maker for about two years now, and I'm not sure anyone can really get into adequate physical condition without a HealthRider. Nothing, however, has held the appeal of a 190-HP, equential-Fuel-Injection-engined, leather-appointed, 4300 V-6-equipped sport utility vehicle.

Something about ridin' high in that split-bench front seat, barreling through snowdrifts and hauling great, ungainly parcels in the seventy-four-cubic-foot rear cargo bay improves my mood and elevates my spirit. I have admired the entire species of Jeep Grand Cherokees, Ford Explorers, and Chevy Blazers long enough to develop an advanced case of genus envy.

This year it took only two Indiana snowstorms to send me rushing into the auto showroom with dollar bills fairly flying from my wallet. I'd been stuck in the snow before—several times that week, as luck would have it. Once I found myself rocking my rear-wheel-drive sedan to no avail at the slight incline where my suburban neighborhood intersects with a major thoroughfare. I had two choices: build up a head of steam from approximately one-fourth mile away and charge blindly into approaching traffic, or inch up to the highway slowly, knowing full well that going forward would eventually be replaced with going backward.

The second time I sat, stuck like a coyote in a trap, far enough from my home to elicit panic. In my passenger seat I carried an adult son fresh from oral surgery, still dazed and babbling from the anesthetic, bleeding profusely from four empty sockets where wisdom teeth once stood. Behave sensibly, I told myself, you can manage this: You won't have to gnaw your leg off. At which point I sprang from the driver's seat and then stopped cold, hollering swear words into the silent snowstorm like a sailor on leave. By this time the drug-addled kid, mortified by his mother's outburst and convinced he could fly, began to walk home, gauze pads protruding from his mouth, leaving a red trail behind as he staggered north.

Precisely forty-eight hours later I drove off the lot of the nearest new car dealership in a shiny, No. 72 Apple Red Chevy Blazer—a moment that literally has changed my perspective, if not my life. It hasn't snowed one inch since then, mind you, but the sheer thrill of seeing the world from the high-riding driver's seat has empowered me beyond my wildest expectations. Where I was once a lowly five-footer staring down the windshield-washer sprayers, I am now Manute Bol, erect in my seat, able to look down at fellow drivers as if they were in Matchbox cars. While the most fun I ever had in my conservative sedan lay in setting my CD player on "random," I'm now Ralph Kramden behind the wheel of a city bus, controlling the lanes, seeing the horizon line stretch in front of me, promising Alice to send her to the moon.

Until you have been tall, even temporarily, you cannot fully understand how miserable it is to be short. Unless you have undergone a knee MRI with your head in the claustrophobic tube because there's not enough of you to extend, unless you have hit every pothole in the street because you can't see over the hood, and unless you have never seen a parade, you may think negative stature is a virtue. I can in great detail describe the person's head in front of me at every movie I have ever seen, and I can state with no reservation that I've never enjoyed an unobstructed view of, well, anything. This new front-seat perch for the first time affords me an unparalleled opportunity to witness society as most people do, to nod at truckers beside me, to actually see the paint color on the hood of my vehicle.

Driving a truck instead of a car instantly transforms one from ordinary genteel citizen to hot-rockin' mama. While my ideal persona consists of an every-hair-in-place, perfectly manicured, Coach-briefcase-slung-over-the-shoulder icon of femininity and class, underneath it beats the heart of a cowgirl. While I'll stop short of stuffing a wad of Red Man chewing tobacco in my cheek or buying Yosemite Sam mud flaps as an optional upgrade, a little Reba McEntire on the AM/FM stereo with graphic equalizer couldn't hurt. Those Goodyear Wrangler tires complete the package, as well as my tough-talkin older brother's assessment that it took me four years, but I'm finally cool.

For some reason most of my friends and coworkers find this turn of events amusing. Is it possible that someone who swoons over diamond watches in magazine ads and judges risotto al funghi as ho-hum could find pleasure in a truck? It is. In fact, with my foot on the accelerator, the truck and I connect and become one. More than just a mode of transportation, it's a four-by-four, standard four-wheel ABS, crash-avoidant, theft-deterrent extension of my soul. Even at just sixty inches, I've mastered embarking and disembarking and no longer require a Rubbermaid stool. Like a ring-tailed lemur in a kily tree, I can hop in and out with grace and am wondering just how tough it would be to maneuver a school bus, ten-passenger limousine, or snowplow. I say you take dominance and strength any way you can get it, and mine now comes from my Chevy truck, complete with standard Vortec V-6 and smart emissions diagnostics. You might never need to haul, tow or pass, but you should utilize any and all opportunities to be tall.

—March 1996

For a college graduation present, we allowed Jonathan and his roommate to borrow the Blazer for a month-long cross-country road trip. Judging by the interior smell, they didn't waste money on motel rooms or laundromats, and even now, air fresheners have no effect. Unwilling to sell it, my husband drives the six-year-old vehicle, whose "service engine" light remains perpetually lit, while on snowy days I commandeer our black Lexus RX 300, an SUV of the highest order.

Screen Gems

WE WERE SEARCHING for the past. My husband's strong memories of his family's summer vacations in Michigan led us to South Haven, and when night fell, we found ourselves at the Michigan Theater, a movie house that hadn't succumbed to progress. Its marquee glittered with the promise of Tracy and Hepburn, although on that evening Antonio Banderas was starring in *Desperado*. Puckered carpeting hinted of a flood or two. A stooped man in the ticket booth took our money, then shuffled into the lobby and tore the same ticket he had just sold. A moment later he scooted behind the candy counter, where he scooped our popcorn into buckets and directed us to the balcony, where my husband, overcome with memories of John Wayne in *The High and the Mighty*, insisted we sit.

Not one for glorifying ghosts of yesteryear, I took my seat with trepidation. While he imagined rowdy boys lobbing Jujubes and shrieking with delight at the pre-movie showing of Woody Woodpecker, I saw dirt, lots of it, stuck to the floor, embedded in the darkened upholstery, eroding the ceiling tiles overhead. Fearful that rats might scurry about the neglected theater and remembering the bats that had swooped down into the gasping theater crowd in my college days, I tucked my feet protectively beneath me and slid down in my seat as far as I could without disappearing entirely. I was set to see the movie in the fetal position, but safe from vermin who would fly menacingly above or click their sharp claws across the sticky concrete floor. You can't go home again, I murmured to myself, the only one interested in my decidedly non-nostalgic opinion.

Movie theaters aren't like they were when we joyfully snuggled up to our fifteen-year-old dates at the Uptown, exuberant at our privacy in the dark, concentrating less on Sidney Poitier in *Lilies of the Field* than on where the hand around our shoulder might ultimately land. As kids, we gathered for Saturday matinees, where we suffered through President Eisenhower on the newsreels in eager anticipation of the feature presentation. My husband remembers waiting in line for more than an hour at the Ritz at Thirty-fourth and Illinois streets. There, he stealthily observed the concessions vendor, judging when the free ticket for the following week's performance might be inserted into the lucky box of popcorn, then pouncing in line at exactly the right moment. Ecstatic at his victory, he rushed into the theater in time for the announcement of next Saturday's show: *Seven Brides for Seven Brothers*, a musical, for crying out loud, a mushy tale of misbegotten relationships to be shown for free to a boy with hopes of *Tarzan the Ape Man*.

Megaplexes are now the Wal-Mart of entertainment, satisfying the masses that choose among the twenty-four screens for their night's ration of passive pleasure. Heavy velvet curtains no longer sweep open in anticipatory drama, and flashlight-wielding ushers in pursuit of hooligans who prop their feet on the seat in front of them have disappeared. You can't twist your neck to get a glimpse of the projector operator anymore, and nobody sings or dances much onscreen. Still and all, I like it. I'll skate like Oksana Baiul across a frozen parking lot to catch a first-run movie on a Saturday night, and happily sink down into my stadium seat with a bale of popcorn and a bubbly Coke before me. I like the previews, word scrambles, comedy countdown, filmstrip roller coaster, movie trivia, classic clips, candy band, and even the popcorn-and-Pepsi date. While I no longer worry about errant hands, I like the cool darkness and the chance to share a straw and whisper seductively into my husband's ear. The movie theater is the only place besides an airplane where I will sit that close to strangers, and I'm happiest if the guy behind me doesn't cough, sneeze, hawk a loogie, laugh too loud, kick, answer his cell phone, or recount the plot to whatever hopeless moron is sitting beside him.

The pastime is not as good as reading but better than *Ally McBeal*. I will gladly pay fourteen dollars for popcorn dumped out of a Sam's Club bag and a Coke the size of a toxic-waste drum. I'll see anything with Meg Ryan and without Julia Roberts, and won't pay to be scared, as I can do that for free every morning in the bathroom mirror. I avoid any movie described as a farce, thriller, dark comedy, or British romp in favor of something to do with love or prison, though preferably not both. I gravitate toward the Castleton Arts, where I am faked out like other patrons by the silly thermos jugs of Starbucks coffee and stacks of yellowed national reviews in the corner, suggesting that something intellectual is actually going on there. Like most of my gender, I'm partial to chick flicks, as long as they have the depth of *Dangerous Beauty* as opposed to *The Runaway Bride*, and star no one who looks better unclothed than I do, which is just about everyone now, save maybe Debbie Reynolds or Jessica Tandy, whom I am pretty sure is dead. Daytime movies are a guilty pleasure, reminding me of seeing *Love Story* the Saturday it opened in 1970, feeling like a pail of ice water was dumped on me as I tearfully retreated from the dark theater into the blinding winter sun.

Sure, I miss the independent movie theaters of my youth, where they made the popcorn fresh and showed romantic kisses instead of graphic orgy scenes. But in my house, Saturday night is still date night, and like millions of other desperate Americans, we line up at the movies with their concierges and coffee stands, and crowd into oblong rooms where we can hear the action in theater twenty-three next door. It's become a way of life, and we'll choose it any day over a marathon viewing of *Emeril Live!* on the Food Network. It gets us out of the house and into contemporary culture, and we can make Academy Award picks the way Stephen Hawking proves a scientific theory. We take our normal seats on the aisle, left-hand side, halfway back, so at a measly five feet in height I can see without bopping the guy on the head in front of me. Although we could easily await the video release, we rarely do. At home, I tend to wear expandable sweatpants, and plop down with a trio of soft pillows behind me. Even with my bag of microwave popcorn as a diversion, I always fall asleep within the first fifteen minutes, ten if there are subtitles. At least at the theater you know that unless you've been wheeled over from the nursing home, the chances are good you'll make it to the credits.

This upcoming movie season, I hear they're showing *The Cider House Rules* and *Angela's Ashes*. The books were great, but it will be fun actually to see Dr. Wilbur Larch sniffing ether and Frank McCourt eeking his way through Ireland. And besides, I don't have any Sno-Caps in my pantry at home.

—October 1999

My favorite movies, in descending order, are:

10. Chocolat
9. Sabrina *(the remake)*

8. Papillon
7. Clueless *("I have an overwhelming sense of ickiness.")*
6. Annie Hall
5. Moll Flanders
4. Braveheart
3. The Out-of-Towners *(the original)*
2. Dangerous Beauty
1. Dr. Zhivago

Technical Difficulties

IT STARTED AS CRACKLING noises, like a radio caught between stations. There were distant voices in the sputter, and I rushed to my office window to investigate the street four stories below. By then it had stopped, and I stood scratching my head, convinced that senility had begun its cruel rampage. A few days later, I heard the static of voices again, only this time a conversation could be discerned: "Shucks, whaddabout that load o' pig feed up yonder?"

"Dunno," came the reply. "Got my own."

The words floated somewhere in the room, and there was only one answer: I was a medium, a direct link to some long-dead farmer who had left his business undone. It would be my job to organize a seance of his relatives, and, with hands joined, we would find the missing cargo and nourish the needy swine. As I contemplated my next move, it began again, but this time heavy laughter punctuated the dialogue, now louder and clearer. "What you up to?" began one exchange. "Just f—g in the wind," the other answered. Alas, it was not coming from the heavens, but from my computer speakers! My sanity restored, I ran for a coworker to validate my experience, but by the time he entered the room, the speakers were silent. Over the next several days my speakers crackled like a bug zapper on a summer night, and then broadcast the conversations, obviously between truckers. I heard about girlfriends and wives and bars, but mostly about loads of hay and grain. And every time I hollered for witnesses, the talking instantly ceased.

Confessions of a Kid at Heart

My office became something of a shrine, and outside my door, lines formed, like when the curious gather around a cornfield to see the Virgin Mary in the crops. And I became an oddity myself, a woman possessed with unexplainable powers, like those goofballs who can open garage doors with the fillings in their teeth. No one heard it but me, and when I called in the company's computer experts to investigate, they felt my forehead for fever and pantomimed a drunk tipping back a bottle to his mouth, wiping his chin with the sleeve of his shirt. The entire experience was the weirdest thing that has happened since my cat Woody learned how to stand on her hind legs and open the laundry room door with her paws.

The problem was complicated by the fact that when it comes to technology, I don't have a lot of credibility. As with most leading-age baby boomers, grasping the art of electronic transmission has been something of a challenge for me, and I have cried wolf one time too many. I can read my e-mail but not with a file attached, and although I have placed award-winning works such as this on the magazine's network dozens of times, I still beg for assistance to ensure that they don't wind up published in *Harper's*, or something equally embarrassing. In my top desk drawer I store piles of notes that read, "Select 'FILE.' Press 'ENTER.' Find 'SAVE AS.' Move mouse there. Click on the right-hand part." When my future grandchildren (God willing) find these notes after I am gone, it will besmirch my memory, but those are the facts. Their granny was a computer dolt described by her own son as the Rain Man as he tried to teach her to surf the 'Net.

Thankfully, I'm not alone. A few months back, I e-mailed a directive to an editor who reports to me at another magazine. Now, I am proud that I know when to hit "Send," and when, lacking sound professional judgment, to press "Cancel." On top of that I've learned to boldface and italicize certain words for emphasis, which I do as often as possible because I can. The memo was full of such verbal punctuation as it detailed the editorial direction I hoped this employee would follow. The editor proceeded to "FORWARD" the message to a coworker, who added some inflammatory remarks about the original sender and then hit "Reply." But even I, proficient in boldfacing and italicizing, know the path that takes, which it did, directly back to me, the last person in this hemisphere the guilty party would want to see such blasphemy. After hearing too many gruesome apologies, I took consolation in the fact that I was called a ditz and the editor in question was the one who lambasted someone two steps above and then sent her the message.

Just the other day two men who looked like the duo in *Ghostbusters,* but without the proton packs, identified themselves as the Y2K team and proceeded to crawl around under my desk identifying computer parts. I am now No. 00084, in case those grandchildren want to investigate after the carnage we expect on January 1. After seeing a sign on Carmel's Faith Apostolic Church, which read, "Jesus is Y2K compliant," I am grateful to be in good company. But I doubt that in the scheme of things, even this exacting preparation will help someone as helpless as I. My computer screen recently delivered the following message: "System has detected a conflict for IP address 192.4741.123 with the system having hardware address 00:60:08:3F:5E:B4. The interface has been disabled." Then it offered me a choice. "Okay?" it asked. "Sounds okay to me," I answered, thinking I might as well be in the cockpit of a B-52 bomber over Kosovo. After all, this is the same computer user who obliterated her toolbar and can't get it back, turned an entire story upside down on the screen for no apparent reason, and unknowingly sent a virus in an innocent document to thirty employees. From here on out, I am to be avoided like one of Moses' ten plagues, lest locusts clatter down upon the heads of my fellow workers like literary hail.

The happy ending reveals that late one Friday afternoon when no other sane person remained at the office save myself and another diehard two offices down, the voices in my computer speakers began to swell. "I got this black box," said one. "Well, sir, then do it," said another. Gingerly approaching the phone, I summoned my coworker quietly, and he came. At long last, a witness, an actual computer geek plus ham radio expert recognized the broadcast as coming from CB radios and explained away the phenomenon with the wave of a hand: My speakers were acting as receivers, not sending me messages from above.

These same speakers are labeled the Genius Hi-Fi Multimedia Booster Speaker System SP-330. I must be more up to date than they are, however, since the last time I saw the term "Hi-Fi" was on the cover of my Henry Mancini album in 1964. And if I can believe more recent correspondence from the sender of the infamous misdirected memo, I'm the genius now.

—July 1999

I no longer share secrets (even with my sister) on my cell phone. It's a radio!

Smoke Signal

WHILE MANY STEREOTYPES represent dangerous oversimplifications of the obvious, some fit so miraculously as to stick in your mind like glue, waiting to be conjured up at the slightest provocation. When I think of a cigar smoker, for example, the image is clear: a short, fat, bald man in an ill-fitting plaid sport coat, with a face monstrously distorted by a TV-camera lens. He is no doubt making loud claims about carpet prices or monster truck shows and even louder admonitions regarding our participation.

The advent of *Cigar Aficionado,* a swanky, oversize magazine devoted to the stinky habit of cigar smoking, or the vision of Demi Moore with a stogie poised neatly between her perfectly manicured fingertips, does little to disrupt that representation. Nope, cigar smokers are named Crazy Al, push racks of *shmatehs* through the garment district, and will smash a half-grapefruit in your face at the very hint of confrontation.

It is difficult, therefore, for me to appreciate the contemporary glorification of these jumbo cancer sticks, much less tolerate their stench or throat-closing smoke. If we believe the statistic that more than ten million people in the U.S. now smoke cigars, we'd better brace ourselves for doomsday: They've entered the workplace, the restaurant, and the party, and they're wearing Armani suits and eighteen-karat gold cuff links. At a recent social gathering replete with such back-slapping corporate cohorts, my buddies and I found ourselves retreating little by little to the outer lobby, while the thick, swirling cigar smoke settled like nuclear fallout over the party. If chic is what we're after, a nice sprig of cilantro or swig of rosemary-scented olive oil might prove less offensive to the rest of us who share the planet.

In an era when sensitivity is key and restaurateurs and hoteliers finally provide a smoke-free atmosphere for us to dine in and sleep, we have taken a giant step backward. Even in our conservative town, an elegant steak house is about to premier the city's first cigar bar, prompting me to wonder what's next. A burping bar comes to mind, along with the host or hostess's requisite request: burping or non-burping? Some of the higher-ups in our normally civilized offices have been known to light one up occasionally in celebration of a particularly fine day on Wall Street, causing us malcontents to cough dramatically, prop open the fire escape door, and beg for sick leave.

Since such corporate moguls like to think they no longer resemble Crazy Al, they are taking their affliction/addiction much more seriously than necessary. They covet four-hundred-and-fifty-dollar rosewood humidors from the Neiman Marcus catalog and admire fourteen-hundred-dollar cigar cuff links with platinum ash and diamond band. They caress each cigar as sensuously as if it were a woman's graceful neck and glide it under their noses like an oenophile judging a rare Bordeaux. Helpless to resist, I once snatched one from the hand of its idolater and dangled it precariously over my half-full Evian bottle. You would have thought I had threatened to smite his firstborn. For some incomprehensible reason, cigar smoking is now being viewed as art rather than addiction, and like the proliferation of the "F" word, we're slipping the offensive element into the mainstream and blaming those of us offended for complaining about it.

Lest I preach about the dangers of cigar smoke (cancer of the mouth, throat, larynx, and lungs; emphysema; chronic bronchitis) without giving the nasty habit its due, I recently tried smoking one. Congregating with office workers accustomed to spending breaks puffing outdoors was an eye-opener itself, like joining your enemies in battle. The fifteen minutes it took to light up against the wind blew my cover, and I wound up borrowing a grill lighter the size of a curling iron from the building restaurant to accomplish the task. By then I felt as comfortable as a librarian at a frat party, adding to the spectacle by spitting grotesque tobacco particles onto the concrete. Finally consummated, the act itself proved at once horrid and bizarre, the smoke tasting like a stale cork, burning the lips and throat like a leftover campfire.

One who joined me found more pleasure peeling apart the cigar like those little umbrellas that adorn exotic drinks, no doubt hoping to find a scroll of Chinese scripture within. Another enjoyed rolling it around in his mouth and finally clamping down on the stub that remained, shouting orders through his clenched teeth like a dockworker. When the ends began to resemble lollipop sticks that had been savored too long, we flicked them to the ground and called it a day. The after-effects included a daylong headache requiring eight Extra Strength Tylenols to quell, and a skin tinge somewhere between The Incredible Hulk's and Kermit the Frog's.

The result of our cigar caper, which proved at least mildly entertaining to coworkers, was simple. I can understand why, considering the frenzy of current trends, someone might smoke one once. I cannot, however, fathom why anyone would do it twice. Maybe it's a guy thing, or a psychotic attempt to orally fixate. If it's just the stench or the bad manners one seeks, however, it might be less of a health risk or social blunder to chew on a clove of garlic and then blow it around. One might not make any new friends, but at least nobody will ask for directions to the carpet store.

—July 1996

The same week this column appeared, I was summoned over the office intercom to the smoking lounge. Everybody's a comedian.

Taking Charge

DEAR ERICA:

You don't mind if I call you Erica, do you? I'm actually unaware of your name, but since you stole my credit card number and went on a cross-country spending spree disguised as me, I feel in some perverse way that we are connected. And I've always liked the name Erica. If I'd had a daughter, I might have named her Erica, as Erica Paul has a nice ring to it. Or Rachel. Dawn is nice, too—Dawn Cheryl Paul.

It all started in a silly restaurant near Atlanta, Georgia, called The Food Business, which is a ridiculous name for a dining establishment anyway. It sits on the town square of Decatur, a historic little burg within a bulging metropolis. I had rejected the first table the hostess offered because of its location at the top of the stairs in the midst of the traffic flow. We were happier at the second table, still upstairs but by the window, which allowed a great view of the square and especially of what I assumed were two homeless people lying together to keep warm. It turned out they weren't homeless after all and were lying together for a different purpose, if you get my drift, but that really doesn't matter.

Our dinner was terrible, by the way. I haven't had beef that bad since the creamed-chipped variety in seventh-grade home ec class. Oh, and by the way, I got an "A" in that class, probably because of my awesome lemon pound cake, which was entered in the 4-H contest at the State Fair and earned a red ribbon. (The blue one went to a show-off with a springform pan.) At any rate, you must be a server or busser at The Food Business, or some perverted patron who lifted my charge card receipt from the table and proceeded to go on a buying frenzy the next day. I found this out nearly a week later at Pottery Barn when I attempted to charge an extravagant wedding gift (eight place settings of Sausalito Blanca dinnerware for the offspring of a lifelong friend), and the Citibank Visa man asked to speak to me personally. I should tell you that I was insulted by this, as I have an excellent credit rating and felt confident that my two-hundred-dollar charge could not possibly be declined. Therefore, I was snotty to the Visa man, who was only trying to help by alerting me to an uncharacteristic spending pattern and asking if I had indeed purchased, among other things, sporting goods, clothing from an apparel catalog, computer software, and lottery tickets, of all things. Who knew you could buy lottery tickets over the phone or computer? What's this world coming to? It turns out you were the one spending my money, and ticked off doesn't begin to describe my feelings on the matter.

Now, this has caused me untold distress. A few days later I received an affidavit, which I must complete in excruciating detail and get notarized. Since you knew how to order lottery tickets by phone, maybe you can help me find a notary public. This isn't Mayberry, you know, and I doubt that a notary is employed at the Western Union office next to the bus depot. After a one hour conversation with a Visa lady, to whom it made perfect sense that they had sent me a replacement card with the same number as the old one (duh), I became so unnerved that I was compelled to consume an entire bag of Nestle's Toll House Semi-Sweet Morsels on a day particularly bad for my diet as it was. You see, I had eaten at Steak 'n Shake for lunch and at Googie's Gourmet Hamburgers for dinner, and had to run an extra two miles on the treadmill to repent. This no doubt further eroded my sore hip socket, which I am convinced is bone rubbing against bone anyway, and causes me to walk like Walter Brennan in *The Real McCoys*.

If you must know, that afternoon I had also been to the eye doctor, who had stuck steel rods into my eyeballs to get a better look at my retinas. My eyes were dilated, causing me to drive home like Mr. Magoo, but with sunglasses placed on top of my eyeglasses, only to have to decipher the blurred mess of my credit card bill when I got there. And this was the same week I had thoroughly cleaned out my closet and discarded anything larger than a size six. Now if my weight balloons, as it surely will after the chocolate chip fiasco, I will be reduced to wearing the drapes, like Scarlett O'Hara in *Gone With the Wind*. Also that week, the landscapers cut our phone line while planting trees to shield our house from a new one that was constructed approximately three-quarters of an inch from our property line.

It took five days to get our phone service back, and I am convinced that my acute forgetfulness is a result of using my cell phone for that entire period, scrambling my brain and causing me to send back a wedding invitation response card with nothing written on it.

Just dealing with the paperwork and the people at Citibank is annoying enough. And why in the world did they change their logo to "citi" in lower-case letters, like something a teenager would write in the margin of her notebook? When I was thirteen, I tried to change my name to Kitti, which my mother forbade. Citibank should have called Mom before they screwed up their credibility, too. She knows better.

Speaking of fighting major institutions, I'm currently battling the Social Security Administration, which has advised me that I was born in 1917 rather than 1947, making me eighty-three. I have called at least a dozen times and never reached a human, left messages but never received a new form, and navigated its Web site to no avail. This reminds me of the time I tried to renew my mother's handicapped-parking tag, and the license branch clerk remarked that I certainly looked good for having been born in 1908. "Lucille!" I remember her exclaiming to her fellow employee. "Look here! This little gal is ninety!" I would be more insulted by the Social Security gaffe were it not for the fact that I should stop working in about fifteen years anyway, when I'm ninety-eight. Then I can collect so much in benefits that a lottery win will seem like chump change.

Speaking of the lottery, thanks for nothing. Since your charges were based in Georgia, I assume those tickets you bought were for the $363 million Big Game jackpot, which you undoubtedly won, knowing your luck. If that is the case, please forward $182 million immediately, and we'll call it even. Minus the hip replacement surgery I need, that will leave me approximately $181.97 million, which will allow me to retire next year, when I'm eighty-four. Then I can pay off my bill, including your charges, plus the one to the Coach store, which charged me for a briefcase I returned, rather than issuing a credit. It required three relinquished lunch hours before they understood that it had to be credited twice (once to negate the mistaken purchase and another time for the original credit). You should have seen the manager's face when, after it was finally corrected, I advised her that, no thanks to your Visa thievery, my credit card had been cancelled and the transaction could not be reported until I got another one, this time with a new number.

Contrary to her opinion, I am not nuts. You are. And immoral, a thief, and probably bad-looking to boot. I hope all the stores that mailed you merchandise you expect me to pay for send representatives to your door at once, like a Publishers Clearing House Sweepstakes gone bad. But as you stand there in your ill-fitting bathrobe with a mud pack on your face, don't expect the Prize Patrol, balloons, and an oversize check. As a matter of fact, I might come myself, just to see who you think you are. It will take me a while to limp there from the car, so be patient. I'm actually in pretty good shape for a plump, blind, destitute eighty-three-year-old wearing cafe curtains and carrying a grocery bag for a briefcase.

Sincerely, Deborah Paul
—August 2000

It took three months for the disputed charges to be removed from my credit bill.

Love and Loss

My father was forty-seven when he joyously witnessed the birth of his little girl. At forty-seven, I came to know the sorrow of losing him on New Year's Day. The oldest and the youngest, we share a heart and own a love that transcends generations. And it lasts forever.

Breathing Lessons

I'VE NEVER UNDERSTOOD allergies. When I was a kid, an allergy was something you said you had if you didn't want the other guy to think he could get your cold. And people are allergic to such silly things. Ragweed and pollen I can understand. But mold, yeast, or house dust?

I have one friend who, every so often, details his reaction to lemons. Lemons, mind you! He puffs up like a balloon and gets sick to his stomach, so he lives his dining-out hours in fear of fish dinners and veal piccata. I remember an old college roommate who was allergic to cold air. On biting Bloomington mornings, she would bundle up to her chin and try to make it to class, only to retreat in failure to the dorm the moment the first blast of winter wind touched her skin. Covered with itchy, swollen hives, she would sink onto the bed to await their collapse.

Having never experienced an allergy to anything save egg rolls (a sorority binge twenty years ago resulted in itchy welts on my eyelids), I approach the subject callously. So who could blame me for ignoring the fact that my twelve-year-old son couldn't breathe through his nose? Even after a cold's natural duration, he continued to make his presence known by a resounding "schnorkk" and a frequent upward swipe of the heel of his hand across his nose.

It was time to seek medical help in the form of an allergist. As the nurse quickly pricked sixty-four holes into a grid drawn on the back of a horrified preteenager, I prayed that he was allergic to Froot Loops, the cherry flavoring in drinks, or something simple like pepperoni or tree bark. I thought of his younger brother, who agonized over the whole prospect, asking, "What if he's allergic to me? Which one of us would have to go?"

Three pricks in a row ominously began to rise and redden: Number 1, cat; Number 2, cat; Number 3, cat. Definitive, unpredictable, dreaded results. He was allergic to my sweet, beautiful, lap-sitting calico cat—a pet whose worst vice was twanging the doorstops. I would be forced to give up a placid puss who put away six cans of Amore a week and snoozed away her days in shafts of sunlight.

I suddenly flashed back to the day I had picked her out at the Humane Society. One of a litter of look-alikes, she set herself apart by licking not just herself but all of her brothers and sisters. She was, in short, an irresistible philanthropist. The day of that joyful shopping spree, a disheveled elderly gentleman stood near the cage that held his mangy black cat. As passersby headed for the cuter kittens, he pleaded with them, one by one, "Won't you please take my cat and give her a good home? I'm old and have to go to a nursing home."

At the time, I didn't want his cat. Now it was I who would become the disheartened beggar. Her selling points, it turned out, were her surgeries. She was like an old lady at a bridge game, defining herself by her operations. She's spayed and declawed, I boasted, which raised her value, but still no one volunteered to take her. Friends who swore they'd always stick by me scattered like chickens with the coop door open, and I was reduced to asking strangers: the grocery checkout lady, the lawn man's wife, a babysitter with a gentle heart.

A haircut at a local salon resulted in the same plea, but this time, a stylist in the next booth quickly leaned in to say she'd love a calico cat and she'd take it tomorrow.

It was joy and sorrow all mixed together. In the car, as the cat mewed mournfully through the holes in the cardboard carrier, I tried to explain the whole miserable situation. But she didn't buy it, and we became the sorriest of partners: cat and cad.

I miss her most, I think, at dinnertime, when no fat feline winds around my ankles, or when the family arrives home and no one greets us at the door. Our fish and chicken leftovers are now dutifully scraped into the garbage disposal, and the milk left at the bottom of the cereal bowl is dribbled down the drain. I don't leave open the window blind to ensure her unimpeded view, and my lap is cold and empty at TV time. Even though the braided kitchen rug is bare, the young man breathes more quietly and comfortably.

A lovely lady recently approached me at a party and—out of the blue—asked if I knew anyone who had a soft, self-cleaning, lovable, one-owner cat she could give to her mother-in-law, a woman who lived alone and yearned for some mature feline company. At first aghast and then just terribly sad, I thought of the desolate man at the Humane Society and wondered what had become of his bedraggled, sorrowful companion.

—May 1986

I used to spy on Paddy-Cat, driving by her new owner's apartment complex to chance a sight of her in a window. Now that our allergic son has left home, our present cat, christened Scooter but nicknamed Woody, lives wherever she pleases.

A World Apart

AS A YOUNG WORKING mother several years ago, I faced the same dilemma as most of my contemporaries: finding babysitters. While searching for someone dependable and reputable, I stumbled onto a unique situation. A professional couple had arranged for Jette, a Danish girl, to come to America for a year to reside with them and babysit for their two children. Their sudden divorce left one frightened girl from abroad without work, and, worse yet, without a place to stay.

Enter one family with no intention of hiring live-in help, whose children probably couldn't even find Denmark on the map, let alone relate to someone who lived there. As the tall, stately young lady with the whitest of hair and the bluest of eyes sat in our living room undergoing our scrutiny, her answers were punctuated with "ems," her way of hesitating long enough to translate mentally and craft the reply.

We were most alarmed when we asked her what her father did, and she answered without hesitation, "He is a beggar." A beggar! We were mortified. Our widened eyes and dropped jaws must have been message enough, and she instantly began to giggle. "A *beggar,*" she repeated, accenting the first syllable. "You know, in a beggary. He begs bread in the mornings." The language barrier was crossed, and our younger son, then four, advanced cautiously to investigate his prospective nanny. They did not speak, but she gently hoisted him up to sit beside her. As our broken conversation progressed, he opened his hand and stroked her forearm. Neither moved, but the bond was unmistakable.

The experience of having her with us was unforgettable. The values most important to her were the ones we overlooked. A tidy house, dinner together with occasional samples of her father's bread, and a bike ride to the drugstore made her stay worthwhile. When the preschooler became ill with pneumonia, the ten-day supply of antibiotic did little to comfort her. Patrolling his bedside, she did not sleep until his breathing no longer rattled and his hot, dry forehead became cool and moist once more.

She was a gem, a modest girl who tolerated children swinging from her arms and legs, and sent tiny folded paper sculptures home to her mother and father. She taught my children love and respect, and we, in turn, forced American culture at her at every opportunity. While she found the olives we enjoy in our salad to taste like, "Em, something rotten from the bottom of the sea," she learned to love *Dallas* and taped Sunday morning radio broadcasts of *American Top 40* to send to her friends back home.

Barely twenty at the time, she was much like all young people, I thought, with one major exception. She was unequivocally and absolutely unspoiled. Desiring a better grasp of our language, she reluctantly enrolled in freshman English at Butler University and, with a crimson face, accepted both her tuition cost and the ride to and from school each snowy Monday evening. When I, often tired at the end of a long workday, would suggest we venture out for dinner, she would order only a salad while the rest of us dined in the limitless American style. While she grew accustomed to our many restaurant meals, she never learned to tolerate the argument that accompanied every where-shall-we-go decision. ("A cafeteria's geezer food, pizza takes too long, we had hamburgers for lunch.") The only time I ever saw her angry was when, squeezed between two spoiled complainers in the backseat, she said sternly, "You should be glad you are going at all. My brother has never been to a restaurant, and he is thirteen."

She and I took long walks and talked together like sisters. For the little one she had boundless hugs and for the often grumpy eight-year-old she cross-stitched a tiny framed message that read, "For every minute you are angry, you lose sixty seconds of happiness." The day she left, the older boy vowed that someday they'd meet again and "dance under the moonlight." I, on the other hand, cried nonstop as she packed the things she wouldn't find at home: carrot peelers for her mother, navy mascara, *Roget's Thesaurus*.

She had never asked for anything before, but I was not surprised when she asked to have our children's baby things—afghans crocheted by a doting grandma, soft, stretchy terry sleepers and warm, hooded sweaters. I gladly complied, thinking how odd it was for such a young girl, with no thoughts of marriage, to think so far ahead.

When she left, her parting gifts to her charges were two hand-painted piggy banks with the message FOR A TRIP TO DENMARK. They were to save their pennies, she admonished, and let her know when they would arrive. The thought of a future meeting provided little solace.

It has been seven years, and we have written religiously. Married two years ago, she and her husband worked and went to school while sharing a tiny flat with no shower. They now have a beautiful infant daughter named Signe, and just last week I received a snapshot of her, nestled in her mother's arms, wearing a blue sleeper that looked extremely familiar.

The piggy banks are full and, with the help of a frequent flyer program, four reservations have been made. Next summer, we hope, we will temporarily trade in our spoiled American ways for the honest, loving values of a foreign girl who changed our lives.

—November 1988

Regrettably, we never took the trip to Denmark. Jette, who just turned forty, has two children, Signe and Simon, and has since divorced.

Fond Farewell

HE KEPT A TERRIBLE secret. Even I didn't know he had AIDS, although I suspected it. We were friends, Graham and I: good friends, and I miss him now that he's gone.

Ours was a professional relationship: two publishers, bound by common problems and separated by distance. From diverse locales, we first met at a magazine conference five years ago. New to the national organization, I sat alone in a hotel lobby in Pittsburgh, hoping for a dinner companion. He happened along, and we chatted about news reports of tornadoes in his home state of Florida. Idle talk, but it got me a partner for the party to follow.

After that it was easy. We met three times a year at national board functions, where we established ourselves as a team. I learned from his successes, he learned from my mistakes. We imitated his computer software, he entered his market with my dining guide concept. And in between endless professional gab, a friendship grew.

With the others, we cruised the Arkansas River and the Caribbean Sea. In a rented car, we got lost on the interstate on the way to a hog roast and circled the highway for nearly an hour, laughing like hyenas. Sympathetic to my pig-on-a-spit aversion, he later joined me in the potato chip line. On a Caribbean cruise, we excused ourselves from a rowdy Conga line and stood at the railing, marveling at the spectacular night sky. Peace and beauty, it said to me. To him it must have signaled an infinity he had no doubt contemplated.

A razor-sharp mind, impeccable style, and rapier wit set him apart. When someone's heyday had passed, he or she was "broken down," and when the meeting got boring, he mouthed, "Let's flee," from across a crowded table. Ever snappily attired, he entered a full seminar by mistake, looked around at the disheveled participants, and declared, "Oops. This must be the *editors'* meeting . . ."

The last time I saw him he looked gaunt and tired. We skipped a meeting and traversed an upscale shopping mall, where he lightly fingered a table of expensive leather goods. A Mark Cross briefcase would be great, wouldn't it? Extravagant, yes, but why not? Still dressed in his suit, he later stretched out on a poolside lounge chair, thin and exhausted.

I knew little of his personal life other than that Amy was his lifelong friend and two Yorkies were the apples of his eye. While more intimate friends and family perhaps provided solace and care at the end, I did not. They loved the side of him with AIDS, and I loved the side of him without.

Graham was not a hero. As far as I know he raised neither money nor society's level of consciousness about the disease that took his life. No one embroidered his name on a quilt, and if he delivered an impassioned dissertation, it was about equal rights for small-market magazines and not about empathy for gays or their plight. Neither Jeannie White nor Magic Johnson will ever know his name; his legacy was silent.

Ever dignified and even vain, he did not share his disease with me. During our last phone conversation, he lusted for gossip and said he felt fine. Because he did not want me to visit, I stood at an airport phone booth in his hometown, and, twisting the receiver cord, searched for a way to help. Upbeat, he chatted and laughed, and—oddly, I thought—wished me good luck in my life and career.

A month later he died. Frantic, I wrote a letter to Amy and to his parents, none of whom I had ever met. He was my friend, I proclaimed. Please be proud of him and know that you are not alone. I called in a hundred-dollar donation to a journalism school fund identified in his obituary and removed his name from my Rolodex.

Then I abruptly left work, hastened to the Fashion Mall and bought a rhinestone-studded dress. Extravagant, yes, but why not?

—June 1992

After his death, a quilt was in fact cross-stitched with simply his name. I sewed the "G."

Friends

IT WAS NEW YEAR'S EVE 1985. While most people we knew enjoyed midnight champagne dinners or rowdy parties, we sat in a knot at the home of our closest friends, gleefully watching each other perform. My own entry in this oddball variety show involved stuffing something approximating Dolly Parton's most distinguishing characteristics into my sweater and singing a duet of *Nine to Five* with my husband. While my younger son shuffled backward across the floor in a feeble attempt to moonwalk, the evening's real star was my then twelve-year-old son, who had perfected an uncanny impersonation of Billy Crystal's Fernando and launched into a cavalcade of obsequious, nonstop talk show banter. "And you," he finally said in the direction of our friends' giggling seven-year-old daughter, "You look mahvelous."

Who else, we couldn't help asking each other, would spend New Year's Eve enjoying a make-your-own chili bar and a talent show whose entertainers won sure approval before they even set foot on the stage—actually the foyer two steps up from the great room? Nobody. This was madness, but as I look back on it, it was the kind of madness I wish had lasted a lifetime.

These rare friends seemed to like everything we liked. Together we ate dinners at six—no later—and caught the seven-thirty movie. We patronized the same restaurants, walked out of the same plays, drank Diet Coke instead of wine, shared vacation condos, and liked our popcorn buttered. When one of us got something new—the first big-screen TV or a house in the suburbs—we gathered together to swoon and approve.

One time, work prevented the husband from joining us for dinner before an IRT production, so we brought him a steak in a bag, something to assuage the *Long Day's Journey into Night* ahead of him. More vivid is my memory of a particularly grueling surgery I endured when my children were small. Recovering slowly, I spent more hours bawling in my hospital bed than I should have, with only one bright spot. Our friend had confided his dream of being a country singer to very few; it was a secret not to be shared. Yet, for me he had recorded an original ballad, "No Letter Today," and sent it over, complete with boom box, for a very captive audience of one. When I think of those dark days, my clearest recollection isn't the hallucinogen that caused me to see antelope on the walls, or the rubber boots they jammed on my legs as I lay wailing on the surgical gurney. It is the strains of those lyrics—"I've waited so long, why dint you write? I know'd I was wrong, nuh, nuh, nuh, nuh, no letter today"—sung in loud and glorious off-key tenor, and how good a fresh belly laugh could feel. Most important, it is the underlying message that if he could conquer his stage fright, couldn't I overcome this?

While we vowed to enjoy at least one dinner a year in the presence of a tape recorder, so that we could one day replay the passages of our lives, we have gradually grown apart. New friends and acquaintances, diverse interests, too much business travel, the rigors of career, the demands of grown children, and the strain of relationships have taken their toll. It isn't a funny break-up, like Lucy and Ricky and Fred and Ethel fighting over who drives to California. It's a mild erosion that feels a little like a divorce: not a vindictive one, just sad.

When we were kids on the playground we could get bopped over the head, bear the hurt with our lips clenched, and finally rush over and make a new friend, whispering cattily about the one that preceded. Before we knew it, we'd be jumping rope in unison, gaily singing, "Bill and Susie sitting in a tree, k-i-s-s-i-n-g." Now it's not so easy, and while we see our present social acquaintances as beautiful strands of silver, we'd probably just as soon have kept the gold.

We can't recapture the good old days any easier than I can reclaim my best friendship with a classmate in whose home I probably spent more nights than in my own. There we whiled away untold hours smoothing our hair onto stiff brush rollers and poking pink plastic picks into our scalps so the unwieldy appliances wouldn't come loose as we slept: two preteen girls who might as well have walked on coals with bare feet. With only a precious few can you share a laugh so intense no breath will come, or practice kissing techniques in the bathroom mirror. I wrote her English themes; she taught me how to gaze up at a boy and say I had a wonderful time and hoped I would see him again. Recently I tried in vain to set up my son with her daughter, with the secret wish we might someday rejoin as in-laws. Fragile friendships can disappear like mist, without your even realizing it.

Recently, we spent a Saturday night with other longtime friends we love. We have a history there, too, of running in our PJs to their neighboring home at two A.M., as fire consumed the garages of apartments behind our home, of calling at midnight after a dinner party to see if any chocolate mousse remained. This was the same man who gathered up an entire party's worth of shoes that littered our entry hall in deference to new white carpet and hid them in various unlikely spots around the house. As always, our evening together was fun, filled with reminiscences and lively conversation. But our dinner reservations were for seven.

—December 1996

Our dearest and closest friends are now separated. We will never abandon either of them, but our foursome dissolved with their marriage.

Hard Questions

THE FUNERAL PROCESSION had lined up in the synagogue parking lot, three cars deep and at least twenty long. As it snaked along a concrete curb, the configuration allowed a view of the limos in front, holding not just grieving, but horrified, family members. Seeing the lead cars so starkly reminded me of the many train trips I took as a child, during which we would press our faces to the passenger car window in hopes of catching a glimpse of the powerful engine as it rounded a curve.

Only this time, a child glanced back. From the darkened limo window you could see her tiny, confused face as she waved continuously at the trailing cars: A princess in a parade, it was at once sweet and embarrassing as any who saw her surely empathized with her mixed emotions.

After all, children should not see other children die, and should not know how to act.

The twenty-year-old young man—clinically depressed and a longtime friend of my older son—had taken his own life, leaving behind incomprehensible frustration and sorrow. His careful note, read in full at the funeral, explained that no one, neither family nor friends, should bear the guilt for his actions. If love and support could heal, he wrote, he would have been the healthiest man alive.

Filing into the service, I was struck by the other boys: a small army of blue sport coats and khaki slacks coming to bury a member of their ranks. Seeing their ashen faces personified the helplessness and despair; the unnatural order of things could not be explained.

None of the boys had seen it coming, and it was too late now to search for signs. They had been wrapped up in ball games and girl troubles and Mexican food. But his life had been troubled, and chronic teenage depression had finally taken its toll. None of these boys had judged; they loved him for his kind, gentle way and unwavering loyalty, and didn't stop to put it in words.

As I sat in the service, I felt my raw emotion rise to the surface and prickle my skin. A mother's pain for another mother erupted, and a mother's pain for her heartbroken son sent welling tears down my cheeks. *How can they survive the agony*, I asked silently, watching the boys a row in front, all lined up in their matching garb, staring straight ahead at the flower-draped casket that held one of them. *What could have been so bad*, I continued to ask myself, *that living could not be endured?*

The poignant scene from *Our Town*, which has haunted me over the years, popped into my consciousness again. The "deceased" young girl, standing in the cemetery, bemoans the fact that she can no longer enjoy her hair ribbons or the aroma of coffee in the morning, life's sweet pleasures that will eternally elude her. Wasn't the end of the school day enough, or a winning hoop? An order of nachos brimming with cheese or the whooping and hollering of five boys together?

But it is not for us to suppose. The young man, whose immeasurable sadness and suffering had become intolerable, hearkened to that in his note. If someone had found him in time, it would have happened again, he explained. Something was amiss, and the thought of suicide was always with him. During the service my mind wandered in a strange, almost selfish direction. As a typical mainstream parent, had I scoffed at this boy's long hair and obvious "alternative" looks? Was I kind on the phone or judgmental? Would his parents find comfort in the notes he left and in the faces of his friends, or would both agonize them even more? When he was missing, how frightening was it for my son to leave messages on an answering machine with his voice—already quiet—issuing its recorded message? Though small concerns of no consequence to anyone, they tormented me as surely as the death of the boy tortured his family and friends.

At the cemetery, as shovels full of dirt were heaped into the grave, his friends stood close. One, wracked by sobs, backed away to prop himself up by a tree while others, their arms draped across each other's shoulders, said goodbye. "Hey, Andy," one said. "We'll see you someday, okay?" A child's salutation to a child, just as deliberate as a tiny princess waving in a funeral procession. Dying is not reserved for the old, and sorrowfully, the young must learn how to grieve.

—May 1994

My son was the one who promised to see Andy soon. I later found Andy's newspaper obituary propped up on his bookshelf, where it has yellowed with time. The memory of a young friendship, however, has not. (Andy's parents ultimately divorced, after which his father also took his own life.)

Help Wanted

MARY'S NOT COMING back. There. If I say it aloud, I can put it in perspective. It's not like she died or anything—if you don't count emphysema and chronic bronchitis, which are stealing her ability to breathe.

Having entered the career force before it became fashionable for women to consider doing something other than answer the door in Saran Wrap, I recognized I couldn't do it all. Small children, a house, and a husband were simply too much to manage with a full work week. With day-care centers just a glint in most entrepreneurs' eyes, the choices were scant: hire a babysitter, drop the kids off at a babysitter, look for a housekeeper.

Enter Mary. You couldn't describe her as a babysitter, exactly, or a housekeeper either. She was more like, well, everything. Having known my husband's family for another entire generation, she was no stranger, simply a pro at holding down the fort, being the boss, keeping everything in incredible order. And now, after seventeen years, she's gone.

Because I left for work each day before she arrived, we didn't see each other much. But when we did, we always had the toughest time getting the laundry folded or dinner prepared. Instead, we gossiped and laughed, complained and cajoled. One Saturday morning we decided to attack the attic, and when the dust proved too thick to manage, we settled on tumblers of grapefruit juice and vodka to "cut the dust," as she put it. Neither of us drinkers, we approached noon in decidedly better spirits, both of us sprawled across the flimsy particle board floor howling and clutching our stomachs as if we would burst.

With a willful young boy to manage, I spent the better part of my off-hours running after him shrieking demands, and shrieking even more when met with a forceful "*No!*" Not Mary. She'd shake her head and mutter, "Hmmph. Just like Rosemary," in reference to her own short-tempered daughter. Then she'd point quietly to a "switch," as she called it, a narrow twig that sat atop a row of cabinets in the laundry room. She never used the switch, mind you, but the very suggestion of it in her no-nonsense hands seemed to straighten out ornery children.

Actually, "hmmph" was an expression used fairly frequently. When I planted pots of impatiens on a Sunday afternoon, her Monday reaction was "hmmph," a signal that they weren't properly spaced or dug, and the sun wasn't hitting them just so. "Hmmph" was what she thought of our new home, located too far away to reach on snowy days, and "hmmph" was how she sized up almost anything I cooked, knowing full well that no one could bake chicken or mash potatoes like her.

Racked by diseased lungs of late, she repeated a familiar chant when asked how she was feeling. "Dyin' . . . slow, but sure," she'd say in a sing-song voice, so often that when we'd ask, we'd all then repeat the response in unison.

After she was recently moved from the intensive care unit, I visited her in her hospital room, where her own children stood by. She was feeling better, and I cheerfully introduced myself to her son from California as his long-lost "sister." While everyone laughed off our differently colored skin, we all recognized the depth of our bond. "Hmmph," Mary said, adjusting her oxygen tube and looking down at the sneakers I wore with my business suit. "Where are your good shoes?"

A later phone call brought what I expected but loathed to hear: At sixty-two and ailing, her working days would come to an end. "I've done the best I could for all my children," she said, "and now I need to rest. But you'll get along fine without me. Remember, I love you."

I love you too, Mary.

—December 1991

Heart and Soul

I DIDN'T STOP the car. I should have, but I was already late for an appointment and could think only of getting there—the sooner, the better. Suddenly, my old friend Jeff was beside me, waving vigorously and signaling for me to pull over. Expecting me to join him, he slowed down and veered into a strip mall parking lot. I tapped dramatically on my watch, made a desperate face, and kept going. Guilt-ridden, I called him the next day, apologizing all over myself. "That's okay," he said. "I just wanted to give you a hug." Jeff and I met in grade school, dated occasionally in high school, and ended up friends. Just this year he suffered two heart attacks and underwent a quadruple bypass; in his delicate emotional state he probably needed to look into the eyes of someone comfortable and familiar, someone who would return his hug as genuinely as he offered it.

For him, these past few months haven't been easy. On the night of August 7, he sat in his family room with his wife, Linda, watching TV. At eleven-thirty he felt tired and ventured to their bedroom, where he sat on the side of the bed. A bolt of pain ripped through his chest, knocking him down. It was followed by the sensation of a terrific weight—a concrete truck, as he describes it—on his chest. He instructed Linda to call 911, then, rallying somewhat, wobbled into the kitchen, interrupted her dialing, and said, "Let's go." His memories of the hospital emergency room are sketchier, but there was the brief moment he slumped over in a chair, was rushed by gurney into a cubicle, and had a succinct conversation with a male nurse. "Am I having a heart attack?" he asked, to which the nurse replied, "I'm afraid so." His wit intact, he instructed, "I just became a grandfather two weeks ago. You better save my ass." The nurse promised, "I'll pull you through."

The weekend in intensive care was spent hooked up, wired, tethered. The emergency room doctor advised him that had he waited another ten minutes, he wouldn't have survived, new grandchild or no. Lying in bed, he had plenty of time to be grateful not only for receiving the clot buster in time, but for having ridden his bicycle nearly a hundred miles a week, which had strengthened him and increased his odds.

Two days after receiving a stent to repair a blocked artery, he was on a treadmill undergoing a stress test when he was struck down again. "Something's not right; here come the pains again," he remembers thinking; then came a hazy recollection of voices: "Get him out of here. People are staring." The next thing he knew, Linda was whispering in his ear, "You've just had a quadruple bypass."

In mid-November, we had lunch on me, to assuage my guilt for not stopping the car. Although he was healing well, he was fragile and emotional. When he told how his son, a fourth-year medical student, stayed by his bedside, his head on his father's chest, Jeff began to cry. More tears accompanied the pictures tucked neatly into his planner—images of his daughter and new granddaughter, Sophia. His eyes welled up again as he remembered the many calls and gifts, and the way he felt the day he returned to daily *minyan,* the Jewish prayer service he attended before his illness.

A hammer did not hit him in the head as a signal to change his life, he says. But nonetheless, his life has changed. He wants to dance at his granddaughter's wedding, consider a new career, redeem his frequent-flyer miles. He laments how it takes a catastrophe before we discover what really matters, and vows to be different. Only now does he recognize the difference between an inconvenience and a problem, and knows how to treat each accordingly. The fact that his wife of thirty years is sometimes late ("It takes her an hour and a half to watch *60 Minutes,*" he jokes) doesn't bother him anymore. Bad restaurant service is just a silly annoyance, and whereas traffic tie-ups could have angered him before, he now abides them willingly. Operating a remodeling business, he once became enraged with unreliable subcontractors, but now just goes with the flow.

Confessions of a Kid at Heart

These are lessons we should all learn, I told myself as I poked at my lunch and tried to understand his struggle. I remembered my college friend, Karen, and how she stood by her friend, Julie, a young mother in the throes of terminal cancer. After Julie died, leaving two daughters, Karen swore she would never again give up a single moment. If there was something she didn't want to do—attend a meeting, a party, a lunch—she just wouldn't do it, she told me. When I see her now, I wonder whether she stuck to her pledge, but I doubt it. In our weakest states, we make deals with ourselves and the Almighty that, when things return to normal, we do not honor.

The other day I took my mother's pearls to a jewelry store to be restrung, and while I was there, admired a gorgeous gold-and-diamond bracelet in the velvet display case. The jeweler let me try it on, cautioning that it had been sold, in case seventeen thousand dollars was burning a hole in my pocket. The new owner had purchased it for his wife, who was in remission from breast cancer. As I unclasped it from my wrist, I wished that we lived every day like it was our last, appreciating our blessed good fortune, bestowing lavish gifts on the ones we love, whether they are sick or not.

As lunch wound up that day, Jeff's mood improved somewhat. He is looking forward to a reunion with his boyhood buddies, including David Letterman, who previously was hard to pin down but now will participate. After I paid the bill, he looked briefly at his watch and smiled. Smack-dab in the middle of the afternoon, he planned to amble over to the IMAX theater to catch the new dinosaur movie and invited me to join him. Naturally, I laughed, feeling like a schoolgirl dawdling on the playground after the bell has rung. "I just couldn't," I said, thinking of the work piled up on my desk. He sat with his arms folded across his chest, realizing that he hadn't gotten through to me at all.

Later, as I sat in front of my computer, I felt sorry: sorry that I didn't stop the car, and sorrier that I wasn't beside him in the theater, marveling at the creatures of the prehistoric age and blowing off the afternoon.

—February 1999

Father Figure

MY FATHER WAS forty-seven when I, the last of four children, was born. I often admired my friends' families, with fathers who coached Little League and hosted nighttime parties, wore shorts and tennis shoes in summer, and joined in the after-dinner neighborhood kickball games.

My father, however, was funny and wise, and I learned to overlook the lack of youthful athleticism, understand the references to grocery wagons and "lessons," and accept the vast generation gap between us. His pre-Depression values did not allow for boys in the house, and when I spent too long saying good-night in a parked car, he ran to the driveway—chenille bathrobe flying—to tap on the steamy window and make certain carbon monoxide had not consumed us. When I slept in curlers the size of juice cans, he assured me I looked better with unset hair, and when I turned my bedroom air conditioner to its coldest level, he tiptoed in during the night to switch it off.

My father offered words of timeless wisdom, like when I couldn't decide which eager young man to marry. We sat across from each other on squeaky Naugahyde chairs in the gritty office of the auto and truck store he and my brother owned, and he said, "Follow your heart." When a higher-paying job outside the world of writing proved tempting, the advice was the same.

My father stacked button-tufted cushions onto the front seat of a 1958 Ford Fairlane and taught a nervous fourteen-year-old how to drive around the parking lot of what is now Hinkle Fieldhouse. Even though he had no inkling of "the new math," I was the only one who knew what a drive shaft was, how fuel lines worked, and when to operate the choke. On turning sixteen, while my best friend shifted her new Corvair from neutral to drive, I sat in the front seat of a used white and red Ford Falcon convertible that had been fished from the bottom of the Indianapolis Water Company Canal and stomped on the clutch until I nearly stood in my seat.

My father called reckless drivers "jelly beans," got his own license renewed when he was ninety, and ventured out on dark, snowy mornings to scrape my windshield and warm up my car. And at camp in my bunk I sobbed with homesickness as I heard a delivery truck crunch over a gravel drive near my cabin—the same sound I heard each morning before dawn as my father left for work.

My father kept his books with the help of an old-time adding machine, complete with paper roll and mechanical arm. When years diminished its productivity, I took it upon myself to replace it, and not with one of those new-fangled solar calculators. Office superstores may be full-service, but none carries—or has ever heard of—such a contraption.

My father shaved with a mug and a brush, and from my perch atop the lid of the commode, I never tired of watching him lather his face, dutifully scrape one stripe after the other, then shudder dramatically with the application of stinging after-shave. Birthday after birthday, he showed consistent delight with the requisite offering of razor blades and Mennen Skin Bracer. And each day, as I waited for him to come home from work from my unlikely seat atop the corner mailbox, I joyfully accepted his "ride home" from four driveways away.

My father frequently told stories of selling newspapers for a nickel and bringing the change home to his family of nine. I, however, had a closet full of pretty matching sweaters and skirts, and my checking account was never in jeopardy. Even after I married, he would wink at me at mealtime, a sign to reach out under the table for a neatly folded stack of twenties to be placed in my palm.

My father walked himself to Methodist Hospital for a tonsillectomy when he was barely five, and walked himself back home afterward. Often to the chagrin of my children and coworkers, I inherited that relentless determination, as well as a never-ending love of words. Tied neatly in a hall closet, purely poetic love letters written to my mother made us weep with joy. Puns were a regular part of any conversation, and his worst jokes he dubbed "Indiana corn."

My father stood at my sister's wedding and announced that he had been told to "shut my mouth and open my pocketbook." When the neighbor children told me I had big feet, he instructed me to tell them I had "good understanding," and a slice from a loaf was never consumed without the accompanying announcement that he was "well bred."

My father stood on the train trestle near his place of business on South Keystone Avenue and waved as my mother and I sped along in the *James Whitcomb Riley* to Cincinnati to visit my maternal grandmother. I pressed my cheek to the window until he grew too tiny to see, but felt secure in his presence. To him, I was always smart, beautiful, and successful, and with his thumb and forefinger aligned in a perfect circle, he'd say I was "100 percent." To my sister and me, he was "Daddy-o," a nickname borne of the 1950s in an attempt to modernize him.

My father was forty-seven when he joyously witnessed the birth of his littlest girl. At forty-seven, I came to know the sorrow of losing him on New Year's Day. The oldest and the youngest, we shared a heart and owned a love that transcends generations. And it lasts forever.

—February 1995

Gone But Not Forgotten

When you take your camel ride, you pay your dollar on the way down, not on the way up.

Accidental Tourist

HE WAS PROBABLY approaching seventy, an aristocrat in an Italian double-breasted suit. Like a cover subject from *Town and Country*, she wore lavish jewels and sleek satin pants with a wide-belted blouse that revealed just a glimpse of expensive lace camisole. They swept across the dance floor alone, flaunting their wealth and style as well as their vast age difference, leaving those of us seated on the outskirts to fantasize at will.

A palace-turned-ornate-hotel in the northern Italian town of Bellagio provided the backdrop. As the string quartet played sweet music, they danced, his arm about her slender waist, touching her only with his middle finger, the others splayed majestically in midair. Well-practiced, she held his shoulder with only her wrist, her graceful hand arched backward like Ginger Rogers. When seated, she tapped the champagne bucket with an exquisitely manicured finger, he returning her obvious favors with one more bubbly glass. Surely he owns a yacht that plies the Mediterranean, while she, of noble European birth, plans charity events for those less fortunate than they.

A spectator, I was grateful that I could only see their lips move, lest the illusion be destroyed. What if she were from south Jersey and not the south of France, or spoke like *The Nanny*'s Fran Drescher? When we departed the inn the next morning, I had to look away as the couple from the night before spoke rapid-fire French to one another and then climbed unglamorously into their Plymouth convertible. This was just one lesson learned from a recent trip to Europe: Life is better without subtitles.

Traveling through Italy in late summer, I expected to get the most from the museums, the landmarks, the centuries-old structures still standing to remind us of not just generations, but entire civilizations past. Some of the things I came away with, however, had nothing to do with the Roman Forum or Botticelli's *Birth of Venus*.

Take Venice, for example. The gondolas so grandly fixed in most people's minds actually feature velvet seats with cheesy tassels, like in Graceland. And when eight or nine cluster together to allow for a serenade of their clientele, who look like refugees from Caesar's Palace, it's more like Benihana on your birthday than *A Little Romance*. Moral Number Two: Imagination beats reality any day.

In that same tourist-intensive town, trust is usually a bad idea. Granted, I'm not gullible enough to really believe those designer bags that street vendors spread out on a blanket (and then sweep up at the first sign of local police) are authentic. I was, however, stupid enough to buy one. I left the street vendor with a trendy Prada bag on my arm, proud that I had talked him down to only eighty dollars. My husband, still reeling from his wife's incredible negotiating ability (yeah, right), did grumble that the bag probably said *Pravda,* not Prada, like the bogus Tommy *Hilfinger* shirts we once saw hanging in a New York booth. I didn't receive my just due until I returned home, however, and discovered that the bag emitted a strange chemical odor, probably leftover from the Hong Kong sweatshop where it was glued together by some unfortunate nine-year-old working for a buck and a quarter per week. The stench was strong enough to make me woozy, and during a trip shortly thereafter I was forced to put it in a hotel room closet so as not to faint dead away. The lesson here is not unlike that provided by the exotic foreign couple: Everything is not what it seems.

When we weren't shopping, it seemed, we were eating. And when it comes to pasta, Americans don't have a clue. There, pasta sauces are lightly tossed with perfect, steaming, *al dente* noodles, not glopped on top like gravy on a beef Manhattan. Italian women eat just as much as their male counterparts, who slurp gnocchi with abandon, butter dripping down their chins. Oddly, they stay slender until they reach the approximate age of fifty, whereupon they begin to don shapeless black dresses to allow for their cheese-induced girth. In Italian restaurants, it should also be noted, when a waiter asks in clumsy English, "Gas or no gas," he is referring to the type of bottled water you prefer, not to how you feel following your second plate of risotto. My favorite meals in Italy and Paris were not those costing more than a hundred dollars per person, by the way, but were a singular plate of tagliatelle with fresh tomatoes in a small northern Italian cafe; and the world's most spectacular crock of French onion soup, enjoyed at a simple bistro. In gastronomy as in life, money doesn't always buy happiness.

Likewise, the best scenery was observed not from expensive hotel room windows or even privately guided tours. Train cars provided views we had only dreamed about: stone cliffs frilly with deciduous trees, clay-colored roofs, ancient steeples, and grapevines draping lushly over wooden posts. This was Italy, we decided, even more than the fancy stores rich with Armani suits, and the frantic streets of Rome.

There were times when culture shocked us, like in the "ladies" room at a railway station, where individual stalls featured nothing but holes in the floor, reducing female visitors to the likes of drunken football fans at halftime. We couldn't get past the language barrier, coming close to ordering cock's comb on a menu in France, and growing alarmed as flight attendants issued lengthy advisories in Italian. But we could get used to leaning up against coffee bars to guzzle our frothy cappuccinos, and strolling through galleries of rare and priceless art at the Vatican and Louvre.

Once in a while, however, we yearned for the trust that comes with familiarity: trust that the bracelet we bought in Florence really was eighteen-karat gold; trust that the Eurostar train engineer knew when to slow down, even in tunnels; trust that the restoration of precious paintings didn't lessen their loveliness or value. Two weeks, we learned, isn't long enough to understand a culture or build relationships. And there were times when we traded our San Pellegrino water for a Coke, just for a hint of home. Something about the tiny curved bottle that just fits your hand, eliciting the gentle tug of a satisfying burp after a healthy swig, lets you know the world is small enough.

—November 1997

Last Resort

For TWENTY-SIX years I have been hearing about Mayman's. A cluster of small resort cottages on the shore of Lake Michigan at South Haven, Mayman's holds the promise of long-ago summers and lost childhoods. My husband, the memory-monger, has regaled us with stories about the globe lights lining the dirt road, fried perch dinners, metal sand pails, and "Apple Annie," who traversed the beach selling her eponymous fruit.

Not only has his current family been privy to *Summers at South Haven:*

The Keepsake Album, we have also seen the movie. Snapping film and flickering images on his parents' living room wall show the suntan mama planted in a low, canvas beach chair, and the daddy, hoisting a boy on each arm—one with a round belly, one tall and lean, both heads brimming with closely cropped curls turning gold in the sun. One of those tykes garbed in square, heavy elastic swim trunks, my husband has lobbied for years to return to South Haven with his own family, to make a new deposit in his memory bank.

Personally, I take pride in never looking back. Old photos and home movies serve only as depressing reminders of how young and thin we once were, and how little we appreciated those days. With our arms full of fat babies we still sometimes wore scowls, and we have already worn well past the age of our parents in the same snapshots. Seeing our unlined faces and thick, dark hair always catches my heart in my throat, making me content with just a mental reminder. A scent or a sound will provoke a long-dormant memory: One whiff of burning leaves and I'm back at the campfire at Camp Dellwood; a rusty roller skate in an antique shop window and I'm circling the driveway, a fairy princess in the clouds waving a twig for a wand.

So why go back and confront it face to face? If everything is as you remember it, you'll choke on the lost years. If it's a new South Haven, you might as well be in Boca or Greece. Nonetheless, the two of us ventured into Michigan's lower peninsula for a last weekend of summer, a final chance for a snatch of the past. Our children, I should add, displayed appropriate remorse at missing this once-in-a-lifetime opportunity and begged to be remembered with souvenirs from Apple Annie.

What we found was as I expected: a reborn, unfamiliar town. Huts on the beach that once offered Coke and ice cream sandwiches were replaced with aluminum-sided stores serving shaved ice and Evian water, frozen Milky Ways and kosher hot dogs. The fisherman's shack that sold smoked fish was replaced by a bar and grill, and a concrete walking pier stood in place of the wooden dock that flooded during storms. Apple Annie was noticeably absent, and shops up the road featured fat-free yogurt and New Age CDs, wrought-iron picture frames and oversize cappuccino cups. In a trendy enclave of shops in the center of town, every manner of logo merchandise was available, so now you carry your memories on your chest instead of in your heart.

While residents remembered the big resorts of Fidelman's and

Mendelson's, nobody had heard of Mayman's. My personal historian, however, seemed to find it at every turn: "Look, there's where it was, just up that road!" Or, "There, where the condos are—that must have been it!"

Now, short-term visitors inhabit B & B's, and instead of slamming the screen door and heading for the shore, you whisper behind wooden bedroom doors and hear classical music tinkling in the hallways.

Groups of partiers who aren't your family gather chattily at mealtime, and when you find a comfortable alcove flooded with sunlight, somebody else is already there. The aroma of cinnamon baking replaces the pungent smell of lake fish, and fringed lampshades and narrow staircases stand in for peeling paint and linoleum floors sticky with Popsicle drippings.

Thankfully for my husband's sake, one village icon remains unchanged: the Michigan movie theater where he thrilled to *The High and the Mighty* from his seat in the balcony. Now home to three screens, the theater nonetheless boasts the same full-size stage in front of the main screen, the same crates and carpet rolls in the corners, the same uneven floors and probably the same proprietor. The rats, I reminded my husband as I sat cringing in the upstairs theater that once served as the balcony, probably had ancestors who either inhabited Mayman's or at least had heard of it.

If the residents, workers, or old newspapers in South Haven, Michigan, are any barometer, Mayman's existed only in the imagination of my husband's family. And personally, I'm grateful. Dredging up memories and then touching them can be as painful as stopping your car in front of your old house and watching as new people go in and out the door. We can probably deal with a fishmarket-turned-hamburger-joint, but a cozy cabin we inhabit snugly with our family—if just for a week—is probably best left absent from the history books, at the end of some nonexistent dirt road.

—October 1995

On the drive home from South Haven, we bought bags full of plump blueberries, which I turned into dense, floury muffins. For a week, everyone I knew got muffins. Oddly, no one asked for more.

On Shaky Ground

WHEN THE HOTEL fire alarm sounded its loud, insistent beep, we awoke with a start and groped for the travel clock, which for some reason not yet understood, had slipped to the floor. Four-twenty A.M. in Santa Monica: a time for emergencies.

I felt both panicked and disgusted. Hadn't the same thing happened at the last magazine conference I attended just a few months before in Toronto? *Another night of disrupted sleep*, I groused to myself. I'll look like hell for the rest of the day. Ever thinking, my husband called the front desk and was advised to evacuate the building—now. I felt the door: cool, a good sign. Get dressed. Glance at the balcony to estimate the jump. Find my glasses. Pull on jeans over my nightgown. *Run!*

As the room door closed behind us, I panicked again. We had left the key, and the balcony, behind, and were prisoners of the corridor. A worrier by nature, I had located the nearest fire escape upon arrival, and was relieved to find it just a few steps away. But as we threw open the heavy metal doors, my heart stopped. A wall of smoke—or was it steam?—prevented our entrance, and we ran again, shouting a warning to a British man coming our direction, eyes puffy, wearing only the hotel terry robe and oxfords. At the other end of the hall we found an exit and swung open the doors. The clear night air was a godsend, and we ran down the metal stairs, the Englishman's hard shoes clacking against each step. No one said a word.

At street-level, at the rear of the hotel, sheets of water spilled from the back door—the result of sprinklers, we guessed. We circled the block and ran up a hill to the front, both shocked and comforted by the sight of perhaps two hundred hotel guests—unkempt and disoriented but wearing the hotel's terry robes—gathered beneath the glass overhang that protected a portion of the circular drive. We joined them, and for a second or two, commiserated. I can't remember whom we met or what we said; we had lost track of the Brit.

And then it hit. A crashing explosion, a jolt that defied description. A roar from beneath, or behind, we couldn't tell which. Was there a noise? Fearing the hotel had exploded, the crowd broke loose and ran screaming toward the street. As the sharp, rocking blasts from the earth below continued, I felt sick, as if I might vomit. My husband's long stride, heretofore an arguing point in airport concourses and shopping mall parking lots, put him ahead of me, our grip slipping. Holding me by the tips of my fingers, he pulled ahead, while I could only think of running with whatever power God had given me, to get out from under the glass overhead.

We gathered en masse in the street, a sea of white terry robes clutching onto one another, some crying, all looking for an explanation. And then the entire city went dark. On a four-lane Santa Monica street we stood, trying to remember what we had once learned about dealing with earthquakes. Stand in a doorway, but there were none. Be prepared for the aftershocks. How? Gas and water lines will burst, and fires will ensue. What should we do? Instinctively, we paraded to a gravel lot across the street from the hotel and waited. With the smell of gas surrounding us, I could only mouth a phrase to my husband: I want to go home.

In a few moments, the disaster scene came to life. A fixed-wing aircraft circled above us, its searchlight briefly illuminating faces here and there. Sirens wailed in the distance, and a man frantically ran back and forth in the street, his hands cupped around his mouth, yelling, "Dee? Dee, where are you?" Over and over he called her name, until a hotel security guard clapped a hand on his shoulder and, with a broad-beam flashlight, assisted in his desperate search. Groups huddled together, awaiting what was to come next. But nobody knew.

Normally the recipient of news via our airwaves, disaster victims are the last to know what happened. Was this the epicenter? Shouldn't we jump into a cab and flee, a conference attendee asked. Flee where? Frozen with fear at the sight of a fire-reddened horizon, we decided to stay. Its siren waning, a fire truck glided into the driveway, surveyed the situation, and left, declaring there were lives to save somewhere else. A reporter appeared from nowhere, her notebook and microphone a link to the outside world. Amid the obvious danger of a gas explosion, some sat on the curb and smoked, and one of our conference group invited us in, one by one, to use the phone in his parked car. Ominously, the man continued to call for Dee.

Led back into the hotel in a single line some two hours later, we studied the dark lobby. No plaster had caved, but bricks lay piled in a fountain, where oversize goldfish (orange roughy, we had joked earlier) still swam. Crystal sculptures lay smashed on the shiny marble floor, and toppled tables lay on their sides. Most odd, I remember, were lamps that stood upright, their shades bent and crooked. Hotel security shrugged off the fire alarm that had sounded prior to the earthquake, blaming it on a broken water main caused by earlier, imperceptible tremors. Although others assembled inside for warmth—and for the cookies, sweet rolls, and coffee the hotel provided—I could think only of the gravel lot and the safety of open space around it, where we returned. Back in the lobby perhaps an hour later, we saw lines at the phones, people gathered around a battery-operated "boom box," and cases of Evian water open on the floor. A movie of the week, the disaster counted us as its stars.

Escorted to our room by a guard some four hours after the quake, we found TVs knocked out of their consoles, drawers open, lamps toppled. Not stopping to collect our sundries from the bathroom, we gathered our bags—already packed for a morning flight—and sped through the hotel stairwell for the lobby. Remotely, I fretted about my appearance: my unbrushed teeth and unstyled hair, face devoid of makeup, shoes without socks. Making our ten-thirty flight took on utmost importance, however, as my children and home, with its trustworthy earth, would await. As unlikely as it now seems, a taxi appeared instantly, the driver a veteran of earthquakes and savvy to the best path to the airport. As we climbed from his cab, the earth rumbled again beneath our feet, causing us to eye each other warily and mount a hasty foot campaign to our plane, scheduled to depart in just fifteen minutes. A nervous flyer, I marveled as we took off that I could ever feel safer in the air than on the ground.

Just twenty-four hours earlier, I had written this column in my mind. In a usual snotty tone, I planned to lambaste L.A. for its lopsided values and cockeyed residents. I would write of the silliness of muscle men with snakes around their necks traversing Venice beach, of dog hat stores, and signs for turtle races and body piercing. Praising my heartland home for its rock-solid morals and lack of oddities, I would ridicule L.A. for its crush of youth in a tattoo store, for the black Mercedes 500 SL wrapped in a large white bow that sat outside our hotel. I would declare that I'd hope never again to eat pumpkin ravioli or rare seared ahi, horseradish mashed potatoes or a grilled salmon BLT. I would chide the town for its twenty-four-hour hair-styling salons, seven-dollar bottles of zodiac oil, and Wolfgang Puck Express. There's no place like home, I would vow, adding punchily that those weirdos in L.A. need an earthquake every now and then to shake their values back into place.

As I watched the TV earthquake coverage from steady ground, my mind changed. Frightened, innocent citizens must reclaim their lives while dreading the next aftershock, or worse. Neighbor helps neighbor sweep up the debris, and makeshift tents are filled with now-homeless families. Nothing, it seems, is really funny anymore, especially the joke "What's shakin',"—with which a fellow editor met me at the door upon my return. Perhaps one must live fear to truly appreciate it, must experience devastation to pity those whose lives are ruined by it. From the safety of my steadfast Hoosier roots, I have been made more humane.

—March 1994

Traumatized for weeks following the now famous Northridge quake, I swore I would never return to L.A. Ironically, our company has since purchased Los Angeles Magazine, *requiring me to visit several times a year. No matter how lavish the hotel, I sleep with one eye open.*

Down Time

NORMALLY, I'M NOT one for getaway weekends. Others probably appreciate the break from the drudgery, but I see it as work. By the time I've loaded down an overnight bag with sundries, curlers, dryers, and shoes, I might just as well shlep it through an airport and head for Florida for a week.

This time, however, I allowed myself to be swept away by the notion of peace and harmony: a weekend at a northern Indiana bed and breakfast where I could curl up by the fire as the Amish clip-clopped by in their carriages. Stress and worries would melt away as thin strains of symphonic music drifted through the parlor, and I'd sleep undisturbed for hours under a puffy down comforter.

All this, I might add, is blasphemy from the lips of someone who judges a vacation by the number of good shops within walking distance. Granted, I stop short of shooting the rapids in the Colorado River, but sit in a Victorian room and stare at the walls? Count me out. I'd be a fish out of water: Woody Allen on the Love Boat, Mother Teresa in Vegas.

Frankly the things I'd heard about country inns left me a little cold. Would I sit around the dinner table with people I didn't know? Would we adjourn to a salon after dinner and try to determine which of us might be a murderer? Because they call it a bed and breakfast, could I expect a really great breakfast? Most important, would Dick and Joanna be in the lobby to greet us?

Thankfully, we had our own private bathroom, and the spacious room resembled a big, comfy bedroom more than a hotel. I felt as if I could amble down to the lobby in my robe (but not enough to actually try it).

After arriving, we felt compelled to scour the area before settling in. Okay, so late morning seemed a little early to start gazing out the windows; maybe we could stir up a little action in Shipshewana first. Scuttling in and out of wagon shops, quilt displays, bakeries, and popcorn stores, we ate up the better part of the day. "Hurry up," we kept admonishing our friends. "We're running out of time to relax." Loaded down with bags of Amish bread, ginger cookies, knickknacks, and fudge, we came back to the B&B at midday, rushed up the stairs to our rooms, and found one another back in the lobby a few minutes later.

"We could play croquet," one suggested. "I saw a course in the front yard." Winter coats dragging, we proceeded to race around with our mallets, furiously competing. "Enough!" I finally announced, tossing my mallet onto the front porch. "I came to sit, and sitting is where I'll be."

Alone in the quiet library, I began to flip pages. Nothing. Relaxation had definitely not set in. Circling the room like a piranha in a fish tank, I lightly fingered the books, antiques, lamps, and tables. Joined shortly by my shivering friends, we plunked ourselves down on facing couches and began to talk, laugh, snort, and carouse, disrupting two ladies at the other end who heretofore had been engrossed in their reading. Feeling guilty, we adjourned to a smaller sitting room, sending our male friend into a knee-jiggling frenzy. "I'm going to the Bag Factory," he announced. "Who wants to go?"

"I do!" I responded, bolting from my chair.

Pushed back down by our mates, we reconciled ourselves to dressing for dinner, an activity sure to fill at least another hour. Eating, it turned out, makes bed and breakfast jaunts worthwhile. With no time constraints, one can slather honey butter on his bread with lusty abandon, stretching three courses into six with little coaxing. Sipping coffee, we sighed a deep, cleansing sigh, one that rid us of our city shackles.

Even though breakfast really wasn't that great, I'd probably go back. This time, however, I'd stay two nights, not one, recognizing that it takes at least twenty-four hours just to unwind. I'm still not sure how good I'd be in a rocking chair, but with a little practice, I'll bet I could clean up at croquet.

—December 1992

Summer Vacation

WHILE OTHERS MIGHT troop to the Grand Canyon or head for the beach, our brood lit out for the Middle East for our summer vacation. Odd, you say? Too close to Saddam Hussein, perhaps? Maybe, but a ten-day guided tour of Israel not only provided a spiritual renewal and a historic awakening, it taught us a few curious lessons about the tiny country in constant conflict, These include:

- Falafel, like 35 mm film, goes bad in the sun—but with more dire consequences.
- At the Western Wall, formerly dubbed the Wailing Wall, men and women must pray separately. Likewise, at the tomb of Rachel, matriarch of the Jews, only men can walk around the monument the traditional seven times.
- The manger where Jesus was born doesn't remotely resemble the wooden artifact constructed each year at the corner of Ninety-sixth and Keystone, but rather is deep in a cave.
- If you bring a beef hot dog into a kosher dairy restaurant in Jerusalem, the owner will chase you out, arms flailing, spewing Hebrew profanities.
- Even though Bedouins live in desert tents with no plumbing, they somehow have access to Taiwanese beads, three for ten dollars.
- Israeli honey is made from date drippings.
- When you take a camel ride, you pay your dollar on the way down, not on the way up.
- The gas masks used during the Persian Gulf war didn't fit civilians, most of whom have turned them in for new models.
- Signs warning of mine fields near the border are written only in Hebrew.

- Eight thousand American and Canadian doctors are signed up to replace Israeli doctors should the latter have to report to the front in the event of war.
- Israelis indelicately call restrooms "toilets." Toilet paper, in the unlikely event that it is available at a public place, is cobalt blue.
- A portion of the highway between Haifa and Tel Aviv doubles as an airfield and can be cleared of autos in an emergency.
- Oriental restaurants serve Arabic fare such as hummus and stuffed grape leaves, not pot stickers. Kosher Chinese restaurants, however, serve vegetarian egg rolls.
- On an El Al aircraft, orthodox Jews pray—facing east—at the emergency door.
- Sandstorms, which whip up in an instant, adversely affect gas-permeable contact lenses.
- Israeli archaeologists, who often live in houses older than U.S. archaeological sites, find it funny that their American counterparts dig up two-hundred-year-old chicken bones at Mount Vernon to see if slaves ate like their masters.
- Tour guides call roadside cows "Goldsteins" instead of "Holsteins."
- If a school group goes on a boat cruise on the Sea of Galilee, it is accompanied by an Israeli soldier armed with an Uzi.
- If it's ninety-three degrees at the base of Masada, it's a hundred and twelve on top. And even sissies who take the cable car up face eighty steep steps to get to the fortress.
- The plural of shekel is shekolim, not shekels.
- Turkish coffee tastes like Chanel No. 5.
- A road regularly traversed by tour buses in the Golan Heights has dynamite buried thirty-two feet beneath the surface, just in case.
- Both male and female Israeli soldiers, who must begin serving at age eighteen, carry their guns with them even when off-duty. It is not unusual to see teenagers gathered at an outdoor cafe, rifles slung over their shoulders.
- Israelis take tremendous pride in their vegetation. Where it's green, it's Israel; where it's brown, Syria.
- When CNN reports that a majority of Americans favor Clinton's surprise bombing of Iraq, you can bet no one polled those of us visiting the West Bank, some four hundred miles from Baghdad.

Also, we travelers in the Middle East don't know what it means when Washington tells us to remain "on alert."

- When you float in the Dead Sea, only your bottom sinks below the surface.
- Because the Israelis insist that McDonald's use their country's potato crop for french fries, the fast-food chain is still negotiating for a Tel Aviv franchise. McDavid's, however, specializes in pita sandwiches, and Burger Ranch in expensive fast-food hamburgers.
- The little really are mighty.

—August 1993

Hmph

Being a woman is like having a boat, what with all the deck swabbing and polishing—more as the wood begins to warp. We strip away unwanted hair with hot wax, poke mascara wands into our eyes at sunrise, stuff ourselves into pantyhose in the heat of summer, and—worst of all—are forced to accessorize.

Howl Be Thy Name

I CAN'T SAY THAT I flat-out don't like dogs, but I can say that I don't understand them—hence my partiality toward cats. You don't have to justify yourself to a cat—they'd just as soon not be bothered. I like that. You live your life; I'll live mine. Dogs are an entirely different matter.

Take the day several years ago when I looked across two backyards and saw my two young sons swinging on a neighbor's swing set, approaching upper-atmospheric heights, which caused the entire steel structure to walk, two legs at a time, with each gargantuan ascent. When the ideal swinging height (perpendicular to the ground) was reached, each child hurtled himself from the wooden seat, flying like a kamikaze pilot to the earth below. Like any other sensible adult, I tore across the acreage that separated us into the fenced-in yard in question, screaming unintelligible orders into the faces of horror-stricken youngsters frozen in mid-air.

He saw me before I saw him—that Great Dane or Greyhound or whatever manner of oversized, bony monster he was—and he misinterpreted my hysteria, or so I was later advised. Charging at me from behind the sandbox like Teddy Roosevelt leading his troops up San Juan Hill, he attacked. Heavy, knobby paws on my shoulders, he barked furiously into my ashen face, missing my eyelashes by mere millimeters, slobbering and growling and prepared to kill. Lion vs. zebra scenes from *Wild Kingdom* flashed before my eyes, and then the children's mother pulled the brute off me, explaining away his behavior with, "He thought you were attacking the children. He loves children." After my breath and the feeling in my arms and legs returned, I sweetly collected my children, smiled plastically at the dog, and tiptoed to the gate.

The next moment of truth came just a few weeks ago, when I came across a neighbor walking a mid-sized black rottweiler with beady, close-set eyes and a curly tail. He strained at the leash and growled, baring his teeth and establishing his superiority. Comforted by the walker that the dog would never attack humans, just other animals—which he was reputed to do viciously and without mercy—I set off to complete my jog.

Just before dawn a few days later, I found myself stumbling down the driveway to retrieve the morning paper. Illuminated by a single street light, there he was, alone and unleashed, making threatening gutteral noises and challenging me to complete my task. "Don't act scared, don't run," I was always told. "They know when you're scared." How am I supposed to act brave and confident when my heart is pounding out of my chest and my knees have turned to Cream of Wheat? Heck with what he thinks; what about what I think?

I crept up the driveway in tiny baby steps, offering placating conversation, as he growled ahead of me. When I was five feet from the door, I catapulted myself inside, arms flailing, and fell into a grateful heap onto the entry hall rug. Another near miss.

A smaller-scale calamity occurred in early fall, when a visit to a friend's house prompted a neighborhood Saint Bernard to bound through the hedge and knock down my eight-year-old son, who lay beneath the dog in horror, while great strings of thick, white saliva drooled onto his face. Once again, a dog mistook the situation, thinking the hot dogs on the lad's breath must mean lunch.

My cat may be more interested in tuna than companionship, but she requires no explanations. She does not run along and bark at car tires; she does not root about in others' trash, tearing up used Pampers and spitting bits of chewed aluminum foil; she does not rhythmically bark the night away because a squirrel has ascended a tree limb a half mile away. She asks only that I change her litter box on occasion and provide her a shin to wind around at suppertime.

Ignorance, say my friends, is bliss. I don't know the joy of an uncontrolled, joyous welcome home or a slobbery lick. I don't know the ever-patient fuzzy ear or the soft, resilient coat in which a kid can burrow when no one else understands.

If I ever do succumb to the curiosity, I think a gentle-faced golden retriever like the one on *Punky Brewster* would be nice. Or maybe one of those miniature yip-yip dogs you can carry in a canvas sling like firewood.

But for now, a feline calico puff ball artistically curled up on a braid rug will do—a non-judgmental friend of sorts who is both dependable and declawed—and who jumps only to the window ledge but never to false conclusions.

—December 1985

Where Not To Eat—Ever

A SURE-FIRE ANSWER for a lull in cocktail-party conversation is the subject of restaurants—good and otherwise. "Where's the best place to eat?" this monthly restaurant reviewer is constantly asked. (Can't pick just one.) What's the worst meal you ever had? (A mushy Italian one that was delivered three hours after we ordered it.) Do they know you're coming? (No. Once they did, and I got four desserts and a serenade by a strolling violinst.) Who do you take with you? (A husband who always disagrees with my evaluation, and two kids to protect my cover.) Tough job, restaurant critiquing, but somebody's got to do it. And it has its advantages. I may not be able to single out the best spot, hands down, but I sure know where not to eat—ever.

Never eat anyplace that has an ax handle as a menu, where waiters wear swords in their belts, or dress as cowboy, pirates, deep-sea fishermen, or milkmaids. Never eat anyplace that serves runny cheese sauce instead of real melted cheese or serves nachos on a paper plate. Add to that anyplace that advertises "Here's the beef," or whose waiters sing happy birthday in a foreign language.

Never eat anyplace that says there will be a thirty-minute wait and would you like to go to the bar, has old catalog pages laminated into the tabletop, or keeps rice in the saltshakers. Never go to a restaurant where the waiters call themselves by their first names (or worse yet, you by yours) or tell you the house specials verbally, putting you in the unenviable position of having to ask how much.

Never eat in a cafeteria that has wet trays, in a restaurant where you have to get up more than twice in pursuit of food, or in one where you have to put a puzzle together to read the menu. Never eat anyplace that has cherry tomatoes on the salad bar, has a help-wanted sign in the window, advertises

"Cool Inside," or has comment mailboxes by the cashier. In addition, avoid any restaurant that sells cotton candy, pennants, and T-shirts.

Never eat anyplace where you can hear Q-95 emanating from the kitchen, where you have to sit at a table with people you don't know, or where there is a sign that says Now OPEN UNDER NEW MANAGEMENT. Never eat at a restaurant that has more than six colors of pancake syrup, where you have to have a friend join you if you want a Caesar salad, or where high-school kids are eating before the prom.

Never eat anyplace that advertises dewy-fresh salad, oven-fresh rolls, ocean-fresh seafood, farm-fresh eggs, authentic spinach noodles, country-style biscuits, or hand-dipped ice cream. And never eat anyplace that labels its bagels, corned beef, cheesecake, and décor as "New-York style."

Never eat anyplace that names its sandwiches after members of the Grateful Dead, has a handwritten menu, or serves after-dinner M&Ms that turn out to be white inside. Never eat anyplace that features a brunch with waffles and rare roast beef next to each other, where the menu is on a blackboard, or where there is a sign that says No SHIRT, NO SHOES, NO SERVICE. Never eat anyplace that serves sandwiches only on pita bread or asks if you want cream for your coffee.

Never eat anyplace where you have to take off your shoes, cook your own meat, or peel your own shrimp. Never eat anyplace that has only a rolling dessert cart, advertises EAT HERE, or has popcorn on the floor. Never eat anyplace that cutely misspells the names of menu items printed in Old-English scrolly type or attempts to rhyme selections like crunchy munchies. Avoid restaurants that name items after political figures—i.e., the "Hudnut Hook Hamburger" or "Dan Quayle Quail." And never eat anywhere where the history of the restaurant and a spot map of locations is printed on the place mat.

Never eat anywhere there is a Greyhound bus parked out front or where the entire dining area rotates. Never eat anyplace that has Coca-Cola sign hung from its exterior or has a sign that says CAUTION, MICROWAVE IN OPER-ATION. Add to that anyplace where you have to stand up to eat or lean on a sort of shelf and act comfortable. And avoid places that have warm-air hand dryers in the restroom, unless you just washed your hair.

Never eat in a restaurant that still serves decaffeinated coffee in crummy little packets or includes caloric information on the menu. And never, I mean never, eat anywhere that gives video-game tokens instead of change and has weird mechanical ape men who have rolling eyes and are singing hit songs.

And, oh yes: Never eat at a hospital cafeteria, the airport, a college dormitory, student union building, or elementary school lunchroom, unless corn dogs and cling peaches are your thing.

—October 1984

This column enraged the restaurant community, which requested my presence at a special meeting called by their professional association. I respectfully declined. And by the way, never eat anyplace that makes you hold a vibrating beeper as you wait for your table, gives kids dough to play with before the meal, or asks you, "Smoking, non-smoking, or first available?"

Friendly Persuasion

JUST AS THE WEATHER turned warm, a funny thing happened at our house. A battalion of carpenter ants, which obviously had lain dormant for the better part of the winter, stormed through the cracks under the baseboard, fairly colliding with one another in their advance.

Nothing we or the pest control company did made a difference. In a macabre dance, we stamped them out one by one, wiping their disgusting antly guts from the bottoms of our shoes. Dressed for chemical warfare, the exterminators bombed them with everything short of Agent Orange, all to no avail. Brushing themselves off, the hideous creatures continued their march, wearing miniature tool belts and, true to their moniker, headed for their daily business of burrowing through the baseboards.

It was then that I discovered the art of complaining. Calling the exterminator repeatedly wasn't doing the trick. Spray defoliants weren't helping. And there weren't enough of us to clobber them manually. In a calm tone I explained that I wasn't interested in someone coming next Tuesday. I didn't care if they'd already tried everything in their arsenal. And most of all I didn't want to know that the culprits probably had nested in a

213

tree uprooted when our house was built and had moved into our crawl space. All I wanted was them gone. So I lovingly wrote a one-page note in which I asked for a drastic and immediate solution or a refund so that I could employ another pest control company.

For the last several days, I am proud to report, we have busied ourselves sweeping up carcasses. Granted, the house smells like a toxic waste dump and probably contains more chemicals than Love Canal, but the ants—at least the live ones—have retreated. There is something unsettling about sleeping atop a mass grave, but we'll adapt.

Which brings me to my mattress. First, allow me to report that I have owned it for approximately five years. It was one of the first "pillowtop" designs, a regulation mattress with a soft, poufy layer stitched atop. Heaven. But it didn't always have two large depressions which perfectly matched our contours. Actually, it looked like Andre the Giant and his wife had slept there, and we were getting pretty sick of it.

Each night as I climbed into bed (literally), I thought of my high school girlfriend, Jackie, whose mother used to sleep with a chair by her side of the bed. This was necessary, Jackie would explain, because her father, a portly gentleman, caused a depression toward the center of the mattress into which her mother, a slight woman, would roll without provocation. Rather than create a fuss, her mother merely slept each night holding onto the chair.

Since I deemed such an arrangement unsuitable, it seemed time to dump the caved-in pile of springs and start over. With my dignity intact, I marched into the store's mattress department, twirled around once briefly in front of the clerk and asked if it seemed reasonable that someone of my diminutive stature could cause a thousand-dollar king-size mattress to permanently disfigure. I didn't even have to get nasty. In a flash I was on the phone to the customer service representative, who advised me to pick out a new mattress, no questions asked. My mastery of the art of complaining remained untapped. No nagging, no elaborate letters, no threats.

Which taught me a valuable lesson: every complaint must be customized. Take restaurants, for example. While I can eat just about anything, I have a problem with chicken that isn't cooked all the way through. I envision myself before Morley Safer describing my bout with salmonella poisoning, and the room starts to spin. So, after holding up my grilled chicken breast to the light recently and finding it pink, I summoned the server, who in turn sent over the manager. By the time I was done describing the possible ill effects of undercooked food I not only got off without paying, I got a chocolate-nut brownie a la mode for my trouble.

To get things done, I've learned to be pleasant but firm. The woman in the billing department of a local hospital and I are on a first-name basis, and I'm counting on a return of a recent overpayment any day now. If not, I'll resort to more definitive measures, assailing her with one of my speeches or letters. I figure if I can wipe out ants, humans should be no problem.

—May 1993

Extra Credit

I'VE HEARD IT SAID that awards aren't all that important unless you happen to win one. That was precisely the spirit as a few of us sat stiff-backed around a banquet table in San Antonio, Texas, about a month back, anticipating the results of the City and Regional Magazine Association national awards. As we awaited the all-important category—General Excellence, our equivalent of the Academy Awards' Best Picture honoree— we practiced deep-breathing, our colons tangled like garden hoses, the chicken Wellington lodged in our throats.

When the screen flashed *Indianapolis Monthly* covers, signifying our first-place win, we leaped from our seats like schoolboys from the bench in a Little League playoff. I had practiced not looking like a spoiled Burt Reynolds when he was passed over at the Oscars, but had no idea how I'd react if we won. The person beside me slapped me so hard on the back I nearly flew from my seat, and as we made our way to the front of the room to accept the Gold in our circulation category, I didn't know whether to laugh or cry.

I have since pondered why the win struck me as it did, and I believe it is because in our busy society, no one offers much praise anymore. When someone says we are good, it's at first a shock, and then an unbelievable salve on our work-weary souls. Stay-at-home moms tending a house with ever-breaking appliances and kids with dirty bottoms rarely get a pat on the back, having not seen their name in lights since their school honor roll was posted in small print in the suburban weekly some twenty years past. Those in the workplace too often function like Dilbert, ensconced in their cubicles, trying to avoid a sexual harrassment lawsuit or the wrath of their boss. Having your mom or your kid or your superior at work laud your performance, tell you flat-out you have won the Gold, would feel like someone giving your tense shoulders a deep and necessary rub.

When I was in fifth grade, I was fortunate enough to be the only one lined up in the school gymnasium who knew that the word "mortgage" had a "t." Never mind that such information was gleaned from overplaying Monopoly, I nonetheless won the School 84 annual spelling bee, and it is not coincidental that I can still remember the feeling as I climbed the stairs to the stage to accept my trophy: a ceramic beagle sitting upright on its haunches, a prize no doubt leftover from someone's ringtoss win at the State Fair. Even after that hapless pooch was retired to a basement shelf, I visited it down there, next to the freezer, my visible proof that I was good.

Years later I was voted president of my high school girls' club, having run against a tall and beautiful brunette at whose lavish and modern home the election was held. So excited was I at the outcome that I ran *thunk!* into a sliding-glass door and had to be carried, cradling my bloody nose with a dish towel proffered by my unlucky opponent's mom, to my mother's car. The only thing more heady than the win itself—that amazing vote of confidence—was announcing the news to my mother, who overflowed with praise, oblivious to the gruesome aftermath.

I guess when our ancestors went about their daily work, the beans brimming in the baskets were proof enough of a job well done. A basketball star is lucky to record his successes in points scored, a doctor in lives saved, an accountant in bucks on the bottom line. It's not so easy for the rest of us, who go about our jobs every day without a peep from those around us. Unless one is awarded a plaque from time to time, he feels like a child who grows up without being enfolded in loving arms at least once a day. You don't realize what you've missed until someone finally gives you that physical validation and you don't know how you've lived so long without it.

If you see someone from *Indianapolis Monthly*, be sure to tell him you knew he could do it. Likewise the bank teller, a fleet-footed restaurant server, someone whose speech you have just enjoyed. I doubt that he's heard it often enough.

—July 1998

Payback Time

THE WAY I FIGURE IT, David Letterman owes me $1,526. Now, in no instance does *Indianapolis Monthly* charge its cover subjects for the prestigious placement, but in this case the rules be damned. And never mind the magazine—I'm collecting this debt personally.

It all started innocently enough on the day before my scheduled interview with Letterman in New York City. Because we had not nailed down a time, it seemed prudent to travel to the Big Apple the day before, to provide a margin of safety. So, the morning of my flight and late as usual, I threw my garment bag into the trunk of the car, manned the wheel, and gunned that baby out of the garage for all it was worth.

Did anyone remind me that because it was Thursday, my housekeeper's car would be parked on the apron of the driveway, clearly in harm's way? Did anyone warn me to slow down, look in my rearview mirror, or modify my usual driving pattern? No-o-o-o. So, in the blink of an eye I careened into the rear of her burgundy Chevy Lumina, never stopping to estimate the damage. Nope, the departure of US Airways Flight 1241 was imminent, and since I had been trying off and on for some fifteen years to spend a little quality time with Letterman (my former high school classmate), I wasn't about to blow it over a little body damage (her car, eight hundred dollars; mine, four hundred and eighty, on a policy with a five-hundred-dollar deductible).

So, deductible or no, I figure it's Letterman's fault. Had his assistant pinned down the exact time, I wouldn't have rushed, wouldn't have crashed into Mary's car, and wouldn't have wasted days and money on estimates and bodywork. As luck would have it, the interview wouldn't take place until one P.M. the following day, leaving an entire afternoon stretched out before me, in a hotel situated dead center between Saks Fifth Avenue and Bergdorf Goodman, hence the additional six-hundred-dollar charge to Letterman for the black Emanuel pantsuit that I was forced to buy in order to look like everyone else in New York. Cost of doing business, I convinced myself, shopping bag gaily dancing on one arm, briefcase dangling from the other.

Lucky for him I couldn't get tickets to *Rent,* or the tab would have gone up at least another eighty-five dollars for an evening's entertainment. No, I spent the night locked in my hotel room, testing my tape recorders, perfecting my questions, and studying maps so I could find the Ed Sullivan

Theater without a hitch. At twelve-fifteen the next afternoon, a healthy forty-five minutes before the scheduled interview, I climbed into a cab that, unfortunately, moved approximately five feet in twenty minutes. "School bus up ahead," I think the driver said, although it sounded more like, "Rule us ah puhd." Panicked and beginning to sweat, I thrust five dollars through a hole in the plastic divider and jumped onto the street, running like Harrison Ford trying to meet Julia Ormond's plane in *Sabrina*. Panting and lathered up like a racehorse, I screeched into the lobby right on time, where I was ushered upstairs to wait (and cool off) in a small reference-library-turned-conference-room near Letterman's office. There I took inventory of the bookshelves, which contained a book called *Beyond Prozac*, almanacs, a nutcracker with the sign "Christmas wouldn't be the same without a few nuts," Cub Foods-sized eight-packs of Hershey bars and Reese's Peanut Butter Cups (Letterman's emotional fuel before a show), and tried to sip my bottled water as if I spent every day in such a place.

The star himself couldn't have been sweeter. A gentle soul who is disarmingly honest, he spent the first ten minutes grilling me about our classmates before laying into the old Broad Ripple High School yearbook. Although I did not look familiar on this day, Letterman recognized my senior picture, especially after I pointed myself out and offered, "See? I was a babe!"

"Still are," he answered, and whether he meant it or not, the compliment propped me up emotionally for the two-day roller coaster to follow.

It wasn't until after the interview that I realized I had been sitting in his desk chair, and he in the guest chair opposite, feet propped up comfortably. And when I accompanied him down to the studio to witness his kissing Dan Rather for part of a fiftieth birthday bit, he invited me up on stage and introduced me to the newsman, who said that since I had gone to high school with Letterman, I probably could best judge the star's smooching ability. Blushing and nearly struck dumb by so many celebrities in one room, I dug a hole on the stage with the toe of my shoe and admitted that no, kissing Letterman had not appeared on my resume.

After having been whisked from the studio, I entered my hotel room to a ringing phone, the hotel operator clearly startled by the message: "Dave Letterman called. *Can that be right?*" A return call provoked his apology that I had been escorted out before a proper good-bye could be issued, and that he wished me a safe journey. A babe to whom Dave Letterman said good-bye without being asked.

So, about the other $446, which, nice guy or not, still appears on his tab: First off, if I hadn't been starstruck, I wouldn't have stabbed myself in the arm with a Deluxe Micro Uni-Ball pen, the black blob spreading on the sleeve of my favorite $375 Dana Buchman suit jacket like an oil spill from the Exxon *Valdez*. And had he not canceled a seven P.M. follow-up phone interview the next week, I would have been home in time to let the cat in, avoiding the hideous aftermath.

Because my cat, Woody (formal name, Scooter; don't ask), spends her days sunning and hunting in our wooded backyard, I feel she needs to be corralled at night, when danger lurks. On this night, however, I sat at the desk of my downtown office, waiting for the phone to ring. When it did, it was Letterman's assistant, advising that something had come up, and could we reschedule for the next day? A business event that evening came on the heels of the phone call, causing me to arrive home well after dark. After we frantically searched for the cat, she finally dragged in somewhere around ten, looking like Mike Tyson after three rounds with Evander Holyfield. The next morning I found her semiconscious, head nodding, eyes slits, jaw ajar, alternately hissing and panting. Clumps of fur lay on the floor around her, and when touched, she growled like a grizzly bear. Unable to place her in her cat carrier, I drove to the vet, picked up two of his assistants and drove them to my home, where they placed her gingerly but firmly into the carrier, and drove back to the vet, where she was examined and pronounced the probable victim of a raccoon attack. A stab wound to the eye and a nasty gash on her front paw left her hobbling for two weeks and left me with a vet bill of sixty-eight dollars, which, if Letterman had called when he was supposed to, would have been zero.

Oh, and since I now hate raccoons, I had to replace the mouse pad (three bucks) by my computer, which featured a cute picture of a raccoon with a little ear of corn in its front paws. Which brings us to the tidy sum of $1,526, acceptable in any form, personal check or cash. Now that I look back on it, however, it was worth the sacrifice. For two days I felt like an exceptional babe even if I wrecked two cars and my cat looked like roadkill. In addition, Dan Rather and I are on a first-name basis, and I haven't had so much fun with a celebrity since my boyfriend (now husband) and I got to drive Simon and Garfunkel to the airport after a college concert. Maybe I'll never be asked to guest-appear on the *Late Show*, but I was privy to a backseat performance of "Juniper and Lamplight" by Art Garfunkel, who, I figure, still owes me six dollars for the tube of cortisone creme necessary to relieve the itchy hives that remained on my neck for a week after the fateful ride.

—July 1997

The most memorable letter I ever received from David Letterman was dated August 11, 1981, before his stints on The Tonight Show *or* Late Night with David Letterman *and in response to an interview request. At the time, he was residing in California. It reads:*

"Dear Debbie:

Thank you for the letter. I am sorry to hear you have been having a bad month. You think you have problems? Just take a look at the size of the left margin. Sure go ahead and feel sorry for yourself, but I'm looking at a huge typewriter repair job.

As it turns out, at this point in my life, I do not have any plans to visit the Circle City before the holidays. This could change quickly, but because of your deadline, it seems silly to bet that it will. I believe that I'm going to be at some college in Kentucky in late September, but again this may be too late. If it isn't too inconvenient to do this thing over the long lines, (oh, great, now the ribbon is going too), I will be happy to make myself available for whatever we need to do.

Well I must go now—the local Girl Scouts are going door to door selling malathion and I want to get a couple of tanks for the big labor day party.

Love always, Dave"

Men Behaving Badly

BRACING MYSELF WITH my knee against airline seat 11D, I clumsily hoisted my rolling carry-on bag toward the overhead bin. I wrestled one corner into the compartment, located uncomfortably higher than my sight line, and stupidly thought I was home free. Predictably, the bag came sliding back down, banging into my collarbone. Worrying about both my injury and my mother's antique lapel pin, I gave the bag one more desperate shove and wound up wearing it on my shoulder like an ungainly boom box. The voice of a burly man behind me thankfully interrupted my Three Stooges escapade. "Ma'am," he said, staring into my hopeful eyes, "I believe I'm in 11E."

Gentlemen, it seems, are at a premium. I navigate the high-rise office building where I work in an elevator where manners are as absent as the Muzak that once made our ride tolerable. Since our offices are on the top floor, I'm accustomed to being shoved to the back and, when our destinations are reached, watching everyone hurtle out, gender be damned.

I'm not particularly spoiled by the kind of treatment I miss. My own husband is not a draper of puddles with overcoats, a "No, you go first" kind of guy. I have withstood this for thirty years because I am secure in his respect, grateful that I haven't had to change a tire on a snowy highway at night. His gait is longer than mine, and I have followed him through airports, on busy streets, and once from a train station in Washington, D.C., to Alexandria, Virginia. He doesn't see his acts as ungentlemanly, but as gallant. After all, doesn't every jungle woman wish to have the overgrown path cleared before her, her man suffering the dangers of the brush before she ventures in? The older I get, the more I think the answer is probably no. Now that we have begun to achieve the kind of equality for which we fought, most of us want to be treated like ladies again, even if we don't want to be called one. As it is, we're lucky a car stops for us at all, let alone that someone opens our door. When I ventured to the South on business, imagine my delight when a companion deftly slid by me to assume a spot on my left, where I would be safe from cars that splash or, God forbid, jump the curb.

The attitude there is as different as the dialect. On one trip, I found myself dropped off by a cab at a building down a steep hill from the site of the party I was to attend. I was dressed formally, and on my bare feet I wore high black sandals, the kind that look better than they feel. On my spike heels I began to trudge, sandal straps digging into my feet, perspiration spoiling the soft folds of my scarf. A young man walking toward the party sensed my predicament, reached out to pick me up bodily, and said, "Little lady, looks like you could use a lift." Of course I was much too proud to accept his offer, picturing myself a worn saddlebag thrown over a pony on the trail. But the chivalry did not escape me, and a lady from the North did not know how to act.

On a rainy day last spring, I joined a group of staffers for lunch at Indy Anna's, located in the lower level of the Scottish Rite Cathedral. One step down the marble stairs and I became airborne, bouncing down the entire flight. No one was more surprised than I when I hit bottom and frightfully discovered that I was wearing one of my shorter, slimmer skirts. Seven people stood frozen, stifling smiles, as if they had just seen the Road Runner bash through a barn. Only one male out of the four present rushed to help, and for that, I paid for his lunch, scoffing at those who had failed me.

When I was in dating mode a hundred years ago, I remember standing patiently by the passenger car door, awaiting my companion's rush to open it. Likewise, he was expected to pay for the evening's entertainment, command the key to my front door and, with a red face, ask for a kiss goodnight. Then came those damned Virginia Slims commercials, and all that stopped. A working woman for most of my adult life, I have struggled on behalf of women's issues and usually agree with feminist doctrine. The dark side of what we used to call "women's lib," however, is a man's excuse to be rude. Maybe it's time for the pendulum to swing back, for the lines between the sexes to sharpen.

If nothing else, women work harder to be women, which should count for something. Not only do we hold down full-time jobs while managing the home and children, but our upkeep is more complex than a man's, and most of it seems to be for his benefit. Being a woman is like having a boat, what with all the deck swabbing and polishing—more as the wood begins to warp. We strip away unwanted hair with hot wax, poke mascara wands into our eyes at sunrise, stuff ourselves into pantyhose in the heat of the summer, and—worst of all—are forced to *accessorize*. Is it too much to ask for a little appreciation in the form of an opened door, an unwanted dessert ordered just so we can have one bite, a hand with our luggage from someone we don't have to tip?

In her legendary cotillion for more than forty years, Mrs. Kenneth Kinnear has taught some forty thousand adolescents how to lead and follow their partners in dance, cut in properly, and offer and say thanks for a cup of punch. Oddly, she thinks boys are more mannerly now than they once were, but for a contemporary reason. They behave differently in dance class because those throat-choking ties, shirts, and blue blazers are as unfamiliar as the white-gloved girl in their outstretched arms. "They're so unaccustomed to being dressed up, they're on their best behavior when they are," she says. Contemporary standards aside, she hasn't wavered from the most traditional male-female interaction. "If you're treated like a lady," she says, "you act like one."

When my father was alive, I experienced a true gentleman's manner firsthand. In his younger days, he would cradle my elbow in his palm as we walked, and would have stripped to the bone if I'd even shivered. Had I been his son and not his daughter, I doubt that he would have warmed up my car on winter mornings; and by watching my mother, I knew how girls were meant to be treated.

One of Indy's top marriage and sex therapists, Dr. Diane Brashear, clinical associate professor of OB-GYN and Psychiatry at the IU School of Medicine, agrees that chivalry died along with traditional relationships. "With today's egalitarian relationship, the man doesn't know which cue to follow," she observes. Gender aside, she feels we don't treat one another courteously, a more profound problem. "We need to have respect for each other," she says.

Brashear believes the decline of gentlemanly behavior is a Catch-22, the price we women paid for our independence. If we act tough, we're treated that way. Since so many of my contemporaries in business are male, I often feel like one of the guys, shaking hands roughly, laughing at their crude jokes, sizing up other women. I can lug suitcases and hail cabs, barrel across freeways, and put together a bookshelf. Sometimes it would be nice, however, to put my macho side away and simply enjoy being a girl.

—November 1998

My husband didn't like this column. At all.

Reality Bites

I'VE DECIDED THAT the things we see every day tell only half the story. I reached this prophetic conclusion during a hectic lunch hour, during which I found myself in a deli line waiting for a tuna sandwich. The sandwich maker, however, was noticeably absent from his post, which gave me a really good chance to observe the color chicken salad turns when it dislodges from its bin. But I digress.

Tapping my fingers nervously on my tray, I craned my neck toward the kitchen area behind the line, hoping to attract the attention of someone in authority. And then I saw him: the sandwich man, leaning against a counter, eating a sandwich himself. Still wearing plastic gloves, he took large, deep bites, leaving his gloved fingers behind in his mouth for the last few. Then, ever so casually, he came forward and asked for my order. Dumbstruck, I thumped my forehead and announced that since it was Friday it must be macaroni-and-cheese day, and what was I thinking, standing in the sandwich line as if I wanted a sandwich. I then proceeded to the potato chip display by the cashier, figuring that anything in a bag was probably robotically assembled and free of saliva-transported bacteria. I haven't been back since.

For some obscure reason probably indirectly related to the movie *Outbreak*, I can't seem to dismiss this picture from my mind. Now that I've related it in print, I take some consolation in the fact that no one else will be able to, either. At any rate, what goes on behind the scenes—in restaurants and everywhere else—has become an obsession, and I am convinced that all of our actions and decisions would be totally different if only we saw the whole picture.

Take the dry cleaner. Waiting for a large order to be assembled not long ago, I was entranced by the man at the pressing machine, visible over the counter. Sweating like an Olympic sprinter, he stood at the large contraption, first smoothing the leg of the trousers on the ironing board and then bringing down the heavy top with a loud hiss. At the completion of the process he retrieved the pants, which happened to be men's jeans, half-folding them over a wire hanger. Momentarily distracted, however, he missed the hanger, dropping the slacks on the dirty concrete floor. Rushing to pick them up, he stumbled onto one pant leg, then picked up the garment quickly, shook out the dirt and wrinkles and hung it under a plastic bag, no one the wiser. Finding that little episode easier to stomach than the glove incident, I was nonetheless alarmed. Some poor shnook was about to pay four dollars for a pair of spiffy, pressed jeans, unaware that the garment was probably filled with hair, spider eggs, smushed Gummi Bears, and dust balls even my cat couldn't digest.

Now, restaurants and cleaners aren't usually life-and-death establishments, mind you, but they seem to bring home the point and cause me a few nights of restless sleep. If I saw those things, I muse, imagine the injustices no one ever sees that are perpetrated on poor consumers like us. All of which is critical to my theory that we'd think and act differently if we really knew what went on. My sister, for example, is not as trusting as I, and after having attended a few cooking classes at a prestigious health spa, is convinced that cooked foods, like grilled chicken, really shouldn't be paired with raw, perhaps unwashed foods, like lettuce. I try not to ponder why. She, however, has reason to be suspicious, having once suffered a horrific weeklong bout of *E. coli* bacteria that her doctor blamed on fruit fertilized with God Knows What that she bought at a neighborhood stand. We both try not to ponder that. So, up to this point, our behavior would already have drastically changed if only we'd known the truth: Pack your lunch, buy fruit at the grocery, launder your own pants.

In real-life emergencies, though, we sometimes have no choice. Take the time a Pyrex measuring cup slipped through my soapy hands, breaking against the enamel sink and slicing my finger from knuckle to knuckle. There I sat in a curtained cubicle in the emergency room, where I couldn't help overhearing the woman's complaint on the other side. "I ran over my own foot," she said, followed by silence. And then, "Yes, I was driving." At that point a clutch of staff stationed elsewhere hastened to my side, where they struggled to stifle their guffaws. *That's it*, I thought, *the final insult*. Our serious injuries provide entertainment for trained professionals, who must later have enjoyed the fact that the reason I was washing the measuring cup in the first place was that I, an avowed career woman, had just baked a cake.

My niece, a fourth-year medical student who has spent a fair amount of time in emergency rooms, advises me that there's a whole side to the business of trauma that the traumatized never see. In fact, she confides, the staff even has a pet name for complaining old people who reside in nursing facilities: GOMER (an acronym for Get Out of My Emergency Room). So, there you go. If you'd known this before you sat with your grandmother in the waiting room for six hours, you might have waited until Monday and seen your family doctor, who probably has lots of patients who run over their own feet. (The accident occurred, by the way, when the woman in question remembered something in the house and forgot to put the car in park. It could happen.)

In the interest of civility, I won't even mention the man wearing a white butcher's uniform who came into the emergency room as I was leaving, complaining of pinkeye. There are some things you just don't want explained. What I've learned from all this is, what we can see is probably all we need to see. Men don't care that half the breasts they ogle are really silicone, and general anesthesia is a welcome relief. Restaurant kitchens are better off behind closed doors, and I intend to forget the picture I saw in the paper of a candy factory with bins of chocolate cooling and hardening in molds on the floor. Fiction is probably better (and safer) than truth, especially if it means we can sleep at night.

—June 1996

Not long ago I found a petrified fly in my salad at a reputable Italian restaurant. After I alerted the management, I heard the chef holler in the kitchen: "I told you to keep that door shut!"

Woman's Work

EVERY DAY ON MY WAY to work I pass a small cemetery. A tombstone once caught my eye, and I can't seem to forget it. Of ordinary granite, it marks a double plot: one side describes Cassius M. and the other, Flora H., his wife. I never knew Flora, but I get sad just thinking of her. Maybe she managed the farmhouse or ran a church office, raised six kids or taught school. Whatever she did, I feel certain she merited better description than just "Flora H., his wife."

With Mother's Day this month, it seems appropriate to discuss not only what Flora probably did when she wasn't "his wife," but what all mothers who are hoping for better epitaphs face. Working outside the home or no, motherhood ranks right up there with the presidency on the responsibility scale. My sister once aptly remarked that it wasn't until her children were grown that she could digest her food, and then it was questionable.

It isn't that dads don't help; I see more and more of them lugging groceries and dragging coughing kids in their pajamas to the pediatrician. It's just that for them, it isn't full-time. Show me a man lolling on the couch watching football and I'll show you a woman sucking dust in some fourteen-year-old's closet, arranging his Hard Rock Cafe T-shirts by city. Likewise, where there's a man leaning back in his desk chair, his conference call on the speaker phone, there's a woman somewhere racing the clock, trying to meet her business appointment and take her kid to the ortho-dontist at the same time. And find a man complaining that the hamburgers aren't cooked all the way through and there's sure to be a woman who tossed around two pounds of frozen meat like a football at five P.M.

Basically, this whole man-woman thing boils down to two points: guilt and dirt. Guilt that dictates that while a baby-sitter or day care center might provide adequate supervision and even transportation, it won't be as good as Mom could do. I had great trust in day care until I picked up my toddler one day and found him asleep on the linoleum under a small chair. Sucking his thumb, he had a tight grip on the small shred of blanket that had survived his two years. Wiping away dirty tear stains on his face, I decided that rather than send him back, I'd figure a way to do it all.

Besides guilt, there's dirt. Dirt that only females see. While men can sit in a leather wingback chair and watch the clutter rise around them, women navigate around the house in a stooped-over position, plucking up piles of newspapers and tennis shoes, sticky Coke cans and empty popcorn bowls.

An old college friend contemplating resuming her nursing career after her children were at last in school once asked my advice on how to manage job and home. After I explained the laws of order, delegation, and self-sufficiency, she scratched her head and wondered, "Yes, but who will clean out their closets?" You will, I thought. Your choice will be simple. Harp on it for six months, or wait until the door won't close and they keep asking for new clothes because they can't find the old ones, and then do it yourself. Take it on some Saturday morning in spring, when you can open the bedroom window and hear everyone outside having fun, laughing and shooting baskets, race walking and spraying each other with hoses.

Credit is all that's missing in this formula of motherhood—someone to say you're just too wonderful for words. But that's okay. Maybe children everywhere will suddenly become adults and appreciate the struggle. I hope Flora's kids are among them.

—May 1991

Personal Foul

OKAY, SO I ADMIT IT. I'm preoccupied with Bob Knight. At IU games I sit on the sidelines and stare at him, waiting for the fur to fly. I write him letters requesting interviews, and he writes me back. No, my wife's not interested in having your readers meet her; yes, I'll cooperate on a piece about Jay Edwards' drug problem.

We came face-to-face once, in 1982, wherein I hammered away at such important issues as whether or not women should work. At that time he not only offered his opinion, he gave me a little unsolicited personal advice about my own home vs. work situation. Needless to say, those choice words never saw print.

I always swore that if given the chance to interview him again, I'd be a little tougher and wear taller shoes. This time, my patent leather pumps sported three-inch heels. The tough part, however, is a matter of opinion.

On the early-morning, one-hour drive to Bloomington I stopped at a Hardee's and two donut shops to visit their ladies' rooms. In the parking lot outside Assembly Hall I dried my palms on the air conditioning vents and reviewed my notes. And then, my high heels and I clicked our way up the deserted ramp to the Basketball Office.

Once inside, we took our positions on two facing card table chairs—he tipping his back with power and finesse, me perched on mine like a bird on a wire. He was Michael Jordan with a home-court advantage, I was the Flying Wallendas without a net.

Discounting a few profane interludes, things went smoothly at first, and we covered sufficient ground to produce this issue's cover article. And then it happened: the eggshells I trod cracked and then crumbled; the mine field that is Knight's mind began to erupt.

"When did the sport coat give way to the sweater?" I asked. "Why did Bobby become Bob?"—questions hardly so nervy as to provoke the explosion that followed. As his face reddened and his voice rose, I kidded offhandedly about "knowing you'd yell at me" sooner or later.

Banter to me, however, was intolerably snotty impertinence to him, setting off a blowup of nuclear proportions. Like an enraged lion he leaped from his chair, his nose less than one inch from mine. "*Yelling?*" he bellowed, with a force that sizzled the skin on my face and sent the ashes blowing to the floor. "*I'll show you (bleeping) yelling!*" An inexplicable two-hundred-decibel tirade of four-letter words and accusations ("Why would you bring up that bleep-bleep? You bleeping bleepers are all alike—just like that bleeper Feinstein!") followed, with me stuck to my seat like gum to the sole of a shoe. I was Isiah Thomas without my teammates, a hunkered-down ref without my stripes.

Shaking off the shock, I prodded him to resume the interview, an offer to which he responded with a heavy pat on the shoulder that signaled the door. Notes and tape recorders flying, I half tripped in that direction, a drunken cowboy tossed out of a Western saloon.

Alone in my car, I flipped down the visor to examine what remained of the skin on my face. My curly hair had become straight clumps that hung in damp disarray. I was Moses after he saw the Burning Bush. My heart in my throat, I lambasted myself for keeping only half my promise via my high-heeled shoes.

I realize now, however, that it wasn't lack of toughness at all that kept me from bolting from my chair and shouting, "Don't you *dare* scream in *my* face, you raving lunatic!" What kept me from doing it was forty years of human decency—a lifetime of learning what's proper behavior and what's loutish theatrics.

You'll easily recognize me on the IU sidelines this basketball season. I'll be the one with the curls in her hair whose eyes are steadily cast on the players on court, confident that while they might relax their defenses on occasion, I really hadn't done so after all.

—October 1990

Five years before this experience, Knight had cooperated with a lengthy story entitled "The World According to Knight." This is the letter he sent on March 15, 1985:

"Dear Deborah:

Let me know if I can ever be of any help to you. You still have the most insight and a better understanding of anyone that has ever interviewed me."

Sincerely yours, Bob Knight"

Trying Day

HAMILTON SUPERIOR COURT 4 Judge J. Richard Campbell was not amused when I told him I couldn't serve as a juror because of my criminal record. He was reasonable enough to excuse me once for a business trip, but this time I pushed my luck. Parking tickets or not, I would appear on July 16, 1998, to perform my civic duty.

The dreaded subpoena was as welcome as the grim reaper, prompting an onslaught of advice from friends and coworkers about how to avoid the unpleasantries. The most useful came from a fellow editor: "Go and get you some potato salad. Then leave it out on the kitchen counter all night. Next morning, eat that potato salad. No jury duty!"

Seated in the jury assembly room of the Hamilton County Government and Judicial Center a few days later, I realized that no amount of squirming and scheming would get me out of this one. Never mind that the large, well-appointed room appeared a cross between my ophthalmologist's waiting room and the lobby of a Four Seasons Hotel. One expects that in Carmel. Just as pandas on the wallpaper don't make childbirth any easier, however, the impeccable surroundings did little to ease the pain. And boy, did the occupants try.

Joe, the bailiff, worked the mostly hostile crowd like a stand-up comic on open-mike night, cracking one joke after another, to the imaginary hollow cough and metaphorical clink of the occasional glass. "Please eat the rolls," he said, gesturing to a tray of mini-muffins and assorted Danish. "I am responsible for the purchase of these rolls. If you don't eat them, I must." He next advised the crowd of some thirty, six of whom would be selected as jurors, that the lucky ones would get forty dollars as opposed to the seventeen-fifty allotted to the dumb clucks sent home. "Where else is your pay doubled on the first morning of the job?" he asked the group, already as edgy as caged tigers at feeding time.

Awaiting the completion of pretrial tasks, I felt like I did the first time I stayed at a bed-and-breakfast inn, where there was nothing to do but look out the window at the Amish passing by in their buggies. "Waste of time," I scrawled on my notepad, each letter drawn and redrawn until an imprint appeared on subsequent pages. Joe then briefed us on whom Indiana law doesn't allow to serve: veterinarians, ferryboat captains, members of the legislature in session, soldiers on active duty, dentists, or firemen. The lunacy of the list fanned the flames already burning in my esophagus, and I looked with rancor upon those chuckling.

Once inside the courtroom, the prospective jurors for the drunken driving case were questioned by opposing lawyers. Pathetic attempts to escape flowed from my comrades, many claiming they could not be impartial, hated cops, had a brother/aunt/stepson picked up for drunken driving. My best shot—that at barely five feet tall I could not see over the railing that separated the gallery where we sat from the bench—fell short. The question that sealed my fate, it seemed, was asked by the defense attorney, a suave, well-dressed man who concluded his declaratives with "M'kay?" reminding me of Mr. Mackey, the school counselor on *South Park*.

"Ms. Paul, how do you define 'reasonable doubt'?" he asked, to which I succinctly replied, "Huh?" With a courtroom of people staring, all I could think was, "What does salt taste like? Salty!" What I answered instead was, "Reasonable doubt means just that: reasonable doubt, er, uh, it doesn't leave room for question."

That incredibly astute reply cost me the next ten hours, as shortly thereafter I traded my freedom for the title of Juror Number One. The judge immediately congratulated our troupe of five women and one man on being selected and assured us that we would not be sequestered, relieving my fears of spending the night at the Carmel Motel. We were shown to the jury deliberation room, which was furnished with a small conference table, a phone, a jar of peanut M&Ms, and the infamous rolls.

Morning testimony came from the Carmel police officer who apprehended the alleged drunken driver at approximately three-thirty A.M. after observing him driving erratically. The deputy prosecutor, a young, very small man, questioned him deliberately and without fanfare. I tried to keep my mind on the proceedings, but couldn't help wondering where he bought his little suits. The facts as he saw them were simple: The driver, unable to walk a heel-toe straight line, failed a field sobriety test and refused a blood alcohol test. His eyes were bloodshot and he smelled of beer. At the police station he called his girlfriend and said, "I screwed up again."

The defense lawyer tried to compensate with style over substance, smiling too much, thanking us repeatedly for our time. "He grasps at straws," I wrote in my notebook, in reference to his questioning the cop's ability to judge intoxication and alleged oversight in not asking the driver if anything were medically wrong with his legs. The officer smirked, further unshaken by the fact that he discarded a faulty videotape of the encounter, which the defense attorney was convinced hid damaging evidence. So far, there was no doubt, reasonable or otherwise. I wondered what the other jurors were thinking.

I scratched notes repeatedly, surprised that I was actually beginning to care more about the guilt or innocence of this man than the fact that lunchtime loomed. Excused for a one-hour break, we trooped through downtown Noblesville to Syd's Bar, a hole-in-the-wall next to Williams' Clothing Store, which was having a sidewalk sale. Earning my reputation of being able to shop anywhere, I was tempted to rifle through the racks but resisted the urge. The low-ceilinged, cramped, smoky, windowless restaurant featured taco salad that day, although most of my fellow jurors opted for the pork tenderloin. Diet in mind, I nibbled on a plain chicken sandwich, eyeing the sign on the wall that read FOOD IS LIKE AMMUNITION. DON'T WASTE IT.

Joe, who was as gracious as a cruise ship director, told cheerful stories of cases past, sharing that the best excuse he ever heard for missing jury duty came from a Carmel housewife who said that her nanny would be off that day. And the only people who are never selected, he confided, were engineers, with their tendency to see things in black and white. When I asked why the judge had a computer on the bench, Joe happily answered, "To check his e-mail."

Recess over, the trial resumed. As the defense attorney droned on, I couldn't keep my eyes off the judge, who rested his chin in his palm, picked at his eyelashes, and scrunched his face like John Cage on *Ally McBeal*. No new evidence seemed to surface, only drama in place of fact. If a newspaper reporter had been present, his version would have read: "Juror Number One took copious notes, fidgeted in her chair, and made occasional slurping sounds when she sucked from her water bottle. After the summation, the jury filed expressionless from the courtroom, at which time Juror Number One dropped her purse, spilling Tic Tacs, cell phone, and car keys noisily on the floor. Fellow jurors scrambled to assist."

Before deliberations, however, we heard a tight-knit conclusion from the prosecution and a long-winded one from the defense. With Johnnie Cochran theatrics, the defense attorney, jabbing at the air before our faces, dubbed each of us a famous movie critic, then gave the case various fictional movie titles, documenting them vertically on a large dry-erase board. He even described his son, who, bless his heart, played such word games to pass the time at church. With much drama, he then circled a line of horizontal letters that spelled "acquit."

Stupidly, I thought the worst was over. That was before we gathered around the conference table in the jury deliberation room, having declared Juror Number One as foreman. Well past dinnertime, it seemed everyone's wish was to wrap this up and present our guilty verdict with as little hoopla as possible. But that was before one fellow juror decided perhaps the defendant was innocent, launching me into a public tirade not seen since a fellow editor and I shrieked at each other over whether the term "walleye" or "walleyed" pike was acceptable usage. It went something like this:

"What part of this don't you understand?" I asked, going over the evidence for the zillionth time.

"I'm not sure he was really intoxicated," she replied, adding that he might have had just one or two drinks.

"So it's okay to drive drunk as long as you're not too drunk," I countered, adding that if that's what she was teaching her kids, I hoped she'd please advise me when they were on the roads.

After what seemed like hours, she relented, and the group filed back into the courtroom to deliver the verdict. Then the judge presented the bad news: This was only part one of the case. The second part would involve recognizing that this was the same man who was convicted for a similar offense five years before. I looked knowingly in the direction of my nemesis, secure that we had found appropriately. The evidence overwhelming, we retired again to the jury room, where I asked snottily, "Does anyone have a problem with this?"

During the reading of the verdict, the defendant, pale in his stiff white shirt and tie, hung his head, making me realize the truth of what Joe had said earlier: "This may be an annoyance to you, but to someone, it is the most important day of his life." Bleary-eyed, I drove home sometime after eight P.M., about twelve hours after I first arrived. I was admittedly slightly sick that I might have sent someone to jail, but nonetheless proud that I helped take a drunk off the roads: a drunk who was drunk enough.

Joe was right. At the end of the day I was glad I had served. The experience was a little like eating Chinese food, however. No matter how satisfying, you don't want to repeat it anytime soon. "After the conclusion of the trial, Juror Number One was quoted as saying she was considering becoming a ferryboat captain."

—October 1998

The defendant was later sentenced to twenty-eight days in jail followed by ninety days of home detention. Other punishments included a temporary suspension of his driver's license, probation, community service, and counseling.

All the Rage

FROM MY AISLE SEAT I could hear the man in the Jetway complaining loudly about the terrible treatment he had endured at the hands of the airport gate agent. As he stepped into the plane, red-faced and boisterous, he was stopped by the flight attendant, who courteously advised him that in order to proceed to his seat, he would have to settle down. Enraged, he advanced, causing the aircraft captain to confront him and issue the same warning. Disregarding him, the furious passenger continued and was stopped a third time by the same flight attendant. At that instant he veered sharply toward her, and, with an outstretched arm, knocked her to the wall in the aircraft galley, where she slid to the floor. The man launched himself down the aisle, pursued hotly by both pilots, one of whom eventually apprehended him and yelled for the crew to call a cop.

I was frozen. The complete stranger beside me reached for my hand, and we gripped one another, half-expecting gunshots to follow. It was as close as she or I had ever come to physical violence, right before our eyes. Even though the perpetrator was handcuffed and quickly escorted off the plane, the incident left a sick feeling in the pit of my stomach. Anything could happen, anywhere. You just had to hope your luck held out.

Rage is, of course, not always deadly. The word itself has become part of our lingo, like the phrases "twenty-four/seven" and "whatever." In an editorial meeting designed to generate new stories for this magazine, someone pitched the subject of the Indianapolis Symphony Orchestra's search for a new conductor, drawing nodding approval. In mock exasperation, one of our editors pounded his fists on the table and lamented that he'd suggested the same story months ago to a lackluster response. When he finished, the editor on my right turned to me and mumbled, "Idea rage." Popular culture not only allows but promotes our venting; short tempers are in.

I'm no stranger to the concept myself. When I recently tried to order sheets from a Neiman Marcus catalog, I asked the operator to explain the difference between king size and California king. "We have both," she answered tersely, raising my ire and causing me to repeat the question twice more. Exasperated, she yelled, "I've told you three times. We have *both.*" After advising her that I was, in fact, the customer, and that she was about to lose a four-hundred-dollar sale, she hung up. My husband, who heard one end of the verbal scuffle from the other room, came around the corner to ask what was wrong. "Catalogue rage," I muttered, shoving the magazine into a drawer.

I have a history of speaking my mind, which I prefer to think of as clearing the air. This can manifest itself in dangerous ways, such as the time I was about to grab the door handle of a small grocery store in Florida when a huge, muscle-bound, tattooed construction worker pushed in front of me and charged inside. Now, I'm a little like the Chihuahua who thinks it's a German shepherd: From the vantage point inside my head, I am sometimes blissfully unaware that I stand five-foot-zero and tip the scales at less than a hundred pounds. "Just one minute," I heard myself say, as he swung around to get a look. At that precise moment, my son, Jonathan, relatively slight of build himself but infinitely more aware of his stature, grabbed me by my arm, shaking his head frantically. "Mom," he implored, "No. Not this time."

He has saved me from myself frequently in the past, with just a hand signal. It usually goes something like this. I will be irritated because we have sat at a restaurant table for nearly fifteen minutes and no one has noticed we are there. I begin shifting in my chair, ready to pounce like a panther at any nearby hostess, server, or manager. Or some smoker waves a cigarette in my face. It is at this point that Jon, who may be across the room, sees the rage rise inside me like the Loch Ness Monster ascending from the the murky depths, and pushes both hands, palms to the floor, slowly downward. "Quell," he says slowly. "Q-u-e-l-l." Since he has moved to another city, I have memorized his subtle refrain and try to live by it. He is right, after all. Such outbursts upset everyone and generally do little to rectify the problem.

Lately, though, rage has become mainstream. According to an Associated Press article, air rage incidents increased from approximately one thousand in 1994 to more than five thousand in 1997. The Transport Workers Federation also reported an increase in unruly passengers, from sixty-six incidents in 1997 to five hundred last year. We are all painfully aware of the Reading, Massachusetts, father who beat to death another father over their sons' hockey practice, but even I was surprised by *USA Today*'s litany of violent acts, including the hurling of a bichon frise into oncoming traffic (killing him) after a minor car accident, and the striking of a teenager with a frozen turkey over a pair of borrowed shoes.

We all become ruffled on occasion. Some merely cloud over, their eyes becoming narrow and dark, or jut out their chins in simple defiance. Others, whose emotions bubble dangerously closer to the surface, erupt. You see them leveling the airport gate agent, demanding answers *right now* from the doctors' receptionist, ripping on the bank teller. After I had traded in a dirty fork twice at one of our favorite restaurants, and had found a large, petrified fly fully coated with vinaigrette dressing in my salad, I reported the incident to both the server and the owner, resisting the urge to march into the kitchen to challenge the chef. None of it, I might add, did an ounce of good, as we were charged full fare for the dinner and given little comfort beyond another salad and a passing apology. The right response, which I since have adopted, is to vote with my feet instead of my mouth, avoiding the place entirely. Knowing our boundaries is what separates us from the badly behaved Bob Knights of the world.

It could be we're so accustomed to getting our own way that we won't accept any other solution. Or maybe no one cares about manners anymore, which explains how easily the "F" word fits into our everyday conversation. Possibly we're in such a perpetual hurry that anything slowing us down is the enemy. The trend toward boiling over, however, is making us look bad and scaring those who still cling to decorum. Revenge, I have come to believe, just isn't worth it.

A few weeks ago, I was driving south on Capitol Avenue, both hands on the wheel, eyes forward, when a speeding car cut me off from a right-hand lane, forcing me to swerve onto the sidewalk to avoid a catastrophic collision. My first reaction was to jump from the car and run after the perpetrator, demanding an explanation and an apology. And then I told myself, "Quell." Anybody who drives like that is probably drunk, on drugs, or even armed. Being right and proving it could be deadly. Sadly, this is what it's come to.

So, I'm rethinking my whole confrontational attitude. Maybe it's time to retire my company nickname of "Xena, Warrior Princess," and mellow out. In this environment of uncontrolled rage, being a fighter isn't funny anymore. I'm practicing pinching my lips tightly together and perfecting my meanest squint. Such techniques don't make you feel nearly as vindicated, but with any luck, you might live to talk about it.

—October 2000

My sheets, ordered from "linensource," arrived as pictured and without delay.

Doctor Dearest

DEAR DR. HEAL-ME:

I've sat in your waiting room for nearly an hour, and, frankly, I'm getting a little miffed. There's not much to look at, save some hotel art and magazines, of which I get my fill at work. The staff's matching polo shirts with your logo on them are cute, however, and I wonder if you sell them, as at Planet Hollywood. I fear they'll call me if I visit the ladies' room, even though I'm certain they've forgotten I'm here. Several people have been summoned, although I was here first. How many patients do you book for each time slot, anyway? I try to convince myself that my time's as valuable as yours, but the truth is it's not. I need you more than you need me.

I guess I shouldn't be in such a hurry. Once I make it to your examining room, there I'll be, legs dangling off the end of the exam table, waiting again. Only this time I'll be exposed, with only a paper drape to shield me from the blast of air-conditioning and, eventually, your knowing eye. I know I don't have anything you haven't seen a million times before, but, hey, these are my bony shoulders, my small breasts, my cold feet. I listen for you in the hall, and my heart skips as I hear folders rattling outside the door. While awaiting my turn, I ponder making a call on my cell phone or eating the peanut butter crackers in my purse. In one hand I grasp my list of questions, because experience teaches that as soon as you walk in, I won't remember why I came in the first place.

My fondest hope is that when you do see me, you'll remember who I am. You see, another doctor who removed part of my bladder didn't recognize me or my scar a few years later. I guess when you say you know someone inside out, doctors don't count. Sometimes, I admit to using this magazine to identify myself in the hope that it will cement me in your mind. The tactic often backfires, like the time I visited one of your cronies for a physical and was asked, "How is your circulation?"

"Not bad," I replied, adding that my hands get numb sometimes.

"No," he pronounced, "I meant the circulation of your magazine." If anything could be more embarrassing than having your naked abdomen plied for abnormalities, it is having it done while making a complete fool of yourself.

I see many doctors for my assorted body parts, so establishing a personal relationship with each may be asking too much. I prefer to get my answers from you, however, and not your nurses, who seem to shield you from everything from drug salesmen to complaining patients. I do appreciate your occasional calls, though, especially those at eight P.M. You're obviously busy, and like a sold-out movie or a crowded restaurant, busy probably means good.

And speaking of nurses, I'd rather they didn't accompany you into the examining room. It is highly unlikely that I will ever sue you for inappropriate touching or lewd behavior, considering I look a lot more fetching with clothes than without. The nurse is just one more witness to my awkwardness, my ridiculous complaints, my unpedicured toes. The resident who sometimes joins you also increases my anxiety, and even though you introduce him as "doctor," I know he was probably carded in a bar the night before. You'll be proud to know that one time I did summon the courage to say no when asked whether the trainee could probe my defective retinas with a steel rod. If you're looking for practice subjects, try the morgue.

But I don't want you to think you are unappreciated. When I awaken from surgery, yours is the face I want to see, even unrecognizable behind scrubs and a mask. Only you can promise me that everything will be fine, even if your fleeting bedside appearance could be mistaken for a hallucination. I like your nice personality, your clean office, and your cheerful staff. I accept the fact that your defective scale weighs me five pounds heavier than I actually am, and that according to your measuring device I am shrinking, which—G-rated movies notwithstanding—must be a biological impossibility. I realize you have bills to pay and that you didn't train your receptionist to ask about my insurance plan before she asks about my symptoms. You have the information I want, and no one follows doctor's orders better than I. I respect you, but I don't revere you and your vast, intricate knowledge the way I do, say, the computer specialist in my office. Sure, you know plenty, but you don't know everything, and this being my body and all, sometimes I think my intuition is just as valuable as your clinical training. If this feels like bronchitis, maybe it is, even though you can't hear the rattle in my chest.

As much as I like you, I can't help missing my old doctors, like Dr. William Wright Jr., who would actually see me when I had an earache, not schedule me three days later. I liked the musty chairs in his waiting room, and the way he would diagnose with, "Well, if it looks like a duck and sounds like a duck, it probably is a duck." Now that my kids are grown, I miss our pediatrician, Dr. James Cumming, who always addressed them and not me, never showed alarm, and always assured me that they were normal, even if they squashed their carpool companions like bugs in the backseat every day on the way to nursery school. I miss my former OB-GYN, Dr. David Copher, who let me kvetch for an hour if I needed it and never backed out of the room in my mid-sentence.

As long as you tell me whether one-forty over eighty is good or bad as blood pressure goes, I'll be satisfied. I prefer that you identify that white blob on my x-ray as an organ or a tumor, and I like it best when you say we'll watch and wait. Besides God or the woman in the health food store, you're the only one who can save my life. But before you do, please allow me to reintroduce myself.

Sincerely, Deborah Paul

—September 1998

Acknowledgments

INSPIRATION RARELY TAKES the place of perspiration. And twenty years of columns—240 in all—don't sort out and compile themselves. Thanks to my assistant, Wendy Jackson, for photocopying, assembling, and transcribing them all, then helping to turn those selected into a legitimate manuscript. Her favorite, "A World Apart," appears on page 175. (I could have lived without it.)

Without Emmis Communications chairman Jeff Smulyan's trust, commitment, and devotion, neither the column nor the magazine could have survived. For that, I am infinitely grateful. More specifically, thanks to sixteen-year *Indianapolis Monthly* veteran Sam Stall, who edited the original columns and created the witty headlines (the lame ones are mine), and then left the magazine to pursue a full-time writing career. Equal appreciation goes to senior editor Brian Smith for ensuring that I made sense and didn't leave any participles dangling. And my work spouses, Emmis vice presidents Jack Marsella and Gary Thoe, who spend more time with me than my husband does, deserve not only my gratitude but a place in heaven.

My literary heroes include Butler University journalism professor Art Levin, my mentor, for his high standards, which I still strive to meet, and *Atlanta* magazine editor-in-chief Lee Walburn, for his encouragement and support. From this master of prose, words of praise mean everything. If he says it's good, you can by God take it to the bank.